TEACHING
the
WHOLE
CLASS

CORWIN
PRESS

The Corwin Press logo — a raven striding across an open book — represents the happy union of courage and learning. We are a professional-level publisher of books and journals for K–12 educators, and we are committed to creating and providing resources that embody these qualities. Corwin's motto is "Success for All Learners."

FOURTH EDITION

TEACHING
the
WHOLE
CLASS

BETTY LOU LEAVER

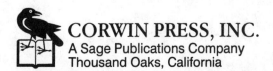

CORWIN PRESS, INC.
A Sage Publications Company
Thousand Oaks, California

For information address:

Corwin Press, Inc.
A Sage Publications Company
2455 Teller Road
Thousand Oaks, California 91320
E-mail: order@corwin.sagepub.com

SAGE Publications Ltd.
6 Bonhill Street
London EC2A 4PU
United Kingdom

SAGE Publications India Pvt. Ltd.
M-32 Market
Greater Kailash I
New Delhi 110 048 India

Printed in the United States of America

Library of Congress Cataloging-in-Publication Data

Leaver, Betty Lou.
    Teaching the whole class / Betty Lou Leaver. — 4th ed.
        p. cm.
    Includes bibliographical references and index.
    ISBN 0-8039-6645-8 (cloth : acid-free paper). —
    ISBN 0-8039-6646-6 (pbk.: acid-free paper)
    1. Teaching — United States.   2. Cognitive styles — United States.
    3. Teacher-student relationships — United States.   I. Title.
    LB1025.3.L43   1997   97-21131

This book is printed on acid-free paper.

97 98 99 00 01 02 03   10 9 8 7 6 5 4

Contents

Preface

This book is a significantly expanded version of a book that literally has traveled the world in spiral-bound form, *Teaching the Whole Class, Third Edition*. The thesis of whole-class teaching and of this book is that all students can learn. Teachers around the world have known this intuitively for a long time. *Teaching the Whole Class* makes conscious those intuitions.

Whole-class teaching is not another method; it is not another syllabus design. Whole-class teaching is a philosophy that puts responsibility for learning back into students' hands and responsibility for the classroom back into teachers' hands, from whence contemporary approaches have wrenched both. Today's teaching practices often place method and assessment of outcome above learning. *This book subordinates method and definition of appropriate outcomes to students' specific learning needs realized within a group setting in order to improve outcomes dramatically—not on tests alone but in actual learning achieved and the ability and motivation to continue learning on a lifelong basis.*

The book explains how to teach in ways that all students can learn, based on an understanding of learning-style differences and how these differences can cause learning difficulties when teaching styles, curricular orientations, or class profiles differ from individual students' learning-style profiles. The book includes information on identifying classroom conflicts in style and provides concrete suggestions for resolving these problems. The purpose is to help teachers accommodate student needs within the classroom for more effective learning in this year's or this semester's class and empower students to learn more effectively for a lifetime.

Although the book is concerned with identifying "the needs of the one" (i.e., the individual learning conflicts), it focuses on meeting those needs while teaching for "the needs of the many" (i.e., the realistic situation in which teachers find themselves: having to take care of individual needs in the larger context of teaching an entire class). Readers are shown how to accommodate learning styles and also how to empower learners to become style-flexible. Suggestions are provided on when to undertake each of these approaches.

The concepts in the book have been tested in U.S. government classrooms, American K-16 classrooms, and classrooms in more than 7 other countries over a period of 12 years. The information has been extensively updated from the earlier edition, based on a quickly and vastly growing theoretical and research base.

WHAT IS THIS BOOK ABOUT?

Twenty years ago Reynolds and Birch (1977) wrote a wonderful book entitled *Teaching Exceptional Children in All America's Schools*. Although they had in mind the concept of mainstreaming special education students in the schools of the 1970s and 1980s, many of their words have even more importance for today's regular education, special education, and gifted classrooms, where, with the exception of some very recent interest in full inclusion of handicapped children in regular education programs, the layering of students into ever thinner slices has often proceeded in directions directly opposed to those advocated by Reynolds and Birch.

Many classrooms today are leaving out more students at the same time that we are making ever more vocal commitments to individualization. Two years ago, in conducting research on gifted dropouts, I contacted the president of Mensa for Children to find case studies. She could not provide any. All the Mensan children she knew were being home schooled! Assuming that these children have the highest IQ (whatever that signifies) of American children and some of the most educationally aware and involved parents in America, the simple fact that nearly all of them are being home schooled is a quiet but deep indictment of American schools and the teaching that goes on in them. At the other end of the spectrum, in developing a research grant proposal, I learned that nearly one fourth of the students in one Salinas (California) high school are receiving some form of remedial education. Salinas may be in somewhat more trouble than many school districts, but it is certainly not alone in having large numbers of students who are simply not learning.

This book refuses to accept the idea that so many students cannot learn. It advocates helping every student learn successfully as a participant in a classroom where students may have very different learning needs from one another. This book is meant to show that (a) selective instruction (grouping by ability) and teaching the whole class are not the same thing; (b) individualization, in its current form, is not the same as teaching the whole class; and (c) current teaching methods meant to improve educational outcomes are not the same thing as teaching the whole class, either. ***Teaching the whole class means that ALL students are learning via their preferred learning styles MOST of the time.*** None of our current teaching methods, including those based on learning-styles research, allows this. The act of leaving method aside and concentrating on how students learn does allow this. This is what *Teaching the Whole Class* is about.

HOW DID THIS BOOK COME INTO BEING?

The first confession I must make as an educational administrator is to admit that most of the effective teaching techniques I advocate have been "borrowed" from an effective teacher somewhere. To admit less would be dishonest.

The ideas behind *Teaching the Whole Class* are based on (a) independent research conducted by me at the U.S. Department of State's Foreign Service Institute (FSI), the Defense Language Institute (DLI), the American Global Studies Institute (AGSI), and elsewhere; (b) research and ideas shared by the Washington-based informal learning-styles group, including, in addition to me, Mary Ellen Alexander (National Association of Secondary School Principals), Eleanor Corbett (consulting psychologist), Dr. Madeline Ehrman (Director, Research, Evaluation, and Development, FSI), Dr. Rebecca Oxford (Associate Dean, School of Education, University of Alabama), Dr. Emma Violand-Sanchez (Director, ESL Programs, Arlington Public Schools), Dr. Thomas Parry (U.S. Office of Training and Education), and Dr. Mary Stuart Woodburn (Professor of Education, Longwood College), which met weekly and culminated in an invitational symposium in 1987; (c) extensive theoretical discussions with colleagues identified herein; and (d) research conducted by others and noted in the references.

Following the 1987 symposium, a number of faculty members at the FSI and DLI enthusiastically participated in researching how learning happens. Many contributed new ideas which have been incorporated into this book. Over a period of four years colleagues at the DLI (Sabine Atwell, Claudia Bey, Dr. Patricia Boylan, Bella Cohen, Grazyna Dudney, Natalie Fryberger, Dr. Maurice Funke, Dr. Neil Granoien, Dr. Nicholas Itsines, Ishka Jenson, Dr. John Lett, Dr. Svata Louda, Hugh McFarlane, LTC John McGhee, Dr. Hana Pariser, MAJ Chester Phillips, USA (Ret.), Stanislas Popov, and Dr. Sofia Thompson) assisted me in identifying and helping at-risk students and crystallizing ways in which to present this information to faculty. My supervisors at the FSI and DLI (Dr. Ray Clifford, Col Ronald Cowger, USAF (Ret.), Ambassador Ray Ewing, Dr. Ronald Goodison, COL Donald C. Fischer, Jr., USA (Ret.), Jack Mendelssohn, and Ambassador Harry Thayer) provided support while allowing me autonomy to discover how the whole class learns. Students at these institutions provided me with many opportunities to research the significance of learning styles. Some of these students have become the strongest proponents of *Teaching the Whole Class*. Many have said that they never found learning a difficult language so much fun or so easy as when they were taught by teachers who knew how to teach the whole class.

The result of the enthusiasm of these administrators, teachers, and students was the first edition of *Teaching the Whole Class*. Responses to that and subsequent editions led to this updated and significantly revised fourth edition. To this book, I have added a number of materials that readers have told me they would have liked to have had in the previous editions.

WHY DID I WRITE THIS BOOK?

I believe that *no student should fail.* In a number of the programs that I have administered, I have made it a practice to teach classes whenever possible. In some cases, I have even learned new content matter in order to be able to teach the class. I have always made the same request of each program's immediate supervisor: Give me those students whom you consider "impossible," "doomed to failure," "untalented," "unmotivated," and so on. In nearly all cases, these students have had cognitive conflicts with some aspect of the program that interfered with their success. In nearly all cases, it has been possible to resolve these conflicts. These students may have had other problems as well (low ability—whatever that is—personal problems, emotional issues, physical impairments, etc.), but the cognitive conflict has been what really prevented them from learning. That conflict allowed all those other problems, where they existed, to creep into the classroom. Resolving the cognitive conflicts permitted the students to block out, at least for the duration of the school day, the after-hours problems they were experiencing.

I use such groups of students as demonstration classrooms. Considered an inordinate risk taker, I prefer to teach most classes in auditorium-sized rooms so that all teachers who wish can observe and, if desired, participate in the instruction, and I compensate for the stress this puts on students by paying even more attention to their individual learning needs. (Sometimes, I have had as much as 10-handed instruction [five teachers] being given in the classroom; other times, I have worked alone in a more traditional demonstration mode.)

Although others consider me to be an extraordinary risk taker, I do not consider my actions to be risks. Because I know that all students can learn, because I can determine their learning-style preferences without instrumentation, and because I can accommodate most learning styles in the classroom, for me there is no risk. All I have to do is apply what I know, and it works.

The purpose of writing this book is to share the conviction that all our students deserve positive and successful learning experiences and to help teachers and administrators develop the skills of accommodation and empowerment. This book is as close as I can come to inviting the world into a demonstration classroom.

Who Should Read This Book?

This book is for any teacher who has ever had an unsuccessful student, as well as for educational administrators and supervisors. According to a recent study, only 15% of teachers feel comfortable in recognizing and teaching to learning-style differences (Snow, 1997). This book is for the other 85%—and perhaps even the 15% will glean some new insights from the case studies and examples provided. The ideas, information, and case studies have been culled from actual K-12 and postsecondary classrooms and purposefully cover the general range of subjects normally taught in these environments.

The third edition of this book has been used in graduate teaching methods seminars. This fourth addition has added a new and comprehensive chapter on style identification (Chapter 3) to facilitate such use.

Although this book is clearly written for teachers, teachers-to-be, and their supervisors, parents who have some understanding of educational issues can gain insights into their children's school performance. Much of what is suggested can be implemented as well in a home, or home schooling, environment.

Some Assumption, Principles, and Faits Accomplis

1. The overall organization of the book is that of a random (nonlinear) author imposing idiosyncratic order on the chaos that characterizes the status quo in research and theory of learning styles. I have tried to make the organization obvious for sequential (linear) readers.

2. In general, gifted education is subsumed under regular education—except in cases where it is more appropriate to provide additional, specific information on gifted learners. Because gifted learners also vary by style, the basic principles apply to them as well.

3. This book does not include special techniques for dealing with specific learning disabilities (e.g., dyslexia or dysgraphemia) because much research is available

elsewhere on techniques that can assist in these instances. However, style issues can complicate the use of these techniques. To that end, examples, where pertinent, have been given from special education and learning-disabled classrooms. Style issues are even more important for students with specific learning disabilities and more involved learning disabilities than for the regular education population. In programs that are not oriented toward capitalizing on their learning styles, special education students are doubly handicapped—the first time for real and the second time by circumstance that does not have to be.

DESCRIPTION OF CONTENTS

The scope of the instructional areas addressed in this book is K-16, any subject. Examples come from elementary school classrooms, high schools, universities, and adult programs.

Admittedly, the topic of learning styles is too broad to be covered exhaustively in one volume. The information presented in this book is meant to provide the blueprint, the foundation, and some of the cornerstones needed for each teacher to continue learning and to begin building his or her own edifice, based on his or her own classroom experiences.

The construction of the book itself tries to accommodate the learning styles of readers. For concrete and inductive readers, who learn by studying, adapting, and applying models, an example is given for each "style war." Throughout the book, these examples follow the theory and explanation that is supplied for abstract and deductive readers, who learn through concept explication. Sensing types, who rely on observable phenomena, might wish to use the learning-styles instruments identified in Resource A or the observation checklists provided in Resource B; intuitives, who trust their instincts, may not feel the need for these.

Although there is clearly a sequence to the book, random readers are invited to read the chapters in any order; most can stand alone. I have tried to make the information within these covers accessible to the kind of visual learner who depends on image, as well as to the kind of visual learner who depends on words. For the limitations of a book format I apologize to auditory and kinesthetic readers, who probably would prefer to receive this information through some other medium; perhaps discussion of the contents with colleagues and completion of the practice exercises will help readers with these learning styles to extract the information that they need. For the intuitives, I have provided ideas, and for the sensing types, I have provided citations, and where available, statistics.

Each of the three main categories of learning styles discussed in this book—sensory preferences, cognitive styles, and personality types—is identified by an icon in the margin of each page where the styles appear. The icons can guide the reader to the discussions in each chapter of the categories of learning style in which they are most interested. Descriptions of the icons can be found in the glossary at the end of the book. Readers new to learning styles may prefer to concentrate on developing skill at accommodating one category of learning styles at first. Readers more experienced in working with learning styles may enjoy having access to the full range of styles presented and so may choose to ignore the icons.

Chapter 1 discusses the philosophical foundations of education in the United States and elsewhere and addresses the question, Why do we teach the way we do? It is presented as a dialogue between a reader of an earlier edition of this book, Dr. Isak Frumin, Director of Universe Laboratory School in Siberia, and me.

Chapter 2 explains the concepts behind the book. It tells why accommodating learning styles is important in today's classrooms and why learner profiling is even more important. It also presents case studies of unsuccessful students drawn from actual classroom situations. It explains how and why their teachers were not able to help them and reveals the source of the real difficulty, giving suggestions on how the situation could have been handled more successfully.

Chapter 3 is optional reading for those not familiar with learning-styles theory. Those who are already familiar with the terms and concepts can check the glossary to see how I have defined the various terms used in this book and skip Chapter 3.

Chapter 4 considers the kinds of activities that typically go on in classrooms of a wide variety of subjects. Activities are identified as either fostering student success or hindering student success.

Chapter 5 explains how to meet the needs of each and every student through style accommodation in the classroom. It also presents questions about learning-style conflicts that have been posed by actual teachers of a variety of subjects and at a variety of educational levels. Not all possible conflicts can be included in one book, let alone in one chapter. The answers to the questions presented in Chapter 5 can serve as models for answering related questions that arise in classroom practice.

Chapter 6 demonstrates how to empower students to become style-flexible. It focuses on learning strategies as the basis of learner empowerment.

Chapter 7 keeps in mind that teachers often cannot write 30 different lesson plans. They need a way to handle a class as a whole. This chapter provides a tested, unique way of doing this, based on class profiles, teaching styles, and orientation of materials.

Chapter 8 summarizes the principles behind teaching the whole class by relating a fable of two military honor guards and how they were trained. This chapter is the epilogue and as such also provides the conclusion to the book.

Resources include an annotated list of learning-styles assessment tools for teachers who prefer to use an instrument to determine their students' learning styles, observation checklists for teachers who prefer to do their own style determinations, and answers to the practice exercises. In addition, a **glossary** of icons, acronyms, and terms; a **reference** section; and an **index** are included at the end of the book.

Reader comments are always welcomed and encouraged! (They may be sent to me at leaver@aol.com.)

Betty Lou Leaver
Salinas, California
March 1997

Acknowledgments

In this fourth edition, I acknowledge a deep and growing debt to teachers and administrators from around the world who have made previous editions of *Teaching the Whole Class* a success. Their suggestions, as well as feedback from graduate students in my teaching methods seminars, have served to make the fourth edition an improvement over earlier editions. So many have helped with this and previous editions that I feel as if *Teaching the Whole Class* belongs more to others than it does to me.

I especially wish to thank those who have had earlier editions translated into Russian (Dr. Elena Lenskaya, Deputy Minister of Education, Russia), Spanish (Dr. Irene Reyes, Director, Centro Colombo Americano, Cali, Colombia, and Dr. Maria Owen), and Belarus and Ukrainian (Soros Foundations and American Global Studies Institute). In doing so, they have made the ideas accessible to many more teachers, who, in turn, have shared with me a wide variety of experiences.

I owe a distinct debt of gratitude to Dr. Isak Frumin (Director, Universe Laboratory School, and Member, Russian Academy of Pedagogical Sciences) for writing the preface to the Russian translation of the second edition of this book. It is with respect and friendship that I have taken the liberty to translate the Russian preface in this fourth edition, and it is with complete faith in the strength of our collegial relationship that I comment on his preface, moving our personal interactions into the public arena.

I further acknowledge the implicit but important contributions of Dr. Madeline Ehrman (Director, Research, Evaluation, and Development, Foreign Service Institute), Dr. Neil Granoien (Dean, Korean Program, Defense Language Institute), Dr. Rebecca Oxford (Associate Dean, School of Education, University of Alabama), and Dr. Karin Ryding (Dean, Interdisciplinary Studies, Georgetown University), who have been colleagues and friends for a decade. Hours of discussions, collaborative professional presentations, and joint publications with them have resulted in my learning more from them than I may have shared with them.

I am also indebted to AGSI personnel, especially my executive assistant, Audrey Duenas, who keeps my work (and life) on the proper tracks. I certainly owe eternal gratitude to the AGSI Board of Directors for their faith in the product and concept of teaching all students and empowering all students to be effective learners. Dr. Dan Davidson (Executive Director, American Council of Teachers of Russian, and

Professor, Bryn Mawr College) has helped forge pathways for sharing the information in this book both here and abroad and was the first to adopt the earlier editions as a graduate text. At a 1993 meeting at Kennedy Airport in New York City, Michael Mears (Vice-President, General Electric Investments Corporation) gave me the confidence to start down this path, and each time the path has turned into a dark area of the forest, he has been there with a light and a supportive word. COL John O'Neil, USMC (Ret'd.) (former Acting Director of the White House Office of Science and Technology Policy) was a military attaché in the first Foreign Service Institute program I supervised; by default I became his grammar teacher and he became my source for learning more about specific intricacies of learner variables. I am still learning from our frequent interactions as colleagues and as friends, and having personally experienced the effects, he is a highly informed, dedicated supporter of teaching the whole class. At times now, he is the one to bring new research in learning styles to my attention. Jeff Munks (Director of Eduventure Projects at California State University at Monterey Bay and Co-Founder, AT&T Language Line) has helped me hang onto what he calls "the tiger's tail," as AGSI explores ways to use technology to make teaching the whole class and understanding (and assessing) individual students easier. Without these very appreciated supporters, *Teaching the Whole Class* would have been impoverished in a number of ways.

This fourth edition benefited from a preliminary editorial reading by Dr. Nicholas Itsines (Chair, Multi-Language Department, DLI); he has never feared to give me candid feedback. The post-Itsines draft was read by friends, colleagues, and helpful souls from many fields and levels of educational administration, teaching, and parenting: Diane Bolduc, Dr. Madeline Ehrman, Dr. Ellen Franke, Laura Hooper, Steven Kemp, Janice Leaver, Roberta Mendler Muse, John and Carol O'Neil, Beth Pemberton, Beth Sterten, and Lisa Thompson. Their comments served to make this manuscript more accessible to readers, especially those with learner profiles that differ from mine, and I thank them all sincerely for their willingness and ability to work with penultimate copy and for their insightful comments, of which I have taken careful note. William Jones (Monterey Peninsula College) provided appreciated assistance with Resource A. A very special thank you is given to the family of Evgeni Khasan, who provided some of the drawings for this edition (Evgeni is the school psychologist from Siberia described in the book as drawing pictures during one of my seminars). Evgeni tragically perished in a car accident in August 1995, but his pictures will always remind me, and now readers, of how one learner with a nonacademic learning style was able to learn in his own way and, in so doing, provided others with wonderful graphic representations of abstract concepts. Any flaws, omissions, and inaccuracies that remain are of my own making.

This book has become a family affair; I thank my family for their support. My mother, Mary Ham, watched my children and did my housework, so that I could complete the first edition of this book. My brother, Kevin Ham, let me hide out at his house in the Maine woods for 3 weeks, where the falling snow and falling temperatures kept me inside on-task during the initial revision of this edition. My husband, Carl Leaver, provided the graphics and typesetting. Three of my children also assisted: Echo helped with library research, Shawn surfed the Internet for the latest information, and Fawn handled bibliographic standardization.

I especially want to thank Ann West for discovering the third edition of *Teaching the Whole Class* and suggesting—rightfully so—Corwin Press as publisher for the fourth edition. The technical assistance of Marlene Head and April Scott was invaluable, and the support of Gracia Alkema, president and publisher, through the rebirthing process was much appreciated.

Credit must also be given to the many faculty members from Belarus, Japan, Korea, Latin America, Russia, Ukraine, the United States, Uzbekistan, and elsewhere who have attended my workshops, often supplying me with new ideas and sharing with me new situations. Also, I owe many ideas to informative discussions on learning styles that I have had with members of the general education and foreign language education profession in the United States and abroad. Not least of all, I acknowledge the teachers of my own children, who have wrestled with some unusual learner preferences in trying to accommodate my children into their school programs.

As an administrator, I have observed some extraordinary teachers in action, and as a student, I have felt the remarkably mathemagenic effect of some extraordinary teachers. To try to list them all here would only result in unfair omissions from faulty memory. These teachers may have preceded the research on learner profiles and the specific teaching techniques associated with them, yet they recognized the differing needs of their students. They exemplified the underlying philosophy of teaching the whole class without knowing that such a philosophy would some day exist and carry a label. They focused on the individual needs of their students, accepted them for who and where they were, led them to where they needed to go, and gave them tools for continuing on alone. Through inspired teaching, these dedicated instructors planted the seeds which germinated into today's learner-centered instruction, facilitative teaching, differentiated instruction, diagnostic teaching, and other learner-focused approaches. They were the people with whom it all started. This book is dedicated to the one who had the most profound impact on my own intellectual development; he provided me with a superb example and bricks for the foundation.

From all these people I have learned a great deal. To them all I gratefully credit much of what appears in this book.

To Jake M. Collins

*I wonder if I would have discovered
how to teach the whole class
without his early influence.*

About the Author

Betty Lou Leaver has been teaching and administering whole classes for more than two decades. She has taught preschoolers, students in an alternative elementary program, secondary students, college undergraduates, graduate students, soldiers, diplomats, and home schoolers.

She currently serves as president of the American Global Studies Institute. Prior to that she was Dean, School of Central European Languages and School of Slavic Languages at the Defense Language Institute; Supervisor of the Russian and Ukrainian programs at the Foreign Service Institute, U.S. Department of State; U.S. Army officer; and Director, Little Bitterrooters Child Education Center.

Ms. Leaver is currently working towards completion of a PhD at Pushkin Institute in Moscow. She holds a BA in linguistics and an MA in comparative literature from Pennsylvania State University, and, with the exception of the dissertation, she completed doctoral work in Russian with minors in Applied Linguistics, Curriculum and Instruction, and International Affairs at the University of Pittsburgh.

She has taught foreign language, teaching methods, and cross-cultural courses at Middlebury College, Monterey Institute of International Studies, Bryn Mawr College, University of Pittsburgh, and Allegheny County Community College. She has provided consultation on general education and foreign language education issues to a number of U.S. and foreign government agencies, universities, colleges, school districts, and individual schools and teachers. She also chaired the Foreign Language Advisory Committee, Arlington (VA) Public Schools.

In addition to conducting more than 200 faculty development workshops, she has authored or edited more than 80 publications in English and Russian. She has made more than 70 regional, national, or international presentations, more than half invited or as keynote speaker, and has chaired more than 40 conference panels.

She has evaluated articles submitted for publication for four professional journals, served on the editorial board of two other professional journals, and cohosted "Ed Talk: The Radio Show" on KNRY in Monterey, California.

Ms. Leaver served as Newsletter Editor of the Alpha Theta chapter of Pi Lamda Theta National Honor and Professional Association in Education, is a member of the Board of Directors of the American Council of Teachers of Russian (ACTR) and editor of the "Front Page Dialogue" of the ACTR Letter, and participates in several other professional organizations: Association in Supervision and Curriculum Development, American Council on the Teaching of Foreign Language, American Association of Teachers of Slavic and East European Languages (where she served as vice-president of the Greater Washington Area chapter), and American Association of Applied Linguists, among others.

She is listed in ten reference volumes published in the United States and Europe, including *Who's Who in the West*, *Who's Who of American Women*, and *World's Who's Who of Women*.

1

Introduction: Dialogue With a Reader

Dr. Isak Frumin's Preface
to the Russian Edition of *Teaching the Whole Class*

S everal years ago during a geometry class I was discussing the conditions for congruency with seventh graders. In the back row, Dennis Burov dozed as usual, paying attention neither to my strictly logical explanation nor to the pictures that clearly depicted the requisite triangles. Unexpectedly, it occurred to me that many in the class could not graphically illustrate the process of overlaying triangles on each other. Then I started to draw these triangles in the air with my hand. The students repeated these motions after me. And then something surprising happened. Dennis roused himself and started waving his hands energetically and in an engaged manner. His smile, his confident and accurate movements — all of this spoke to the fact that the image had become consolidated in his hands. Many times after that I used as many real motions as possible in geometry class, and these occasions were always a holiday for Dennis. They were also a holiday for me because I had found the pedagogical key to this, as it turned out, lively and bright boy.

I remembered this story when I participated in a seminar, "Whole Class Work." An American educator, Betty Lou Leaver, conducted this seminar in the fall of 1993 at the Krasnoyarsk Center for the Advancement of Education. The seminar materials and a careful reading of this book, which you also can now read, explained to me what had happened to Dennis, or more accurately, what had happened to me, the teacher, having discovered that children are different. That which is clear to Yulya is not always clear to Dennis, and vice versa. Betty Lou Leaver's book helped me polish this profound pedagogical discovery.

I write about this with no sense of irony; rather, with sadness. After all, *the Soviet tradition out of which we all came always focused on teaching everyone alike*. Of course, people talked about the individual traits of students and about a differentiated approach. But the talk, as a rule, was only about how much a given student corresponded or did not correspond to accepted methods and content of instruction. There was even born the concept of a "difficult student." In actuality, differentiation of instruction led to (and, alas, often leads to) the selective instruction of those children who can adapt to the characteristics of our pedagogical system. There is no way I can forget how one teacher of Russian, when asked the reasons for a student's failure, replied simply, "He has no ability; he does not understand what I say." Well, *what can we say about entrenched teachers, if many recently graduated school psychologists find the reasons for school difficulties to lie in children's "incorrect" ways of studying and understand pedagogical intervention as adapting the child to our system of requirements and techniques?* This generation of educators and school psychologists sees the resolution of all school problems in the selective instruction of children, in the creation of classes for "strong" and "weak" students. Their number is growing, signifying the triumph of educators who favor group learning and who have written on their shields: *"Children are different; this impedes teaching."* For them, teaching to differences means the necessity to teach well those children who have adapted to the system and the possibility of teaching the "difficult" children, who have not adapted, poorly (with lowered expectations).

We do understand the ideological and sociological roots of this concept. It is no accident, after all, that in our country the psychology of individual differences has significantly lagged behind the majority of other psychological disciplines.

So how does humanistic pedagogy contradict this group learning approach? First, it conceives of variation in children not as an impediment but as something positive. Second, while recognizing the commonalty of educational goals, it calls for the teacher to find different approaches for different students.

One version of such a multivariate approach is suggested by the author of this book. Betty Lou Leaver looks at the class not as an aggregate student body but as an ensemble of learning styles. Students with different learning styles differ from each other by the way in which they acquire new information, the way in which they relate to peers and teachers, and many other parameters. The author provides clear techniques for identifying various learning styles and recommendations for teaching various students in one class.

However, although ending this preface with an expression of confidence in the indubitable usefulness of this book for any educator or administrator, I must express one reservation. It appeared after a seminar on this book when one of my teacher-colleagues began to explain his professional difficulties and the limitations of his own learning style. In essence, he was treating psycho-pedagogical diagnostication as medical diagnosis, individual traits as individual limitations.

If one were to transfer this attitude to students' learning styles, then new possibilities arise for selective instruction: the idea of separating students into different classes in accordance with their learning styles. This danger is often felt distinctly in the country that spawned learning style theory—in the United States. Many critics there contend that the identification of learning styles is often perceived by teachers as the identification of the limits of a student's potential. My experience in sharing and discussing the work of Betty Lou Leaver shows that such a perception is characteristic only of those teachers who remain religiously mired in selective instruction. Humanistic educators—educators who are growth-oriented—look at the idea of learning styles, the idea of individual differences, as increasing the possibilities of true pedagogical work. It is for them that this book is intended.

Dr. Isak Frumin
Director, Universe Laboratory School, Krasnoyarsk, Russia
Member, Russian Academy of Pedagogical Sciences

AUTHOR'S COMMENT TO DR. FRUMIN AND READERS

Of all the people with whom I have shared the ideas presented in *Teaching the Whole Class*, no one has understood them better or applied them more conscientiously and creatively than Dr. Frumin. His Universe Laboratory School is one of my favorite institutions. The remarkable innovations of this school, situated on the banks of the Yenisei River in the wilds of Siberia, where 10-year-olds set about solving novel physics problems with delight and insight, speak to the power of teaching the whole class. Anyone who needs reassurance that the future of education can be bright should visit that school for a day. Although the building may be old and the supplies from an earlier decade, the learning I have observed taking place in that school is unparalleled. I remember an American colleague looking at me with tears in his eyes as we observed one group of eager middle schoolers planning the hypothetical reorganization of an entire community. Neither the cracked blackboards upon which writing was impossible to read nor the need for someone to constantly race to the bathroom to re-wet the rag used to wipe the board slowed down the lightning-speed mental activity and learning that was taking place in all of these students' heads.

I know where the tears came from. I look around me just in my own small region of California (for which parallels can be found all over the United States) and am appalled by the amount of learning that is not going on, the amount of time that students simply waste in classrooms of teachers who do not know how to reach them, and the lack of concern by administrators that only a small portion of each class of students is being taught. Those teachers, principals, and (rare) superintendents who are dedicated to reaching whole classes of learners too often labor alone without collegial, administrative, or financial support. Upon occasion in my own town of Salinas, I have been given to understand by some county educational administrators that (a) literacy is not a public education goal for all students—social skills are the goal and literacy a by-product; (b) students need not understand how they learn—this is the teacher's job, (c) hopefully, the very next method coming out of a big name university will be the ultimate—we just have to wait until someone gets the perfect system that orchestrates what teachers must do in the classroom; and (d) understanding how all students learn may be too sophisticated an expectation or too much information for teachers—my suggestion that this information is not only accessible to teachers but can and should be accessible to parents and students at all grade levels unnerves such administrators. I wish that some of these schools with their newfangled white boards, contemporary construction, polished floors, and impeccably coifed superintendent's staff would create the focus on successful learning evident in the classrooms of Universe Laboratory School!

Yet in spite of such classroom successes, Dr. Frumin found *Teaching the Whole Class* and the seminar at the Krasnoyarsk Center for the Advancement of Education epiphanic. His experience was neither unanticipated nor unique. In conducting many such seminars, not only in Russia but in other countries as well, I have found epiphanies to be a common outcome of the first day.

The discoveries of Dr. Frumin and his international colleagues do not come as a result of information that is extraordinarily novel. Rather, ***this is knowledge that talented teachers already have on some intuitive level***. Some, like Dr. Frumin, have already made this finding on a conscious level and have tried to define and articulate it. The content of these seminars simply confirms for them intuitions which they already possess but for which they have had no theoretical construct, let alone support to test their intuitions.

The educational climate in Russia that is bemoaned by Dr. Frumin is akin to the educational climate in just about any country one would choose. *In most places, to be different is to be wrong or untalented.* All students are supposed to march to the same beat, regardless of whether or not they hear the same drummer.

The drummer may play a different beat in one country or another, so that the student who is out of step in Europe may well be in step in Asia. Nevertheless, the concept is constant: *Students who are out of step are trained to march properly, and if they cannot do so, they are segregated, expelled, allowed to drop out, or punished.* The only difference between countries lies in which kinds of students are punished.

Why do we do this? Why do we teach the way we do, whether we are in the United States, Russia, Latin America, or some other part of this globe? Why did Dr. Frumin have one set of teaching experiences and his colleagues in the United States another? The answer is simple. Education does not stand apart from the rest of society. Rather, *the desired adult product sets the tone for education within any given civilization* (Leaver & Granoien, 1997).

As Dr. Frumin has pointed out, the ideological underpinnings of Soviet society could not permit certain kinds of instruction. The adult product of an autocratic society is one that recreates, obeys, and otherwise safeguards that society's values. The underlying educational philosophy in such a society is one that Miller and Seller (1985) would label "transmission"—the passing on of knowledge and values from one generation to the next. It is no surprise that I routinely find almost no intuitive thinkers among large groups of Russian teachers. Intuitive thinkers question authority, and in an autocratic society, such children will be punished, will not be successful learners, and certainly will not be promoted into the teaching ranks.

In the United States, we have been in an information age for some time. We need adult products who can solve problems, especially technological ones. We need particular (detail-oriented), sequential, analytic learners. We use methods that evolve from an educational philosophy of "transaction," and we reward those students who can learn problem-solving techniques, rather than those who acquire esoteric knowledge or challenge our assumptions. The latter students are punished, including the same intuitive thinkers who were not welcome in Soviet society.

Russia today is replacing a traditional educational philosophy of transmission with an educational philosophy of "transformation," in which the goal of education is highly individualized growth of students leading to the transformation of society. Because mature cultures do not promote the development of adult products bent on changing, or destabilizing, the culture, it is not surprising that a transformation philosophy usually arises only when cultures are in crisis. (The United States went through a similar phase in the 1960s. Our Rogerian methods were based on an educational philosophy of transformation and aimed for an adult product that would change a society split asunder by reactions to the conflict in Vietnam. American students who had not fared well in earlier settings, the intuitive thinkers and intuitive feelers, fared better in the transformation classrooms, where their creativity and unique approaches were prized. However, students who preferred rote learning or were better equipped to take in and pass on established values suffered.) What Russia will become is far from decided. Dr. Frumin is already in the forefront of the efforts to define the new Russia, to provide her with support pillars, and to prepare a generation not of students but of learners. He is doing that in a very simple way: He is creating the conditions in which all of his teachers can teach all of their students.

Teaching the whole class frees the teacher from methodological scavenger hunting. Once the notion that no method (even a method that claims to account for learning style differences) works for all students all of the time and the notion that all students have a right to learn are concurrently accepted, we can put aside methodology and the teaching of subject matter and start teaching students. After all, it is the students, not the teachers, who do the learning. *Teachers who orchestrate the pieces of clever methodological activities are too busy to know whether or not their students are learning*, and even if they ascertain this much, they have no time to determine the source of difficulty or to treat students as individuals. Teachers who stop teaching long enough to begin to facilitate learning—those teachers whom you find perpetually moving around the classroom, who listen rather than talk, and who give independent learners uninterrupted time on task—are the ones who have the most realistic opportunity for understanding each of their students. Those teachers have time to observe how and if each student is learning. Those teachers are learning about learning, are teaching diagnostically, and are turning classrooms into learning laboratories for themselves and their students. Those teachers may use parts of one method with one group of students, parts of another method with another group, and parts of a third method with another group of students, while allowing yet other students learning time away from the classroom. Those teachers are teaching the whole class. *All students may be learning the same information, but they are not doing it in the same way.* There may be venues for all students to share newly acquired information with each other in the classroom, but their interpretations of the information differ. Such differences are accepted in classrooms where facilitative learning is going on, and they are used in the development of critical thinking skills, in strategy training through peer collaboration, and in the acquisition of new information and skills. Unlike the teachers described by Dr. Frumin, facilitative teachers carry shields with the words, "Students are different; this liberates teaching."

Teachers who facilitate learning, rather than directly instruct students, give their students an important gift; they show them that they can be successful learners on their own. This, in turn, creates the motivation to continue learning. Still, this is often a gift that lasts only until the students return to a class where all students are considered the same, a specific teaching method (often the latest fad) dominates, or a conflict between teaching and learning styles erupts. At this point, students' newly-found self-confidence erodes. This does not have to happen. Teachers who facilitate learning can also empower their students to manage style conflicts.

They can help students understand how they learn best and how to adapt their behavior when encountering a style conflict from teachers, peers, a specific method, or even text materials.

There are schools and districts where such activity is taking place, where all students are considered worthy of an education and capable of learning. Some of the programs in Arlington Public Schools (Arlington, VA) have pockets of it, as do Portland Public Schools (Portland, OR), Lawton Intermediate School (Essex Junction, VT), East Lansing High School (East Lansing, MI), Elkhart Community Schools (Elkhart, IN), and a very occasional public or private school or classroom in the Monterey area (Monterey, CA). Accelerated Christian Education as implemented at the Lower Burrell Wesleyan Academy (Lower Burrell, PA) is a fine example of it. The foreign language departments of a number of leading research and Ivy League universities are becoming strong enclaves of facilitative learning, and the foreign language proficiency of their graduates has taken a giant step forward. Conversations with the principal of a Native American school on an Alaskan island and with a remedial reading teacher in Appalachia indicate that, ironically, more interest and expertise can sometimes be found in remote, culturally diverse or challenging, and resource-poor regions than in larger, resource-rich, and unwarrantedly complacent school districts. For more than two decades, the National Association of Secondary School Principals has tried to support a countrywide understanding of the significance of learner variables, and a few schools have begun to apply the concepts formed from the emerging research. Where I live, community colleges, such as Hartnell College and Monterey Peninsula College, which handle the academically limited student products of a school system that for the most part did not teach the whole class, are finding that even this late in the learning process, teaching the whole class can help their students. On a regular basis, I hear from individual teachers in a wide range of locations, from the remote corners of the earth (the lone voices in the wilderness) to the middle of metropolises (the lone voices in the crowd), who are finding success and fulfillment in letting go of their need to instruct and moving on to assist students with learning.

In conclusion, I would say to Dr. Frumin: Do not consider that your Soviet experiences differ all that much from our experiences in the United States or experiences in Asia, Europe, or Latin America. You may well be leading the world into a tomorrow where we begin with the learner and end with the learner, a tomorrow where all students are learning.

Betty Lou Leaver
President, American Global Studies Institute, Salinas, California, USA

2

Rationale for Teaching the Whole Class

In supervising a couple hundred teachers, visiting many hundreds of classrooms, and graduating thousands of students, many of whom I taught personally at some point in their career, I have reached the conclusion that all students, given the right support, can learn. My additional experience in working with students, teachers, and administrators from a variety of other kinds of programs ranging from pre-school through college in a number of countries serves to confirm that conclusion.

REASONS FOR TEACHING THE WHOLE CLASS

There are many reasons for teaching the whole class. The most important is: "because we can." Sixteen other reasons are presented below. At least as many more reasons could be added to this list; every teacher every day encounters possibilities for teaching the whole class and the reasons for doing so.

☞ *All students can learn.*

Students can learn foreign languages, math, and science. They can learn to read. They can learn to write. All students, even learning disabled ones (with the exception of those with extensive brain damage), can learn all these things. What they may not be able to do is learn in the way prescribed by a specific program, textbook, or teacher.

☞ *Not all students can learn in a prescribed way.*

Since the dawn of the age of schooling, students have more often than not been taught in prescribed ways. Teaching methods courses have focused on how best to teach specific subjects. Few have focused on how best to teach specific kinds of students. The search has always been for a magic method from which all students will learn. Teachers have found some methods more useful than others and have gone on to make fantastic claims for one or another specific method. Often, teachers have intuitively taught individual students, adapting the method for the students in their classroom, yet they have claimed that their success is due to the method itself. The reality is that no one teaching method fits all students, and it is not likely that such a miracle method will be discovered or invented.

☞ *Unmotivated students do not exist.*

*Un*motivated students do not exist. Some, if not many, students have become *de*motivated by teachers who do not understand them, parents who do not know how to help, peers who learn faster, and curricular materials oriented toward another kind of learner, but initially they want to learn. When barriers to learning are removed, their motivation often returns (Dunn & Griggs, 1995; Holt, 1989).

All too often, today's students grow up in home environments that are less than ideal. Many come to school without the external motivation of the home upon which previous generations of teachers have been able to rely. For those students who have not become demotivated by schooling itself, the school is a haven, proven on a routine basis in classrooms across the United States where students from broken homes, impoverished environments, and addicted parents graduate at the top of their classes and become first-generation college students. More students could experience such achievements if they were taught in ways that helped them succeed rather than ways that made them struggle (Dunn, 1988, 1992, 1993; Sternberg, 1997).

☞ *Teachers must help students,*
not give up on them.

The fact that students can learn means that teachers must help them. The longer we wait, the harder it is. Demotivated students who reach high school present greater challenges to their teachers than demotivated students at an earlier age. High school teachers who are not successful at preventing demotivation or at remotivating students do not create any challenges for their successors; there are no successors. Demotivated students do not enroll in college. It is time for success for everyone.

☞ *Student success may have more to do*
with how students are taught than with innate
ability.

Gifted students may drop out of school. Learning disabled students may learn well in spite of predictions to the contrary. Students who perform well in one classroom may perform abysmally in another classroom. In many cases, the cause of poor performance lies not in the student but in a conflict between the learning style of the student and the style of the teacher, the materials, or the majority of the student's peers. In other words, "style wars," a term first used by Oxford, Ehrman, and Lavine (1991), are being waged in our classrooms.

☞ *Style wars can be won.*

Winning the style wars first requires an awareness of learning styles. Two students can be very much alike yet very different. For example, Shawn and Shane (see opposite page) are twins, but in the classroom, that relationship is far from evident. Being aware that students differ creates a requirement to arrange the input and activities so that they can learn differently. Reacting to the awareness of learning differences sets up the conditions needed for success.

WHEN TWINS AREN'T TWINS

Shawn and Shane are twins. They look alike. They talk alike. Often, they dress alike. People even say they walk alike. Their parents sometimes cannot tell them apart. They are in the same class. They have the same friends. Their friends cannot tell them apart. But their teachers can tell them apart.

Shawn finishes his work very quickly. He sometimes makes mistakes. His teacher asks him to check his work more carefully. Shane labors over every answer. He wants to make sure it is absolutely correct before he goes on. His teacher sometimes lets him take his work home, so that he can finish it.

On tests, Shawn answers all the questions quickly and finishes first. Often, he has many mistakes. On tests, Shane usually finishes last. Often, he does not complete the whole test, but most of his answers are correct.

When Shawn looks at a picture of woods, he sees a forest. When he learns something new, he understands why the information is important and where it fits with other information he knows. When Shane sees a picture of woods, he sees all the different kinds of trees that are in the woods. He does not see a forest. When he learns something new, he understands what the information is and how to use it.

Shawn is a good reader. He understands everything very quickly and thinks about how the new information from the reading fits with what he already knows about the subject and what the information means to him. Shane is a good reader, too. He thinks about what the author wants to tell him about the information and remembers very well all the details about what he is reading.

Shawn remembers best by keeping pictures in his head. Shane remembers best by keeping words in his head.

Shawn learns new words when he sees them in a story. Shane learns new words by looking them up in the dictionary.

Shawn is learning French. He likes to talk to his teachers and friends in French. If he doesn't know every word he needs, he will make up words or find some other way to express his ideas. Shawn likes to make up stories in French. Shane is learning Spanish. He doesn't like to talk to anyone until after he has learned all the right words and the right ways to put together a sentence. Shane prefers to translate stories.

Shawn likes to figure things out for himself. Shane likes to have things explained to him.

Shawn makes models by looking at a picture. Shane makes models by following instructions.

When people ask Shawn what it feels like to be a twin, he tells them how much alike he and Shane are. When people ask Shane what it feels like to be a twin, he tells them how different he and Shawn are.

Shawn and Shane are twins. And they are both good students.

☞ *The chaos in the field of learner differences can
be organized.*

In general, the field of learner differences is relatively new, the terms in flux, and the organization, if an organization of any sort can be claimed, chaotic. Dozens of systems have been proposed. These range from three kinds of brain dominance proposed by Torrance (1980), to four kinds of cognitive styles suggested by Gregorc (1982), to seven multiple intelligences proposed by Gardner (1983). These older systems are still in use today, and many educators are just beginning to implement them, although we now know that these very simple designs inadequately describe the complexity of learner differences. Some of these designs, such as whole brain learning (Hermann, 1983) and multiple intelligences (Gardner, 1991), are prescriptive approaches, dictating classroom practices. My preference is for a descriptive approach (i.e., providing information about learner differences, not preformatted lesson plans); *when teachers develop the ability to facilitate learning, they usually find solutions to the style wars that are more situationally appropriate and more effective than a priori practices.*

Some teachers find the broad array of learning styles easier to understand and to manage, if the various systems are grouped by type. The grouping that I have found most useful clusters learner differences into four overarching categories, which are described in detail in Chapter 3:

1. Sensory Modalities
2. Cognitive styles
3. Personality types
4. Environmental preferences

☞ *The miracles reside within the students.*

Learner-centered instruction goes beyond system, beyond method, beyond textbook, beyond classroom, and beyond teacher to the source of success in learning or failure to learn—to the student (Aliev & Leaver, 1993; Nunan, 1988). If there are to be miracles, those miracles will reside within the individual students. The teacher's role is to orchestrate the miracle by focusing on the student who is not learning and rearranging the environment, task, or subject matter so that the student can learn. By accommodating learning-style profiles (see Chapter 5) and empowering students (see Chapter 6), teachers can "deconflict" the conflict in teaching and learning styles that interferes with students' ability to learn.

☞ *Learner-centered instruction is not an easy
answer, but it is an effective approach.*

Paying attention to individual learning need is far more effective than searching for a perfect teaching method. Looking for answers from the outside—a book, an authority, a method—may seem easier than looking for answers from the inside—analysis of students' mental processes and classroom interactions—but the time spent searching for external solutions to internal problems is usually wasted. Ultimately, an internal search must be undertaken to effect any miracles.

☞ *Learner-centered instruction can resolve style conflicts.*

An example of a learning-style conflict is the fourth-grade spelling student who was required to repeat third-grade spelling because she could not pass a placement test. The test required her to circle the misspelled words in a list. Like other global (big picture-oriented) learners, she did not pay attention to details. She would be more likely to look at a misspelled word and in her mind's eye see a correct spelling than she would be to notice a missing or incorrect letter. Fortunately, her parents understood learning styles. They asked the teacher to allow their daughter to write the words. On this test, she received a score of 100% on both the third-grade and fourth-grade lists and was advanced into the fifth-grade spelling book. Later that year, she placed fourth in the school spelling bee. That teacher became a believer in the necessity of testing to a student's learning style.

Likewise, a foreign language student was failing because he could not remember vocabulary. He was clearly an analytic learner, one who learns from breaking new information into its component parts, but he tried to remember words by marching around the room shouting them aloud. Why? Because his roommate, an oral learner (one who learns by talking) and an A student, did this. The difference was remarkable. The analytic learner spent up to 3 hours on this deafening activity in order to maintain a D average. The successful oral student spent 10 to 15 minutes. When the analytic learner was presented with analytic strategies for word recall, he began to spend much less time with individual words and to recall many more of them. His grades improved from D to B nearly overnight, and his teachers became believers in the power of learning via one's learning-style preferences.

Similarly, a high school student was failing Spanish but needed to pass a difficult entrance exam in Spanish for another school. His Spanish teacher, who was teaching him in direct opposition to his learning styles, gave him no hope. With only 16 hours to work with him, a foreign language tutor knowledgeable about learning styles helped him with learning the kinds of strategies needed to pass a test based on details, not with his language skills. He possessed the language skills but was unable to show them because the testing methods required the use of strategies associated with a learning style oriented toward details, whereas he had a learning style oriented toward "the big picture." He passed the test.

☞ *Learner-centered instruction can increase success rates and lower attrition.*

When learner-centered instruction was introduced into one foreign language program, the percentage of students reaching professional levels of proficiency during the course rose from 52% to more than 90%. Similarly, when learner-centered instruction was introduced in another program, attrition fell from 32% to 3% at the same time that competency increased from 44% to 81% over a 3-year period. Of course, other variables, as always, were present in both instances. However, a significant change in the programs was the increased attention to student learning styles and general needs. Elementary schools committed to teaching to students' learning styles have reported similar results.

☞ *There are tools for teaching the whole class.*

There are no miracle methods for helping all students to learn. But there are tools. And there are tremendous rewards for both students and teachers who are willing to invest the time needed to learn to use these tools.

These tools are not ready-made lesson plans. No class is the same as any other. No lesson plan fits all classes.

These tools are not learning-styles tests, although a list of extant learning-styles tests and where to obtain them is provided (Resource A). Although learning-styles tests can be helpful for providing objectivity, giving credibility to student feedback on learning styles, providing corroboration of observation (especially for teachers with learning styles that seek external evidence for intuitions), and facilitating quantitative analysis, nearly all the learning-styles tests on the market today, including my own, are flawed in a number of ways. First, students often answer questions in a "wannabe" mode, presenting themselves as they think their teachers want them to be, as they think their parents want them to be, or as they themselves want to be. Second, there is no way to prevent misinterpretation of questions by students. Third, none of the current tests considers that some students' styles may differ, depending on whether they are acquiring new information, storing that information, or using that information. The result of most tests is the identification of one style, a composite of styles used for all these activities. The composite style may not be the style to which the teacher needs to teach at any given juncture in the educational program. Moreover, with students of high school age or older, the use of such tests is sometimes mistaken as a "contract" to provide individualization beyond that possible, needed, or even desirable.

These tools are basic understandings of possible permutations in the learning processes that allow teachers to observe and ascertain how their students are learning. They provide teachers with the strategies and the tactics needed to develop a battle plan for winning the style wars in their classrooms, but teachers must write their own operations orders. Only they know all the details needed to reach their objective.

☞ *All teachers can teach all students.*

Sometimes, teachers have told me, "I know all about learning styles, and they don't work." My response is usually that something is terribly wrong with this statement. First, no one knows "all about" learning styles. We are still learning new things every day about how students learn and about how learning styles fit into the memory and learning picture. Second, paying attention to how students learn does help students learn more effectively. Unfortunately, much theory has been sold to school districts in the name of learning styles without the means of implementing the theory usefully. Sometimes practitioners of learning styles will propose a conceptual framework, suggesting that if teachers will simply teach to those several styles, all students will be "covered" and therefore, all students will learn. This is the same process as throwing paint against the wall and about as effective. Many optimistic teachers have become bitterly disappointed when these models that "cover" all the students with some paint fail to paint any one student in full.

Learning-styles systems that promise seven-stop shopping miss the mark. In such systems, most students are working out of their preferred style most of the time, as teachers break the teaching hour into segments, with each segment presented in a different style. Furthermore, selecting only a few styles out of the dozens that exist means that the style that is causing the classroom conflict may be overlooked. McCarthy's 4-MAT system, for example, focuses on two sets of cognitive styles (McCarthy, 1987, 1997) and systems proposed by Gregorc (1982), Hermann (1983, 1984), Kolb (1984), and Torrance (1980; Torrance, Reynolds, Riegel, & Ball, 1977) on one set of cognitive styles (see Chapter 3 for a discussion of all of these styles).

Giving teachers a prescribed set of activities that teaches to all the styles in a given system can be a step in the direction of reaching more students, but it will not result in teaching the whole class. Moreover, such ready-made lessons contain the subtle insult that teachers are not capable of developing individualized strategies for teaching all students. I believe that teachers *are* capable of this level of sophistication. In fact, I believe that *all* teachers are capable of this level of sophistication. *To provide teachers with yesterday's bronze tools rather than today's more sophisticated laser instruments does them a disservice.*

☞ *Learner profiles, used in teaching the whole class, describe how students learn.*

Teachers who have used a specific learning-styles system may need to reorient themselves to a different concept of learning styles if they are to teach the individual students in their classes (Hatch, 1997). This concept looks at learner profiles as complex descriptions of how each student learns.

Developing learner profiles is not new. As early as the late 1970s the National Association of Secondary School Principals (NASSP) advocated a learner profile approach (Jenkins, 1989-1990; Kiernan, 1979): understanding the range of learning styles that exists and how the resultant profile can explain how any given student learns best. That knowledge is the most valuable information that a teacher can have in teaching successfully. It is not easy or simple work, but it is feasible work.

With time, practice, and experience, the effort becomes much simpler because each teacher builds his or her own system for evaluating and implementing knowledge of learner differences. Over time, observational skills can be honed to the point that it only takes a few minutes for a teacher to determine the learner profile of each student in the classroom, and that can be done while teaching.

☞ *Parents can understand their children.*

Learner profiling need not lie in the exclusive domain of teachers. Parents who understand how learning occurs can prepare learner profiles on their children using similar techniques. They can adapt the information in this book to understand the uniqueness of each of their children and use that information to help their children complete their homework more successfully and to discuss their children's learning needs more articulately with their children's teachers. It is fair for them to expect their children's teachers to account for the learner profiles in their classrooms.

☞ *Students can understand themselves.*

With the help of teachers and parents who understand learner profiling, students can adapt the information in this book to understand their own strengths and weaknesses as learners (see Chapter 6). They can use that information to become better learners, to develop learning-style flexibility, and to identify and resolve classroom conflicts between their own preferences and the learning-style preferences of their teachers. We call this learner empowerment. Empowered learners do not need their teachers to account for learner profiles; they are able to take care of themselves.

WHAT'S WRONG WITH THESE STUDENTS?

A fact of life that most people wrestle with, successfully and unsuccessfully, sometimes for years, is the knowledge that things are not always what they seem to be. The same is true in the classroom. Students are not always what they seem to be, and their behaviors do not always stem from the sources from which they seem to stem.

The four situations described here are all real examples of students who were not learning. For the behavior of each, there could have been several explanations.

In each case, the first set of explanations offered represents the typical responses given by teachers before the situations were explored in depth. These explanations fall into at least six categories:

1. The student was not capable of learning better.
2. The student was not applying sufficient effort.
3. The student was learning disabled (LD).
4. The student was physically disabled.
5. The student had emotional, social, or home problems.
6. The student was hyperactive or had attention deficit disorder.

All of these can be accurate explanations and should be explored, along with learning-styles issues. All of these are also frequently assumed to be the correct answer, and teachers look no further, to the detriment of their students. A look at what lies behind each of these responses can help us to understand why they should not be both the first and last suggestion.

Response 1, the student is not capable of learning better, places the student into a position of not ever being asked to learn better. *Chances are that if the problem were removed, the student could learn better.*

A related, easy explanation of poor performance is to assume that the student has limited talent in this particular subject matter and, therefore, more practice will be needed. Teachers who make this assumption often simply exhort students to "study harder." (Although this is a common exhortation, no one usually explains what the word, *harder*, means in conjunction with studying—longer? more often? in more effective ways?) Exhortation to study harder provides the student with absolutely no good advice; empowering the student through strategy training is a much better answer (see Chapter 6).

Response 2, the student is not trying hard enough, certainly removes the onus for teaching from the teacher. However, that's not going to help the student. *If the student really is not investing an appropriate level of effort, there usually is a reason for this, and ferreting out the cause is worth the time and effort.*

A corollary is the response that the student simply did not prepare for the class or the test. A better response would be to look at *how* the student prepared for the class or the test and determine whether the strategies used were appropriate (Chapters 3 through 6 discuss such situations).

Yet another related response is that the student is unmotivated. In reality, most students often are initially motivated. However, the more frustrating they find classroom learning experiences, the more demotivated they become. Lack of success leads to demotivation, which leads to lack of interest. Students who are successful learners rarely become demotivated, disinterested, and troublemakers. Observation can confirm whether students are disinterested and not listening. What is each student doing during classroom activities? Taking notes? Doodling? Daydreaming? Talking? Listening? Making a puzzled face? Asking questions?

Response 3, the student is learning disabled, is similar to Response 1. The expectation is that the student will not learn better, so at best, the student is not asked to learn better, and at worst, the student is placed into a program with lower expectations. Students who fail to learn to read rapidly are at risk for special education placements. So are students who fail to learn to calculate rapidly. In a society that puts special emphasis on the ability to work rapidly, students who take a long time to complete tests and in-class assignments are often thought to be learning disabled. In such cases, the "problem" may simply be a mismatch between the tempo of the teaching and the tempo of the response (see the discussion of reflective learners in Chapter 3). *Assessments for LD placements are often based on a student's ability to learn in the same way as other students, not on the generic ability of the student to learn.* Thus, the formal assessment confirms the classroom teacher's informal assessment, but neither may be accurate. Bandler (1985) looks at LD determinations somewhat differently than do most educators:

> "Learning disabilities," "minimal brain dysfunction," "dyslexia," or "educational handicaps" . . . are very important-sounding words, but what they all describe is that *the teaching isn't working.*" (p. 125)

Even where students are learning disabled, lowering expectations is less helpful than maintaining expectations and changing the conditions, teaching, or support to enable students to meet the higher expectations.

Response 4, the student has an intervening physical problem, is one that tends to be overlooked. The student who cannot hear well is not likely to answer oral questions well. The student who cannot see well is not apt to be a good reader. The underlying physical cause needs to be eliminated. Physical handicaps, however, are another issue. Often, the assumption is that a person who cannot walk also cannot think. Making this correlation often results in accommodations well beyond those that are needed or that are beneficial.

Response 5, the student has social, emotional, or home problems, is a reality. However, this response is too often used as an excuse to exempt students from learning. History shows that external problems can and will be set aside in the classroom as a result of school success. *Successful students are rarely attracted into anti-social behaviors*, and self-esteem developed in the classroom can often cushion blows to self-esteem from outside the classroom. Every teacher has seen instances of this.

Response 6, the student is hyperactive (a neurological condition whose symptom is uncontrollable activity that interferes with learning, with interpersonal interactions, and with daily life) or suffers from attention deficit disorder (inability to focus or attend for more than a very short time), is a very typical response to highly active students. Certainly, there are very real cases of hyperactivity that are resolved via medication. However, the real cases may be far less common than the number of students currently being treated as if they were hyperactive (McGuinness, 1985). Parents and teachers should both be aware that *"guessing" at a diagnosis of hyperactivity and medicating is a crude approach from the past* that is still the most prevalent way of dealing with hyperactivity. When the presence of hyperactivity is a question, then more sophisticated means, such as brain-wave tests, can be used to determine whether a child is hyperactive, very active, or a kinesthetic learner (D. Davis, personal communication, January 1995).

In each of the case studies below, the above traditional explanations were incorrect; the "problem" was a matter of conflict between the learning style of the student and the teaching style of the teacher, the orientation of the curriculum, or the learning styles of the student's peers. These students come from a variety of states and school districts across the United States. Teachers from foreign countries who have used these case studies frequently find similarities between these students and their own students.

◆ *McCorkle: Hooligan? Disinterested? Lazy? Victim?*

Third-grader Mac had moments of sheer brilliance in class. His homework was nearly always perfect—when he completed it. The work he did in class was among the very best. His memory on tests was phenomenal. However, from time to time he showed up without his homework done or with the wrong pages done. He claimed to have "forgotten" what he was supposed to do? Why was Mac's memory so fickle?

Some teachers have suggested that Mac was a hooligan. Was he? His behavior in class did leave much to be desired. However, Mac had not always been a hooligan but he had always had homework problems. Therefore, the chance that Mac was just a "bad apple" was unlikely.

Mac's teacher complained that Mac was disinterested in schoolwork, and she was correct. However, disinterest was not causing his difficulties; it was the result of his difficulties. After constantly being reprimanded for poor performance for diligent work, Mac began to care less. After being accused of having a bad attitude, Mac began to develop one. Assuming that the problem lay in Mac's attitude made the teacher overlook the real cause of Mac's troubles.

Mac's teacher also complained that he did not study hard enough. Perhaps sometimes he did not. He certainly started to give up after months of being reprimanded. When he did his homework conscientiously, he was often told he had completed the wrong assignments or the wrong problems on the page. Why would he want to study more, when the result was the same regardless of effort?

History ultimately showed that a learning-style conflict was at the root of Mac's classroom wars. Mac was a visual learner; he needed to see in order to learn, but nearly all homework assignments were presented orally. When Mac did not write down the assignment accurately, he would turn in fully completed homework *as he had written it down.* The teacher did not understand why the homework completed did not match the assignment given and assumed that Mac was not trying.

To complicate matters, Mac had a personality type that required a sense of competence for a healthy self-image. Because he received a near-constant stream of negative input about his competence from his teacher, his self-esteem suffered. A vicious downward spiral was in effect. This was of no benefit to Mac, his teacher, or even his peers, who had to deal with his temper outbursts.

The tip-off lies in the unevenness of Mac's performance. Examining the conditions of poor performance versus the conditions of good performance produces a uniquely uniform graph. Classwork was uniformly good. Answers were uniformly correct on the homework, but the homework itself was sometimes from the right pages and sometimes from the wrong pages. Homework assigned in written form came back accurately prepared. Homework assigned in oral form was inconsistent in accuracy. *By missing the style war raging in the classroom, the teacher unwittingly exacerbated the problem.*

Mac's case creates sympathy on the part of a number of teachers who hear it. One of the most responsive reactions to Mac's predicament was a comment that often, homework tracking is equated with "responsibility training" and that maybe Mac is a good case for not placing roadblocks where they are not needed (J. Leaver, personal communication, March 28, 1997).

◆ What is Rory's story? Bad boy? Hyperactive? Victim?

Rory, an eighth grader, was a real plague in the classroom. His legs were always bouncing and his eyes dancing. In physical education classes, his energy was appreciated, and he received excellent grades. In his academic classes, however, his grades varied from day to day. His highest grades were in shop, followed surprisingly by Spanish. His math grades rose and dipped from topic to topic; he especially liked pregeometry topics, although there was the usual clatter of pencil dropping, protractor tapping, and noisy compass swirling, not to mention the five-times-an-hour trek to the pencil sharpener. After being placed on medication for hyperactivity, the leg bouncing, noisy math lessons, and pencil-sharpening trips eased considerably. Rory now seemed much more a part of the quiet, diligent group of students in this class. However, his grades did not improve. Even though he actually completed much more written work, his test scores were lower, especially in the classes in which he had received the highest grades. His best subjects remained his best subjects and his worst subjects his worst. Did Rory need more medicine, or was there more to Rory's story?

The immediate thought in trying to solve Rory's problems was that the amount of medication was insufficient. If a little did a little good, then a lot should do a lot of good. The oddity between completing more work and receiving lower test grades should have led someone to understand that there was not a clean link between medication and learning performance. Obviously, the answer was not in medication. The question, of course, is, Was the answer ever in medication?

Rory could well have been hyperactive, and if the medicine did calm him, it may be that perhaps he was. But hyperactivity was clearly not the full answer in terms of his learning difficulties because his grades went down, not up, after being put on medicine.

One of Rory's teachers finally realized that Rory was a kinesthetic learner. When he was presented with physical activities associated with the learning of new ideas, he understood and remembered remarkably better than at any other time. She tested out her theory a number of times, and it proved true every time. She had to wonder whether medication could have been avoided had someone earlier realized that Rory was a kinesthetic learner and involved him more deeply in the learning process.

Kinesthetic learners are frequently mistaken for hyperactive students. Their need to store and recall via physical activity is often interpreted as the inability to control their own activity. Furthermore, when they do not receive input via physical activity (and they rarely do), they often fidget or find some kind of physical activity which they can do to somehow deal with input that is being presented in a nonpreferred form. This activity is often interpreted as the inability to sit still, that is, as hyperactivity. With kinesthetic learners, learning needs via physicality are usually ignored in favor of some kind of therapy or medication that calms their behaviors.

The tip-off in Rory's case is the lack of improvement in his performance when treated for hyperactivity. His teacher, once cued in, noticed many other things. When he was taught via action, he remembered best. When he was taught via sight or ear, he remembered least.

Before medicating Rory, someone should have checked for a kinesthetic learning style. If Rory is still on medication, someone should evaluate him for the possibility of taking him off medication. It does not seem to be of great value in his academic work!

◆ *Eliza: Disinterested? Poor note-taker? Victim?*

Eliza was always a good student. She really enjoyed her community college courses, until one day she just could not seem to get a handle on one of her psychology classes. This especially perturbed her because she was a psychology major. Well-organized by nature, she just could not figure out how to organize her notes from the class; they made little sense to her, once she returned to the dormitory. She read the book chapters in advance and could follow the lecture itself, but by the time she returned home, her notes were meaningless. This would not have been so disturbing if the teacher had not put questions on the test that included material covered in class only. As a result, Eliza's 4.0 grade point average was in danger of falling by the wayside. What was happening with Eliza?

The first thought that comes to mind when an otherwise good student starts to fail in any given class is that some aspect of the course does not attract him or her. On the contrary, Eliza really enjoyed the subject matter and did well on all the test questions that were taken from the book. In class, she was able to hold her own in discussions with other students. Her only difficulty appeared to be taking notes.

Clearly, Eliza did need assistance with note-taking in this class. However, why would this be the case, when her note-taking skills in other classes and in previous psychology classes had served her just fine? Obviously, the whole answer did not lie only in the way in which she took notes.

In reality, Eliza was a victim of a conflict in styles, although this may well have been the first time that she got caught in a style war. She had mainstream learning styles, the styles for which most textbooks are written. Not surprisingly, most of her school experiences were with teachers who had mainstream teaching styles, because these are the styles that are generally rewarded and, therefore, are the styles of most people who are attracted to teaching. Eliza had become accustomed to sequential, or linear, presentations of new information. She was used to "step 1" being presented before "step 2." She was used to information being written on the blackboard from left to right, from top to bottom, from beginning to end. However, she had landed in the classroom of a professor who imposed nonlinear, idiosyncratic structure on new information. The professor moved around the room and wrote on the part of the blackboard near wherever he happened to be standing. He went through principles (and wrote them down) in whatever order they happened to come to mind by association and diversion. For Eliza to succeed in this class, she would have needed to develop a method of superimposing sequential structure on the random fallout that she was simply copying straight into her notebook.

The tip-off to Eliza's problem was in the discrepancy in her answers on the test, depending on whether questions related to the classroom or the textbook. Eliza's good note-taking in other classes also indicates that her note-taking difficulties must have something to do with the teacher's lecture characteristics.

◆ Heather: Learning Disabled? Superhuman? Victim?

Heather was a pretty good student, but she was physically handicapped. Therefore, school administrators frequently suggested placing her into special education. Because she maintained a grade point average that was slightly above average, no one could force her into special education until seventh grade when she started to fail mathematics. Quick to spot a "learning disability," school administrators insisted that Heather be placed in special education classes for her math disability. Once placed in a learning disabled (LD) classroom, Heather's grades fell rapidly, and her mathematics scores rarely rose above 10 to 20 points out of 100 on any quiz, test, or homework assignment. Had Heather reached her peak? Was she now destined to permanent placement in LD classrooms?

Because Heather was physically disabled, administrators expected her to be learning disabled also. Unfortunately, sometimes expectations are self-fulfilling. However, in Heather's case, there was no learning disability. Once her seventh-grade mathematics problems were resolved, Heather returned to regular education for the remainder of her high school and college years.

Closely related to the incorrect assumption that physically disabled students are learning disabled is the assumption that physically disabled students only keep up with their peers through superhuman efforts. It was not surprising to hear the suggestion that Heather could just not keep up the pace of intensive study. As a matter of fact, Heather's study habits were no better and no worse than those of her peers. Mathematics, however, had suddenly become very difficult for her.

In reality, Heather was a victim of a conflict in learning styles. Heather required context for learning. She needed to see mathematics in a meaningful, applied way. The elementary school textbooks had used pictures and word problems. These things made sense to Heather. The seventh-grade textbook presented mathematical concepts as rules and exercises. This meant that Heather had to perform calculations and draw graphs without knowing the purpose behind them. The teacher tried to help by breaking down the concepts and calculations into ever-smaller pieces of information—precisely the opposite of what Heather needed.

Heather's family hired a math tutor from a local college. He did not use the materials provided by the school but took examples of graphs from the newspaper with full articles attached. He asked Heather to collect her own data, evaluate it, write it up, and prepare a graph to go with her "article." Within two months, Heather's math skills were on a level with others in her class.

The tip-off to Heather's problem came from the sudden drop in performance in just one subject area. Had administrators not been poised to move Heather into special education at the first sign of any trouble, someone might have noticed how radically the orientation of the textbook and class differed from Heather's learning-style preferences.

One of the signs of the times has been the frequency with which students are labeled "learning disabled" and passed on to a special education teacher, even through the filter of assessment batteries. In many cases, these students can perform as well as peers in the classroom if their learning styles are taken into consideration. *A nonmainstream learning style should not be considered a disability.* Unfortunately, the number of students in LD classrooms with nonmainstream styles is evidence that it is. (Fortunately, graduate schools of education now promote the full inclusion of students with disabilities in the regular education classroom. Emphasis is on altering curriculum to accommodate learning styles [B. Pemberton, personal communication, April 1997]. It may take some time for this information to cause a countrywide change, but at least there is hope. Community colleges have been a bright spot in this respect for several years. A number of community college counselors, versed in learning-style theory, have focused on learner empowerment issues with disabled students, opening more opportunities in higher education than were previously available to them.)

There is nothing inherently "wrong" with any of these students. However, in many programs they might be counseled for lack of effort. In other cases, they might be labeled learning disabled, mentally retarded, or emotionally disturbed and remanded to programs that teach less information *in the same style* as the classrooms in which they were performing poorly, and a lifetime cycle of failure might be initiated. *The astute teacher asks not what is wrong with my student but what is impeding my student's ability to learn.*

The cases presented here are the "easy" cases. With students who really are learning disabled, the complication can be much greater. First, the learning disability itself can get in the way of determining whether the problem is a learning-style conflict or something else. Second, the available research implies that learning-disabled students may be less flexible than other students (Lester, 1974; Naigle &Thwaite, 1979). Third, there is emerging evidence that indicates that perhaps many learning-disabled students have discontinuous learning styles. In other words, the learning style that they use for comprehension may differ from the learning style used for storage into memory and for recall from memory (Leaver, Jones, & Johnson, 1996). All these complications are discussed in further detail in the following chapters. It is possible to work with the complicated cases.

The first step is to determine whether a learning problem is due to learning-style preferences or to some other cause. The key to making this differentiation is to look for discrepancies. When things don't seem to add up—a good student takes a nosedive, someone is significantly better in one subject than another, medication does not have the expected effect—look for a learning-style conflict.

In short, students can learn. They may need support from lessons that accommodate their learning-style preferences. They may need help to understand their own learning processes and strategies for increasing their style flexibility. Teachers can help learners in these ways, leading them to a high point where they all learn and enjoy learning.

TAKING THE RISK

Can all teachers really reach all students most of the time? Can they really teach the whole class? After reading even part of the plethora of information available on learning styles, many teachers feel overwhelmed. The same feeling occurs after a week-long seminar on this topic. The effect is a little less pronounced when the seminar sessions are broken down into weekly or semiweekly meetings because teachers have a chance to try out the ideas a little at a time. I suspect the same feeling will occur as readers proceed through this book. Very likely, the question will arise: Can one person really do all this?

My answer is yes. I have seen many "one-persons" doing all this. Yes, all teachers really can teach the whole class. In fact, nearly everyone over the age of 8 can understand the concepts that lie behind this book. These concepts are not artificial constructs. They are known by everyone at some subconscious level.

When these concepts become conscious understandings, they seem overwhelming at first. In making concepts conscious, it becomes necessary to label them. It is the proliferation of labels that is overwhelming, not the understanding of the concepts or the teaching of the whole class. *Many good teachers have taught the whole class for many years intuitively.* (Chapter 6 describes one such situation.)

Today, we are more fortunate. We have keys to these concepts and keys to the students who populate our classrooms. People are complex structures, and many different keys are needed to unlock their mysteries. However, the mysteries can be unlocked one door at a time. Therefore, using one key at a time is okay. *Teaching the whole class need not be overwhelming if it is done one student and one key at a time.*

Looking at the task another way, the first step up the mountain trail is often the most difficult to take and, for new hikers, the most frightening. After the first step, the other steps begin to feel a little more familiar, and soon the path is comfortable. So it is with teaching the whole class. To try to implement all the ideas in this book concurrently can be daunting. My advice is to pick a specific subset of styles and start to accommodate student learning styles in that dimension. The icons that represent the various categories of learning styles provide a "trail" through the book for each style. Choose any one icon and ignore the others, until ready for a more difficult trail. Work with that dimension until comfortable with it. Then, add another dimension. And another. Or begin to empower students to style-shift and become more flexible learners one dimension at a time. Success at teaching the whole class—accommodating learner profiles and empowering learners—takes time, patience, and perseverance. No one can start the hike up the mountain at the top. A step at a time, however, takes every hiker there.

Along the way hikers will learn much about the trail, much more than I could put in a book. Every group of students is different; every teacher is different; every classroom interaction is different. The kinds of terrain one might meet along the trail can be shown in advance, but all of the different permutations of that terrain and the way the land, rocks, and vegetation will come together to make hiking easier or harder cannot be predicted, especially because each hiker will have different strengths in hiking. The same is true with academic classes. I can present the kinds of traits typically found in classes and those combinations that can make a journey easier or harder (and strategies to deal with the difficult spots). However, each teacher must do his or her own "hiking" (experimentation), and each will have to apply those strategies in unique ways as unique "terrain" (each new combination of students and materials) is encountered.

I hope this book can serve as a hiking staff for those just starting out on the trail—something on which to lean, something with which to probe, a means of defense. Likewise, the concepts (and, I hope, some of the aids, such as the checklists and the practice exercises) in this book may serve as resources for more experienced hikers as they make their way through new terrain and new challenges.

It is possible to make it to the top of the mountain. Others have done it. Many of them started with less information. Successful whole-class teachers find these others and hike with them. In stumbling, they reach out for collegial support. Once, in hiking a trail along Crimean cliffs, I slipped and dangled above sharp rocks in the Black Sea, held momentarily in place by the strong grip of a Ukrainian prison instructor. Had I been hiking alone, I might not now be writing this book, but fortunately a half-dozen colleagues came to my rescue. The same thing happens when I take intellectual and methodological "hikes" (i.e., risks). Colleagues always pull me back as I slip off the edge of a cliff. Teachers, even such independent types as introverted intuitive thinkers and accommodators, may find that they reach the top of the mountain more swiftly and more certainly when they seek and accept such collegial support.

In sum, the hike does not have to be made in 1 day, and the hike does not have to be made alone. What is essential is making the commitment, planning the route, getting prepared, and most important, taking the first step.

3

Styles and Profiles

This chapter is intended for those readers whose background in learning styles may be somewhat less comprehensive than they would like. Although there is not space enough here to include every style that has ever been suggested, I have described in some detail those styles and types that seem to create the greatest impediment to successful learning (admittedly based on my own experience, as well as the experience of my colleagues).

Although I have included information on instruments associated with various styles in Resource A, in my experience, the seemingly ad hoc estimates based on observation by skilled teachers are no less accurate than the spiffily-boxed instruments—and a lot faster. (My colleagues in psychology will likely disagree with me vociferously, but I stand my ground.) Estimates by observation are fairly easy to do. They require only the understanding of the construct being measured and observation skills. *Students reveal their learning style preferences by everything they do and do not do and by everything they say and do not say.* Most people most of the time act in accordance with their preferred learning styles. When we observe what they say, how they behave, and how they perform, we can begin to isolate their styles. Clues can be found in behaviors, performance, words, and feedback. Techniques for style identification include direct observation, feedback forms, written work, listening in on student conversations, and experimentation. For each learning style, I have included information on how to work with these clues and techniques.

Given the page limitations of this chapter, some readers may want more information than I am able to provide. I have identified additional reading for each of the specific styles. Readers are encouraged to go to the original sources for more in-depth information.

LEARNING STYLES: WHAT ARE THEY?

To date, no single definition of learning style is commonly accepted. The best definition, in my opinion, was offered years ago by Keefe (1979): "Learning styles are characteristic cognitive, affective, and physiological behaviors that serve as relatively stable indicators of how learners perceive, interact with and respond to the learning environment" (p. 4). Most researchers and teachers working in the area of learning styles tend to use this definition or one that parallels it.

As mentioned in Chapter 2, the system I use to impose order on the current chaos in the field of learning styles divides learning styles into four areas:

1. Environmental preferences
2. Sensory modalities
3. Personality types
4. Cognitive styles

Teacher accommodation of the latter three kinds of learning styles (described later) benefit students in all subjects and at all levels of study. Environmental preferences are much more difficult to accommodate. However, students and parents can implement adaptations at home that take into account environmental preferences.

Environmental Preferences

☞ *Physical surroundings and physiological conditions influence student learning.*

Students differ in the kinds of physiological conditions they need for optimal learning. These needs include biorhythms, digestion, and atmosphere, among other conditions. (As they say, "some like it hot, some like it cold...") Although teachers may not be able to make extensive adaptations for environmental preference, they can advise parents and students how to take advantage of environmental preferences rather than be captive to them. Typical parental guidance includes the following: (a) Sit up straight at the desk; (b) turn on the light so that you can see; (c) work in quiet corner of your room; (d) do your homework right after school and get it out of the way; and (e) if you are hungry, eat your snack quickly and get down to work. That is the conventional wisdom.

Example. I never had the sense to follow conventional wisdom. For that I was lucky, because conventional wisdom would not have worked for me. I recall my most effective periods of studying during my college days in the following way: Around 10:00 at night I would run into the library and check out an armful of books. I would carry them, along with a candy bar, a drink, and a blanket, to the rec room in the basement of the dorm, find a comfortable spot on the floor out of reach of the ping-pong players, and then hunker down to do some serious work. My best writing was done there, as were test preparation and preparation of oral reports. The oldest of eight children, I found being alone distracting. Studying made me hungry, and the night hours inspired me.

We now know that I am not simply weird. There are many others who learn best under these same conditions. Researchers have identified a number of environmental variables (Dunn, Dunn, & Pizzo, 1990). Some students do learn best with background music; others need silence. Some students need food; others are distracted by it. Some students need warmth; others want cooler temperatures. Some students need bright light; others need dim light. Some students need to be alone; others need to be in groups. Some students are early birds; others are night owls. Some students learn better sitting; others learn more effectively standing or prone.

Our schools are not organized to accommodate environmental preferences. Classes meet during the day. (Sometimes, there are two shifts, giving students the opportunity for afternoon study. However, the decision on who attends which shift is not made based on environmental preferences, although it could be.) Schools are quiet. They are brightly lit. Food is served between classes, not during classes.

Obviously, incorporating environmental needs into the classroom is quite complicated. However, some teachers have been able to do it in a number of elementary school programs (Carbo, 1997; Dunn, 1988, 1993; Hodgin & Wooliscroft, 1997; McCarthy, 1997). At higher levels of education—high school, college, graduate school—the task of incorporating environmental preferences is much more difficult because teachers do not have the same students all day, and they have limited control, if any, over the physical appearance, temperature, and layout of their classrooms. My advice to teachers is to *incorporate where possible, and where not possible, teach the students (and where appropriate, the parents) to make the adaptations for themselves, especially for homework and study time (and place).*

Identification. First, environmental needs must be identified. Several means for doing this exist. Interviews with students can be very revealing. Parents are also a good source of information. They are often painfully aware of differences among their children—those who from infancy were most active in the middle of the night, easily overstimulated by simultaneous input to more than one sense (T. Brazelton, personal communications, June-July, 1980), needed more clothing, or did not notice lack of light. The signs often are there as early as in the hospital nursery!

For more information on this topic, readers are invited to consult any of Dunn's books. Several are listed in the references.

Sensory Modalities

> ☞ *Students perceive and take in new information through different physical channels.*

The most common of the sensory modalities are visual, auditory, and motor learning styles. Each of these categories has two possible variants. Most people have a primary modality and a secondary modality through which they learn. Some even have a tertiary, and a few people have no preference—all the modalities work for them. *Difficulties in school arise when a student has a strong preference in one modality and learning is required through a different modality.*

Visual learners acquire new information through sight. Distinctions that are important to visual learners include brightness, size, color, saturation, distance, clarity, contrast, texture, frame, and symmetry (Bandler, 1985). Visual learners can be subdivided into two groups: **verbalist** (they see words) and **imagists** (they see pictures). For example, in learning English as Second Language (ESL) or a foreign language, verbalists use different strategies from imagists. If verbalists want to remember the French word *soleil* for the English word *sun*, they see the letters *s-o-l-e-i-l* in their heads. If imagists want to remember the word, *soleil*, they associate it with an image of the sun.

Example. Jacqueline, a very good fourth-grade visual learner, maintained a high average, except for arithmetic. State law required all students to recite basic facts aloud and calculate simple arithmetic problems in their heads, giving the answer to the teacher orally, and Jacqueline just simply could not do this. The teacher knew that knowledge was not the problem, because Jacqueline's tests, classwork, and homework were usually correct. So, what was going on? Jacqueline had memorized her math tables well, but she could not convert her visual memory of these facts into auditory memory. Jacqueline's mother ultimately resolved the problem. She noticed the discrepancy between Jacqueline's written and oral work and realized that Jacqueline needed to use visual strategies. She had Jacqueline visualize the problems as if they were written on the ceiling (yes, sometimes the answers *are* on the ceiling). When Jacqueline "wrote" the problems on the ceiling, she was able to "see" the answers underneath them. Overnight, she went from being unable to solve single-digit problems to being able to solve multiple-digit problems.

Auditory learners acquire new information through sound. Distinctions that are important to them include pitch, tempo, volume, rhythm, timbre, and resonance (Bandler, 1985). Auditory learners can be further divided into two groups: **aural** (they learn by listening to others) or **oral** (they learn by talking and hearing themselves). Aural learners need auditory input; when they read instructions, they often become lost because their patience for visual input is limited. On the other hand, oral learners need auditory output. As children, they usually frustrate both parents and teachers because they just cannot keep quiet. Once parents and teachers learn to listen to oral learners, they realize that these learners are the easiest to understand because they tell whoever is listening just what is going on in their minds.

Similarly, students who practice spelling words aloud at home and then take a written test at school often receive a poor test score (D. Bolduc, personal communication, March 31, 1997). Just as Jacqueline could not convert visual knowledge to an auditory system, these auditory learners may be unable to convert auditory knowledge (the practice) to a visual system (the test). For this, they may need to learn phoneme encoding strategies (see Chapter 6).

Example. Frances was a typical auditory learner. Her oral reports were wonderful, but her written reports were atrocious—full of errors. "Write the way you talk," her parents advised. She did write that way. Because written and oral speech have different characteristics, she needed to develop visual strategies for reading, so that she could later reproduce the same information in writing accurately. Too often, she subvocalized, slowing her reading and derailing her thought.

Motor learners acquire new information through movement. Distinctions that are important to them include frequency, pressure, duration, and intensity (Bandler, 1985). Motor learners can be subdivided into two groups: **kinesthetic** (they learn through the use of gross motor muscles) or **mechanical** (they learn through the use of fine motor muscles).

Example. An example of a motor learner is someone who learns telephone numbers by dialing them. Often, such a learner cannot tell someone else the number without picking up the phone (or an imaginary phone) and pretending to dial.

Identification. The first step to accommodating a modality is to determine each student's preference. Identification can be accomplished by modality tests (see Resource A).

Identification can also be made through observation. As an initial model for determining preferred modalities through observation, let's use me. Here is how I prepare a lesson plan (or outline a book). If possible, I walk and write down my ideas along the way, organizing them later. If I am at home, I play the piano, stopping periodically to write down ideas. Once my ideas are on paper, I enter them into the computer, organizing them as I do so. What type of learner am I? Anyone who thinks anything except kinesthetic needs to reread the preceding paragraphs! Did I have trouble sitting still in school? Yes! Is this a difficult style for an academic? Yes! For an educational administrator? Yes, yes! I survive classroom environments because I have a strong visual secondary preference and because I have developed style flexibility. We can even tell that I have a secondary visual preference, if we observe what I do when I am not moving: I read. When I lecture, I use many visual aids and paper handouts because I feel the need for them myself. This is another clue that I have a visual secondary preference.

This same approach can be used in determining students' preferred sensory modality. Let's take a look at some theoretical students, who have been asked to write an essay about the first day of spring, and see how *they reveal their sensory preferences in writing*. The chart below shows how three students, each with a different modality preference, might describe the same scene:

A bluejay appeared outside my window this morning. A glimpse of its broad, blue wings spread under the early rays of the sun caught my eye in the dim ether between sleep and wakefulness. I watched as it landed on the barren ground, its head cocked, and its eyes seeking out anything that it might see in the grass for breakfast.	The lilting song of a bird rang in my ears this morning, its melody waking me gently from quiet sleep. I heard the soft folding of its wings, as it plopped onto the quiet earth, cocking its head, and listening for sounds in the grass—a potential breakfast.	A bird swept past my window this morning. The flash of light that slid over its wings as it glided past the window grabbed my attention, jolting me to full wakefulness. I walked to the window, just as it alit on the ground, its eyes darting across the grass in search of sudden movement —the slithering away of a potential breakfast.

Do modality preferences show up in these writings? Of course! Each learner expresses "reality" through the sense he or she uses to perceive and interpret it.

The visual learners "see" a picture, and they paint a picture (left column). Based on the visual learner's description, the reader can paint the same picture. The visual learner includes visual detail, such as color, hue, shape, image, and brightness. The nouns relate to sight: *glimpse, bluejay, rays*. The verb forms relate to seeing: *appeared, watched, seeking, see*. The bird is trying to find worms with its eyes.

The auditory learners "hear" the sounds of the scene, and they write a song (middle column). Based on the auditory learner's description, the reader can write a song, too. There is insufficient detail—no mention of color or surrounding objects—to paint a picture. The nouns relate to things that are heard: *song, melody*. The adjectives are musical: *lilting, soft, quiet*. The verb forms relate to hearing: *rang, heard, plopped, listening*. The bird is trying to find worms with its ears.

The motor (especially kinesthetic) learners feel the scene, and they relay the motions and the physical feelings associated with those motions (right column). Based on the kinesthetic learner's description, the best that the reader can do is to reenact the scene through action. Everything relates to movement. The nouns are associated with activity: *flash, wakefulness, movement, slithering*. The verb forms are all energetic actions: *swept, slid, gliding, jolted, walked, lit, darting*. There is a greater emphasis on verbs, as well as a greater quantity of verbs than in the other two essays; even some of the nouns are actually gerunds. The bird is poised to pounce.

Obviously, these samples have been constructed for instructional purposes. In real life, the preference may not be quite as obvious, but the clues are still there. Visual learners describe pictures that can be painted in glorious color and detail. Auditory learners describe music that can be written, sometimes with a cacophony of sound in the background. Kinesthetic learners describe actions, often leaving the reader feeling stressed or tired and rarely with any way of relaying the same information other than through reenactment.

Another way to determine modality preference, according to proponents of neurolinguistic programming (NLP), is to **watch students' eyes** (Jacobson, 1983). Visual learners look up, auditory learners to the side, and motor learners down when either recalling old information (eyes to the right) or creating new information (eyes to the left). In my experience, this "test" often does provide a clue to modality preference and can be used with other measurements fairly reliably, but as a stand-alone instrument, it is not accurate enough.

Using eye movements has inherent problems. There are more reasons than learning modality for how people move their eyes. Sometimes, there is a distraction that catches one's attention, and that distraction can be on the ceiling, out the window, or on the floor. Behaviors associated with cultural norms also dictate eye movements. Members of some Asian cultures, for example, look down out of deference; they are not all motor learners. In the United States, we believe direct eye contact to be a sign of honesty; we are not all auditory learners (and conversely, the kinesthetic learner who stares at the floor is not being impolite or dishonest). There are many reasons why someone's eye movements may not accurately reflect that person's modality. However, consistent eye movements while performing assigned academic tasks can provide a clue as to modality.

Another way to check for modality is to *listen to what students say*. After hearing verbal instructions, visual and motor learners invariably raise their hands and ask, "What are we supposed to do?" (Remember the line, "If I've told you once, I've told you a hundred times?" With visual and motor learners, one could tell them 200 times; they still may need the information in a modality which they can more readily process.) Likewise, after reading written instructions, auditory and motor learners are likely to ask, "What are we supposed to do?" In both cases, students may understand the input just fine on the "bottom-up" (word and sentence) level, but they are not processing it well on the "top-down" (general meaning) level. What they do not do—or process—signifies a nonpreferred modality.

Yet another way to determine student learning style is to *judge by their success in task completion.* Visual and motor-mechanical learners perform well on written tasks, auditory learners on oral tasks, and motor learners on performance tasks.

Sensory modalities have been researched for well over two decades. Readers are invited to consult Bandler (1985), Dunn (1992, 1993, 1996), and Griggs (1985).

Personality Types

> ☞ *The ways in which learners relate to other people and to the physical and intellectual world around them influence their learning.*

Interest in personality variables dates to the days of ancient Greece. Hippocrates posited four temperaments: sanguine (optimistic, energetic), choleric (irritable, impulsive), phlegmatic (calm, slow), and melancholic (moody, withdrawn; Itsines, 1996).[1] Today's personality types derive from the work of Jung (1971). The two most commonly used instruments are the Myers-Briggs Type Indicator (Myers & Briggs, 1976) and the Keirsey Temperament Sorter (Keirsey & Bates, 1988).

The Myers-Briggs Type Indicator (MBTI)

The MBTI describes 16 different personality types. These personality types come from the combination of traits found in four personality type domains. (Jung's psychological type model is a complex system, and the information provided below is not even the tip of the iceberg.)

Introversion-Extraversion, a continuum, is one of three domains suggested by Jung. In MBTI shorthand, introverts are identified by the letter I, and extraverts are identified by the letter E. According to Jungian typology, introverts' energy emanates from within; they lose energy in interaction with large numbers of people and tend to have a few close friends. After a party, where they have had to associate with many people on a superficial level, introverts often feel exhausted. Their interests, like their social relationships, tend to have depth. Extraverts gain energy from interaction with people. When alone, their energy dissipates. They tend to have a wide network of acquaintances. After a party, extraverts want to go to another party. Their interests, like their social relationships, tend to have breadth.

The lay terms *extroversion* and *introversion* do not fully coincide with the meanings attributed to the terms *extraversion* and *introversion* as used by Briggs-Myers (1980), Jung (1971), Keirsey and Bates (1988), and Myers (1993). In lay terms, extroverts are usually gregarious and introverts diffident. However, in the way these terms are used in personality type circles, shyness is not a factor. Both extraverts and introverts can be shy; both can be not shy.[2]

In a classroom, extraverts seek opportunities to interact with their peers. Introverts seek opportunities for independent work.

Example. The most vivid example of introvert-extravert differences that I recall occurred when I was working at the Foreign Service Institute. The computer laboratory used for course development was nearly filled one morning with introverted writers, all quietly typing away on their keyboards, when a very extraverted teacher came in to talk to me. As she crossed the threshold, she called out in a cheery, loud voice, "Hi, everybody!" None of the introverts responded.

Sensory-Intuitive differences in approaches to life form the second Jungian domain. In MBTI shorthand, sensing types are identified by the letter S, and intuitives are identified by the letter N. Sensory people focus on details, facts, reality, probabilities, and the here and now. They work with their five senses. To convince sensing types, one usually must present them with empirical results and other forms of hard evidence. Intuitive people focus on intuition, possibilities, and the future. They are comfortable working with their "sixth sense." To convince intuitives, one must inspire in them a "gut feeling" (forget the data—they are often suspicious of it and can find many ways to interpret the same information).

Example. An example of intuitive-sensing differences comes straight from today's movie screens in the interaction of Captain Kirk and Mr. Spock in the *Star Trek* series. Mr. Spock, the sensing type, is always looking for the details, the numbers, the data. Captain Kirk finds Mr. Spock's statistics mildly interesting, if not amusing, but puts his life on the line over and over again based on a hunch.

Thinking-Feeling differences comprise the third domain. In MBTI shorthand, thinkers are identified by the letter T, and feelers are identified by the letter F. Thinkers generally place principle over people. For thinkers, then, being fair is very important, as is being treated justly. Thinkers build systems and usually need to feel appreciated for their competence. Feelers, on the other hand, generally place people over principle. Rather than focusing on justice and fairness, feelers show compassion and want mercy. Feelers build relationships and usually need to feel appreciated for their efforts. For these reasons, style-aware supervisors motivate T employees by praising their work and withholding praise until they have accomplished something worthy of praise. (If they do otherwise, they may lose credibility with the T employees.) They motivate F employees by praising their efforts. Whereas T supervisors are still focused on a good product, they know the Fs will give it to them if they encourage their efforts right from the start. It is important to note here that the idea that only feelers experience emotions is widespread but inaccurate. Both feelers and thinkers experience emotions, but they express them in different ways. Feelers use words and touch; thinkers use actions and deeds.

Example. I once heard my daughter, a feeler, interpret this difference with unsettling clarity. Noticing that the feelings of her popcorn-loving brother, also a feeler, had been hurt, when I, a thinker, fended off what I would label a "kiss attack" by him, she told him, "You know, Mom really loves you, but she doesn't let you know that by lots of kissing; she lets you know that when she always checks to make sure that you have enough popcorn and buys more when it is low."

Judging-Perceiving differences were added by Myers and Briggs. In MBTI shorthand, judgers are identified by the letter J, and perceivers are identified by the letter P. Judgers tend to plan and to be decisive. Their need for closure makes them comfortable working to deadline. Typically but not always, they are mono-active, starting a new activity only after a previous activity has been completed (resulting in neat, organized offices and rooms). Perceivers are more likely to be adaptable and tolerant. Having a need for freedom and flexibility; they want to explore options before deciding on an action. They tend to be polyactive; due to simultaneous work on multiple projects, their rooms tend to be cluttered.

Example. I remember a series of meetings I had with the faculty of one department in the process of developing a new curriculum. The plan was to brainstorm the problems with the current curriculum during the first session (P work), then, based on the results, define a new curriculum during the second session (J work). Although I warned the Js in the group that they would feel a certain amount of discomfort during the first session, one could not contain himself after the first 90 minutes. Frustrated, he suddenly jumped up and nearly shouted, "Look, you're the expert; just tell us your opinion."

The MBTI combines these four domains into 16 personality types.[3] Their significance for the classroom is summarized briefly in the chart below.

TYPE	HOW THEY LIKE TO LEARN
ESFJ	cooperative groups
ESTJ	organization, clear instructions, deadlines
ENFJ	one-on-one or with peer groups
ENTJ	leading a group of peers in a project
ESFP	activity with a group and with choice
ESTP	games, negotiations, simulations
ENFP	real-life applications, projects
ENTP	analysis, invention, develop new procedure
ISFJ	manuals, assisting others
ISTJ	details, calculations
INFJ	plays, poetry, visual images, archetypes
INTJ	manipulation of theory, logical problems
INFP	creative writing, metaphor, impressionism
ISFP	practice, play, action, concretization
ISTP	outdoors activities, artwork
INTP	research, systematize, theorize

ESFJs (extraverted-sensing-feeling-judgers) are cooperative learners. As SJs, they listen to authority, and as EFs, they relate well to peers. They work happily in small groups, seeking praise and harmony.

ESTJs (extraverted-sensing-thinking-judgers) are administrators by nature. They organize things and learn best with clear instructions, overt organization, and deadlines. They seek utility.

ENFJs (extraverted-intuitive-feeling-judgers) are like the ESFJs in terms of being cooperative learners. Natural teachers, they enjoy assisting teachers in their work. They seek feedback on what others think and want.

ENTJs (extraverted-intuitive-thinking-judgers) are natural leaders, but more than one ENTJ in a group can be a natural disaster. They vie for leadership of the group. The ENTJ whose modality preferences and cognitive style needs are met can be a strong positive force in the classroom and an assist to the teacher. However, the ENTJ whose learning-style needs are not met can make everyone miserable with his or her defiance or acting out.

ESFPs (extraverted-sensing-feeling-perceivers), like other SPs, are often present in the classroom only physically. The ESFPs, because of their EF nature, are likely to join in group activities, especially if those activities are active. They tend to be friendly and popular, often earning their claim to fame through sports.

ESTPs (extraverted-sensing-thinking-perceivers) like hands-on activities in which they are required to think. For them, games, negotiations, and simulations represent ways to actively apply their thought processes with other students. They are natural problem-solvers.

ENFPs (extraverted-intuitive-feeling-perceivers) like activities that relate to real life. For them, applications of principles are more important than the learning of principles themselves. Projects have more meaning than exercises. They have great imaginations and are usually ready to help anyone in distress.

ENTPs (extraverted-intuitive-thinking-perceivers) enjoy complicated ideas and systems. They are entrepreneurs by nature. They enjoy analytically creative processes, such as evaluation, invention, and the development of new procedures.

ISFJs (introverted-sensing-feeling-judgers) are thorough and accurate in their schoolwork. Details neither attract nor repel them; they manage details. They like to pass on values, but they want to make sure that the methods they use for doing so are well-researched.

ISTJs (introverted-intuitive-thinking-judgers) are also characterized by thoroughness. Organization is a forte, and they are able to focus on a distant goal and march toward it, regardless of external distractions.

INFJs (introverted-sensing-feeling-judgers) work for the common good. Their work is usually quietly well-done. Whatever is needed to succeed is what they will do. They tend to be good students who display creativity in their work.

INTJs (introverted-intuitive-thinking-judgers) expect people and activities to have a purpose. They develop theories and build models. They follow classroom procedures if they find them useful. Like other NTs, they do not particularly consider a teacher to be an authority figure. Their ideas come from within, and they do not change those ideas simply because someone says that they are incorrect.

INFPs (introverted-intuitive-feeling-perceivers) prefer independent projects. They may be full of ideas, but they do not usually share these without prompting. They may appear oblivious to possessions or physical surroundings. In general, they are enthusiastic, loyal, and capable of independent work.

ISFPs (introverted-sensing-feeling-perceivers) need harmony and avoid disagreements. Socratic approaches puzzle them at best and frighten them at worst. Deadlines amuse them. Even when very talented, they are typically modest.

ISTPs (introverted-sensing-thinking-perceiving) are nature-lovers. They seek the natural world, are physical risk-takers, and often choose professions such as forestry and zoology. Many are artistic and combine their love of nature with artistic form, such as nature drawings and nature photography.

INTPs (introverted-intuitive-thinking-perceivers) focus on thought and ideas. They enjoy research, instinctively systematize the chaotic world around them, and theorize readily. They look for logic and expect intelligence from their teachers. They concentrate well and are good at remembering new information once they understand it. Their preference is for quiet, uninterrupted, independent work.

Some teachers (I suspect mostly those with a psychology background or interest) prefer the full MBTI system. Readers inclined to work with the full system are encouraged to seek assistance from colleagues working in this area.4

The Keirsey Temperament Sorter

For those preferring to wade, rather than to dive, into cold water, Dr. David Keirsey proposes a system that some teachers find easier to incorporate into lesson planning (Keirsey & Bates, 1988). My recommendation is to start with the Keirsey temperaments and work up to the MBTI, for which a fair amount of training and experience is required.

Keirsey and Bates (1988) define four temperaments: sensing-judging types (SJ), sensing-perceiving types (SP), intuitive-feeling types (NF), and intuitive-thinking types (NT). These are the combinations they have found to be most salient at school, at home, and in the workplace.

The **SJ**s (sensing-judgers), or "guardians," have a need for organization, rules, and order. These are the people who ensure that cultural values are passed from one generation to the next. They obey authority, and when they are in positions of authority, they expect obedience.

The **SP**s (sensing-perceivers), or "artisans," cannot be tied down. They have a need for freedom and choice. In many ways, SPs are fearless, especially in physical risk taking and, as a result, may seem "larger than life" at times. They often are artisans and artists in real life, and most have a strong affinity for nature.

The **NF**s (intuitive-feelers), or the "idealists," are involved in growth activities, enjoy developing relationships with other people, and are often flamboyant. They are "people people," emitting "warm fuzzies" and expecting them in return.

The **NT**s (intuitive-thinkers), or "rationals," put principles first, build systems, and question authority. NTs, who are frequently college professors but rarely K-12 teachers, must teach, even if they are not teachers. If they are in business leadership positions, they mentor and train middle managers. Ensuring that their subordinates have the opportunity to reach their full potential is important to NTs.

If we look at each of these types as different kinds of creators, here is what the distinction among the temperaments might look like:

WHAT THEY DO		HOW THEY APPLY IT
NT	Create Systems	ENTJ - get others to implement their systems ENTP - get others to buy their systems INTJ - write books about their systems INTP - invent systems that others may (not) use
NF	Create Friendships	ENFJ - support and nurture friends ENFP - influence and understand friends INFJ - empathize with friends INFP - sacrifice for friends
SJ	Create Order	ESTJ - administer organizations ESFJ - nuture organizations ISTJ - preserve organizations ISFJ - implement procedures for organizations
SP	Create Artistry	ESTP - play games ESFP - play with friends ISTP - play risky, physically challenging games ISFP - play music (or some form of the arts)

NT students want a "hands-off" approach, "figuratively and literally" (Keirsey & Bates, 1990, p. 152). They like to control their environment through understanding it. "Scratch an NT, find a scientist," claim Keirsey and Bates (1990, p. 64). As for teachers, NTs do not feel any particular need for them. They certainly do not consider them authority figures simply because they occupy a position of power. NTs frequently do not care what will be on a test or what a teacher considers important. Scholars by nature, they prefer to decide for themselves what to learn.

Example. Three years ago, I visited a physics class in which four boys were quickly convincing the teacher to change her occupation. Three were kinesthetic learners and SPs (see description below of SPs). They all sat together, encouraging each other to engage in any activity other than that conducted by the teacher. The fourth student was clearly an NT. The teacher expected students to copy down notes from the board. The NT did not. He doodled. He made it very clear that he was in control of the information that he took in. The SJ teacher (see the SJ description below), frustrated beyond patience, required him to stand up at the end of the class and summarize her lecture. This is always a dangerous tack to take with the NT. The student did precisely as he was asked—then he proceeded to analyze the (in)significance of what the teacher had presented!

The **NF** student is self-reflective and dedicated to growth and self-actualization. NFs want to establish rapport with their teachers, and they want to be noticed. They expect to like their teachers, and they want their teachers to like them. NF students want harmony with their peers as well. They strive to please and, to some extent, will adjust to the teacher's style or the styles of their peers.

Example. One teenage NF was accidentally registered for two social studies classes her freshman year. She stayed in both courses because she did not want to choose between the teachers and break off a relationship.

The **SJ** student wants to preserve tradition. They respect authority figures. SJs like to know what will be on the test so that they review what the teacher considers most important. The want deadlines in advance, policies, and explicit expression of expectations.

Example. When my older daughter, an SJ, was small, reacting to two non-SJ parents, she would frequently ask, "When can we have a real family?" meaning when would Mother stay home, when would supper be on the table at the same time every night, and when would the Christmas tree go up before January 1 and come down before July 4? A real family to her was one that respected social norms.

SP students want freedom and choice—and to be out of the classroom. More attracted to nature than to the barren classroom, they want to make things and to do things. Several SPs have informed me that their favorite school activity is recess.

Example. At a seminar that a colleague and I led for 100 K-12 educators in Russia four years ago, one school psychologist, Evgeni Khasan, sat isolated in the rear of the room. Quickly determining that he was an SP (and an introverted one at that), we ensured that the applied component of the seminar was of sufficient quantity to keep him involved much of the time and left him to his own devices for the rest of the time. Neither of us had any doubt that he was learning in his own way. Had we had any doubts, they would have been allayed at the end of the seminar, when he handed us a set of cartoon drawings—drawings that captured the very essence of each learning style so aptly that he may well have understood the content better than many of the other, more "involved" participants. (As an example, the drawing he did of the Keirsey temperaments is shown below.)

Identification. It may be easier to determine student personality types by first observing how personality types influence teachers' lesson planning. The lesson plans on the following pages are reconstructed from a faculty development seminar. I have collected examples of such lesson plans from many places in the United States and abroad. Wherever I have been, culture notwithstanding, SJs write the same kinds of lesson plans, and these lesson plans significantly differ from the lesson plans prepared by NTs, NFs, and SPs.

AN SJ LESSON PLAN

Students should arrive at the school early because we must take attendance and make sure that everyone has brought everything that they are supposed to have. Students will be paired with buddies. They will sit with them on the bus and stay together at all times. We will board the bus precisely at 8:00 and will leave the school parking lot no later than 8:10. We should arrive at our first stop no later than 8:30.

At the television station we will be met by the station manager who will escort students through the studio. If anyone must leave the group for any reason, permission must be obtained from one of the adult chaperones. Students are expected to be quiet and attentive at all times, except at times when the station manager indicates that it is permissible to ask questions. Following the tour, students will be permitted to listen to a show in progress. They should sit in reserved seats on the left side of the studio.

For lunch, we will walk to McDonald's across from the town park. The staff is expecting us at 12:30. Students should line up and order as a group. Students will be given 45 minutes for lunch and for rest needs. No one is authorized to leave the restaurant.

At 1:15 we will be met by the editor-in-chief at the newspaper office. He will escort students through the office, pointing out various aspects about publishing. Following the tour, students will be provided the opportunity to ask questions.

We will leave the newspaper office at 2:15 and arrive back at the school at 3:00. Students will return to their classrooms for home room and will be dismissed at the normal end of the school day at 3:10.

Note: Well-behaved students will receive a candy.

SJ teachers invariably prepare long, detailed lesson plans. This is in keeping with their "S" side, their focus on the present moment and all the physical details associated with it, and their fascination with facts, statistics, and numbers. Organization and order permeate the SJ lesson plan, regardless of topic or grade level. The words selected by the SJs give them away immediately: *should, expected, will, must, well-behaved.*

AN NT LESSON PLAN

The goal of this excursion will be a comparative analysis of the various media, focusing on the relative effectiveness of the various media for specific purposes. Students will undertake in-class projects, using various media to share information on a topic of their choosing. They will conduct the background research prior to the excursion. The excursion will provide them with insight into turning information into an effective production. We plan to have in-class discussions on this topic, following the excursion, and students can make an informed of media format for their own projects. When projects have been completed, students will have the opportunity to provide feedback on the relative value of the excursion for producing a good product.

NT lesson plans are usually shorter than those of SJ teachers, partly because NTs do not focus on all the details but rather on the general purpose and goal. NTs want students to learn, and they want that learning to come from within the students. Their lesson plans are filled with ways to create learning. They are less concerned with whether students arrive on time for the bus and bring the right clothes than that they prepare in advance and bring the right information in their heads. The kinds of words they use include *goal*, *opportunity*, *research*, *informed*, and so on.

Only once in having NT seminar participants present their lesson plans did I encounter a group of NT teachers (in this case, academicians from the Belarus Academy of Sciences) who did not mention the word *goal*. Quite surprised by this, I nevertheless said nothing and moved on to the next group of participants. I was still puzzling over this oddity when I saw a piece of paper being passed from row to row. The folded paper eventually reached me. It was from the leader of the NT group, and on it was written the following words: " We forgot to mention the most important thing: the goal of this lesson. . ."

AN NF LESSON PLAN

This will be a fun day for the students. They have been cooped up in classes for too long. The excursion will provide them with a new, personalized experience, related to the media topics that they are studying in class.

In class, students are working in cooperative groups. These groups will stay together for the field trip. Since these groups were not selected through normal friendship channels, the field trip will allow students to get to know the others in their cooperative group better and perhaps foster easier working relationships after the trip.

Students will be able to visit a television station and newspaper. At each place, they will be able to see shows in action and to talk to personnel working there at length. They will be able to see the working relationships of the personnel in each place and the teamwork that goes into putting together a show or issue of the paper.

After the trip, they will prepare group projects, using the information that they have gained from the field trip. They will emulate the same working relationships that they observed on the trip. The projects will be shared with the class by each group.

NF lesson plans focus on group and interpersonal relationships. (Sometimes, groups of NF teachers, working with colleagues they have never before met, do not complete a lesson plan during a seminar session—they are too busy getting to know each other!) The need for harmony, rapport, and collective work is clear throughout many NF lessons. The lesson plan invariably includes interpersonal work; here, the teachers are planning to have students interview media personnel, an interpersonal activity. The length of NF lesson plans is usually shorter than those of SPs or SJs, because, like the NT, the NF does not dwell on detail. The words of NFs quickly identify their personality type: *fun, cooperative, group, friendship, shared, working relationship*.

AN SP LESSON PLAN

This excursion will allow the students to have some fun and experience how the media works. In planning, students can use the map skills from their social studies classes to select the route. Students will be divided into three committees by type of media: television, radio, and newspaper. Each committee selects what to visit. Students may choose to talk to personnel, tour facilities, or watch programs in progress. The establishments have promised to provide students with take-home mementos.

Students are asked to come attired in comfortable clothing and bring a sack lunch, which they can eat on the bus, at the station, or in a nearby park. The bus will be here at 8:00. Therefore, students are asked to be here sometime earlier than 8:00. We will return to the school before the end of the school day.

SP teachers reveal their need for freedom by providing it to their students. They offer choices in just about anything—preparation for the field trip, conduct of the field trip, lunch, and a rather "loose" timing of the return. Their sensing natures do focus on details, and their lesson plans tend to be more in-depth and longer than those of NTs. They also focus on hands-on activities and the development of skills (e.g., use of maps). The words they select identify them as SPs: *choice, recommended* (rather than *required*), *select, experience.*

Although observation can tell us much and, in general, I clearly prefer it to testing, the MBTI test for personality types is reliable, has been well-validated over a period of time, and is inexpensive (see Resource A). There are a number of versions, and some are short enough to be taken and scored quite quickly. In this case, unless a teacher is very skilled at observation and understands personality types very well, the test results may be more accurate than the observation.

For more information on personality theory, readers might turn to Jung (1971). A wide array of books on the MBTI exists. Some authors whose writing is accessible for teachers just starting out include Lawrence (1993) and Kroeger and Thuesen (1988). The only book on Jungian-based temperaments, as far as I know, is Keirsey and Bates (1988); an updated edition is in progress. In some localities, MBTI discussion groups meet regularly.

Cognitive Styles

> ☞*The ways in which people perceive and process*
> *information affect how they learn.*

Cognitive styles refer to thinking processes, a complex set of actions that takes place in the mind. To think, intake of information must first occur, followed by processing, storage, and reconstruction of that information, as well as the generation of unique thought. Cognitive styles shape one's way of perceiving, processing, and organizing the world (Claxton & Murrell, 1987; Cornett, 1983; Entwhistle, 1981; Hashway, 1992; Lewis, 1991; Reiff, 1992; Saracho, 1988; Solomon, 1989). According to Messick and Associates (1976):

Cognitive styles bear on the how—on the manner in which behavior occurs... with the emphasis upon process . . . [They] differ from abilities in their breadth of coverage and persuasiveness of application. . . They appear to serve as high-level heuristics that organize lower-level strategies . . . They function in part as controlling mechanisms determining an individual's characteristic . . . impulse, thought, and behavioral expressions. (pp. 6-9)

A great many systems have been developed to explain differences in cognitive processing. New systems appear on a regular basis. In this book, we will discuss only the better-known ones.

It really does not matter which systems we use. *Teaching the whole class means looking at each student and seeing how that one student learns, then considering that student's needs in conjunction with the learner profile of the entire class (class profile).* The description of one student learning is highly individualized. Usually, the cause of the conflict that is preventing success in school can be identified by one of the well-known systems of learning styles. However, the problem could be something else, and teachers need to be aware of those possibilities as well, such as a learning-styles domain not presented here, affective variables, motivation, physical health, real learning disabilities, and outside pressures.

Global-Particular Differences

One of the most significant cognitive style differences, in my experience, is the holistic (global) and discrete (particular) approaches to learning. Frequently in learning-styles literature, the terms *global* and *analytic* have been used to refer to opposing learning styles. This has created a serious difficulty in learning-styles application. Recent work has developed a profile of 10 style dimensions associated with what have been previously called "global" and "analytic" processing, labeled for now the "Ectenic-Synoptic Construct" (Ehrman & Leaver, 1997).[5] In this construct, analytic is not the opposite of global; the opposite of global is particular, and the opposite of analytic is synthetic (see discussions below of these differences).

Global processing attends to gestalts and the "big picture," is aware of "forests," and focuses on overall meaning first (Ehrman & Leaver, 1997). These students try to put meaning to whatever they are doing, but they may miss some of the details in so doing. If they miss enough details, the meaning that they "invent" can stray quite far from reality. These tend to be the students who are accused of having their "heads in the clouds." Actually, depending on their personality type, global students can be very well-grounded. Sensing types who are globals (global-sensing is not a contradiction in terms) are very much focused on reality. The critical element is that for a global learner, the big picture is almost always the center of focus.

Example. When my children were young, getting four children ready for school while working full-time took its toll on a global learner who paid scant attention to details. One morning, I had all four washed, dressed, breakfasted, and standing in line with backpacks 15 minutes early! I dressed quickly and headed off to the bus stop on the nearby main thoroughfare. As I arrived, a kind lady looked at me and asked, "Haven't you forgotten something?" A quick inventory revealed that I had my purse, briefcase, shoes . . . "What about your skirt?" she asked.

Students who display **particular processing** are attentive to discrete items and details. They are aware of "trees," rather than the forest. They see the form first and the general meaning second (Ehrman & Leaver, 1997). Sometimes the details become important to them independently of any relationship to larger concepts, creating a different kind of difficulty.

Example. Covey (1990), paraphrased here, gives an excellent example of particular behavior (although his intent in reciting the story is something quite different). According to this story, a work crew is chopping down trees, cutting a path through the forest. They work long and hard, and toward the end of the first day, the boss sends one worker up a tree to check on the progress the crew has made. The worker surveys the scene from the tallest tree and calls down to his fellow workers: "Hey, guys, great progress; wrong forest."

Because the Ectenic-Synoptic Construct, of which global-particular is a subscale, is new, readers may need to wait a few months for more information. Forthcoming articles by Ehrman and Leaver are planned to address this learning style domain.

Leveling-Sharpening Differences

Leveling and sharpening represent a second important difference in cognitive processing. Leveling and sharpening differ from each other in how students perceive and remember information (Holzman & Gardner, 1959; Messick, 1984).

When learning new information, **levelers** meld together information that may be distinctly different and come from a number of sources. Therefore, when it comes time to retrieve specific information, the details of the pieces that formed the melded concept are no longer available to the learner (Lowery, 1982).

Levelers remove distinctions instinctively; frequently, they see only similarities. They look at an apple and an orange, and when asked what they see, they respond, "fruit." Contrastive analysis is difficult for them, as are analogies, because these test items are based on differences. College Board test scores, dependent on understanding analogies, often convey inaccurate information about levelers. Low scores of levelers are less likely to reflect their verbal knowledge than their ability to find a common thread among any two items; in an analogy, they can make a case for every answer being possible, regardless of how farfetched that might seem to a sharpener. Given two writing assignments, one to liken objects and one to contrast objects, a leveler might receive two different grades, with the higher grade received on the description of similarities.

Letteri considers leveling to be a style that hinders good school performance (Lowery, 1982). If true, then it is principally because *we expect students to sharpen and do not recognize the talents of the levelers*.

Example. Once, a leveling friend and I went shopping. We both put "food" into the cart, then checked out. When we arrived home, our sharpening children looked at the unusual items (not our normal fare) and asked which of us had selected them. Neither of us had. We had apparently exchanged our shopping cart for someone else's (to a leveler, there are no distinctions among carts), and had purchased someone else's food (to a leveler, there are apparently few distinctions among food items).

Sharpeners look for distinctions among items. They readily retrieve details because they store them in different compartments. They notice differences, and they write well when the assignment allows them to use this ability. Their College Board test scores, assuming that other style issues are not in conflict with test design, are usually accurate.

Example. I happened to see the note left for other hikers at an Appalachian Trail shelter by my older son, who spent 6 months hiking the trail when he was 10. A sharpener, he had written: "For those who need water, there is a running stream located approximately .33 miles from this shelter on an azimuth of approximately 87.8 degrees."

Identification. Levelers and sharpeners are spotted by the kinds of things they write in essays and by the kinds of tasks they succeed at. An informal teacher-made test can identify whether students are paying attention to similarities or differences.

For more information on leveling and sharpening differences, readers are directed to works by and about Letteri (Lowery, 1982; Keefe & Monk, 1989), styles definitions by Messick (1984), and the original description of these learning styles by Holzman and Gardner (1959). These sources are listed in the references.

Synthetic-Analytic Differences

Synthetic-analytic difference is another important domain. This difference refers to the directionality of processing: putting together or taking apart. Synthesizers assemble new models from known information. Analyzers disassemble known information into its component parts (Ehrman & Leaver, 1997).

Synthetic students use pieces to build new wholes. They develop new models from disparate ideas. Synthesis as a learning style has several characteristics:

1. Hypothesis formation is experienced or intuited.
2. Processing is unconscious and product conscious.
3. Process and product are experienced as simultaneous.
4. The synthetic learner goes from insight to construct. (M. Ehrman, personal communication, January 3, 1997)

Example. John's classmates loved to hear him read stories because he read with expression. A synthetic learner, John was a voracious reader and an outstanding writer, using a wide range of stylistic devices. However, since third grade, he had received poor scores on silent reading tasks. On diagnostic reading comprehension tests of the multiple-choice format, he missed many answers.

The problem was the test, not the reader. When John read, he subordinated input from reading to information he already knew, then combined this with other information to form new ideas. Therefore, when he was asked details on the reading tests, he could not provide them; they were interwoven within an entire field of new information and irretrievable as discrete items of old information.

John obviously could read: He read well orally, and he wrote well. These are not the attributes of a student who is a poor reader. John simply did not possess the appropriate test-taking strategies to perform well on analytic tests.

Analytic students break wholes into parts. They see that the big picture is composed of small pieces, disassemble with alacrity any product that falls into their hands, and like rules because they can break them down into component parts and use them to explain phenomena. They like word study because they can break words into etymological pieces: roots, stems, affixes. Analysis has several characteristics:

1. Hypothesis formation is built.
2. Processing is conscious, and the product is held in abeyance.
3. Process and product are experienced as consecutive.
4. The analytic learner goes from construct to insight (M. Ehrman, personal communication, January 3, 1997).

Example. I will never forget one analytic "stuck" in a foreign language class, where emphasis was placed on synthesis—use of authentic materials and acquisition of meaning through context. His need to break words down into parts and to understand reading passages through their componential structure was so strong that he hid a dictionary and a grammar reference book under his coat, which he put on the empty desk beside him. Whenever the teacher turned his back, the student quickly looked up words he did not know. He became quite proficient at rapid location of information, not within the authentic materials, but within the dictionary. (The instructor for some reason never questioned why the student needed a coat in sunny California in the spring.)

Identification. Synthetic learning styles can be confirmed by asking students first to read two paragraphs of an article or two pages of a story, then to predict what will occur next. Synthetic learners will make sensible predictions but have difficulty recalling specific details. Their knowledge of vocabulary, if this is important, can be tested by forcing them to extract the details from the context. This can be accomplished by telling them beforehand just which details will be asked for. However, teachers should not be surprised if the students can then tell them the details but not be able to explain the meaning of the text.

Analytic learning styles can be determined by the ease with which students handle discrete-item tests. In addition, they often pencil into texts the definitions or translations of "words"—even ones that they already know.

There is a large amount of literature on synthetic and analytic learning styles. Some of it is mixed together with the work on cerebral dominance, but the information on synthesis and analysis can be sorted out from it. There is also a problem with some of the literature in that often global-analytic opposing styles are described, but with an understanding of the global-particular and synthetic-analytic domains, readers should be able to sort out those distinctions, too. Readers might consult the following researchers: Huber and Prewardy (1990), Froumina and Khasan (1994), and Oxford, Ehrman, and Lavine (1991).

Impulsive-Reflective Differences

Impulsive-reflective differences are yet another learning-style domain important to the classroom. This concept relates to the speed and manner of processing a response to a cognitive stimulus (Messick, 1984).

Impulsive learners think and respond nearly simultaneously. Impulsive learners tend to complete their work more quickly but with less accuracy than reflective learners. They often give facile answers.

Impulsives frequently can be found on quiz shows, such as *Jeopardy*. More than once, an impulsive contestant has rung the bell, only to ask for a repeat of the question or to respond to a piece of information in the question while missing the essence of the question itself.

Example. In graduate school, I took a final exam in Old Church Slavic. I sat beside a friend, an emigre from Russia, where sharing answers on tests is accepted practice. He looked over my shoulder frequently. Being impulsive, I finished the test quickly, checked my answers, and turned in my test booklet. Later, my Russian classmate approached me and asked why I had failed to complete Part V of the test. I was certain he was incorrect. However, I was reminded that impulsives are, indeed, fast and inaccurate, when the professor called me at home, asked me why I had omitted all of Part V, and then had me conjugate aloud the aorist form of several verbs in a language that is no longer spoken!

Reflective learners think, then respond, showing more involved and deeper levels of thinking. They work accurately, but their slowness sometimes means that work is incomplete. Teachers often think of impulsive learners as smart, and reflective learners as not smart. After all, in our American society, unlike many other societies around the world, is *quick* not a synonym for *bright* and *slow* a synonym for *stupid*? Before Super Bowl IX, Terry Bradshaw, quarterback for the Pittsburgh Steelers, commented, "People are funny. If you talk slow, you're dumb. If you talk fast, then you're a sharpie" ("Quotes," 1997, D1).

If we have any doubts about the relative intelligence of impulsive and reflective learners, we have only to look to works on intelligence. Reflecting the opinion of many psychologists, Muriel Beadle (1970) wrote in *A Child's Mind*: "The greater one's intelligence, the faster and better one does [cognitive tasks]" (p. 191).

Example. Mark, a delightful extraverted reflective student in class who enthusiastically participated in classroom discussions but who always had to take classroom work home to complete, might well have been labeled "slow" by the criterion suggested by Beadle. Mark rarely finished a test on time; however, the completed portions were usually correct.

When speed and knowledge are erroneously equated, reflective learners lose. Some reflective learners have been able to improve scores on College Board exams significantly, not through further study but through extensive practice in filling in dots faster! When teachers and administrators define intelligence in Beadle's terms, they deny students like Mark a chance to succeed. Worse, these students can confirm their own failure. They cannot finish tests on time; they must be slow learners.

Identification. Teachers can confirm reflective and impulsive learning styles by giving students two tests on the same subject matter, a power (untimed) test and a speed test. Reflective students perform better on the power test than on the speed test. Impulsive learners turn in the tests early, often with careless errors. When told to check their work, they do it quickly and turn it in with many of the same errors.

Identification of impulsive and reflective learners through observation of behavior is usually easily accomplished. Impulsive learners, upon hearing the first few words of a question, begin waving their hands energetically. Reflective learners rarely have their hands up early, participate less in discussions (the impulsives have gone on to another topic while the reflectives are still formulating their responses), and often turn in incomplete tests.

Observation of performance can also help identify reflective learners. This might be accomplished by letting students work on individual projects or in small groups on a task; when the task is completed, the suspected reflective learner can report on it. If a student is truly a reflective learner, his or her oral performance posttask should be better than his or her oral performance pretask. The oral aspects of pretask and posttask performance for impulsive students rarely change.

Students also often articulate their impulsivity or reflection. Impulsive learners will beg peers to "hurry up." Reflective learners will ask peers to wait. Several years ago, a teacher of Russian asked me to observe one student in her class. This student did well on tests but poorly on classroom performance. During the hour I visited, the student identified himself as a reflective learner this on no less than three occasions. Three times when the teacher called on him, he responded, "Let me think." Three times, the teacher, an impulsive learner, encouraged him to respond right away. The teacher needed to let him think.

Given the importance of impulsive-reflective differences in the classroom, there is a surprising dearth of information on the topic. Some information may be found in Ehrman (1996), Keogh and Donlan (1972), Messick and Associates (1976), Naigle and Thwaite (1979), Zelniker and Jeffrey (1976).

Inductive-Deductive Differences

Induction-deduction, as terms, are far from uniformly understood. Sometimes, two sets of researchers will define these terms in opposite ways. When reading research about this learning-style dimension, it is always important to first determine how the researcher is defining the terms. Here, I am defining induction as using examples to figure out rules and deduction as using rules to figure out examples.

Inductive learners form hypotheses, then test them. In doing so, inductive learners rarely seek teacher support. They enjoy seeing a multitude of examples and intuiting what the rule should be. Inductive learners often cannot get enough examples during class and, worse, the teacher's explanations fill the quiet time they need for thinking, so they have to do their inductive learning at home. As a result, they often have better control of their classroom output the following day.

Example. Mary Jane was a typical inductive learner. She never seemed able to follow an explanation in class. She took notes, but she did not ask questions. She certainly could not handle the exercises that followed the explanations. However, after taking the work home, she could do the exercises. The difficulty was that the teacher wanted the students to follow the development of the rule being explained as she worked it out sequentially and logically on the blackboard.

Conversely, Mary Jane needed to see the application of the rule in several environments, from which she could figure out the rule herself. The teacher wanted to go from the whole to the part; Mary Jane wanted to see multiple parts so that she could understand the whole. At home, she had enough information at hand to process the material inductively.

The teacher would have known that Mary Jane was an inductive learner if she had been listening carefully. Mary Jane frequently asked for several examples, and she asked for time to spend on the materials alone without explanations. Neither request was considered appropriate by the teacher. Inductive learners can become frustrated enough to stop listening, doodle, start working on their own, and otherwise involve themselves in activities that teachers generally do not appreciate if their inductive needs are not met. Checking that learning has occurred with inductive learners depends on teacher observation, but *sometimes teachers are too busy teaching to notice that students have already learned*! It is unfortunate that many inductive learners never get the opportunity to use their learning preference to their advantage because there are marvelous advantages to this particular learning style.

Deductive learners study the rules, then practice applying them to examples. They do not instinctively know what to do with a multitude of examples. For that reason, they do want the teacher to explain the rules to them.

Example. During the six-year period I supervised the FSI Russian language program, I found that nearly 75% of the students enrolling for training were deductive learners. I inherited a textbook, based on the Natural Approach, that was highly inductive. I also inherited a group of students who were vocally displeased with the program and poor performers as well. Both the complaints and the poor performance could be traced to deductive students being forced to learn in an inductive program. (As a U.S. Navy Captain told me: "I did not become a Captain by guessing.") The very first action I took was to add deductive classroom work and teaching to the program without removing the inductive elements needed by the 25% of the class who were inductive learners.

Identification. Confirmation of an inductive learning style can be obtained by giving students the opportunity to see applications of the rule in use before they are asked to follow a deductive explanation. If the students are indeed inductive learners, they will respond by understanding the concepts before they are ever explained. Deductive students will usually reveal themselves by asking for explanations, rule books, and reference materials. Here is where eavesdropping comes in handy. If students are working on an assigned task in small groups and the teacher is walking around the room, facilitating the learning process, the teacher will be able to overhear the deductive students asking the inductives to explain to them how and why something works. The inductive students can be heard making up their own, often unique and frequently feasible, processes for understanding and applying new information.

For more information, readers might turn to works by Ehrman (1996), Leaver (1996), and Messick (1984). These works are identified in the reference list.

Concrete-Abstract Differences

Concrete-abstract differences, like visual-auditory differences, promote or impede learning, depending on grade level. In the early grades, much of the classroom work tends to be concrete in nature. As students progress into higher grades, however, the work becomes more and more abstract. It should not be a surprise, then, to discover that the majority of elementary school teachers are concrete learners and the majority of college professors are abstract learners.

Concrete learners use real materials and examples for learning. They are hands-on, experiential learners. In early grades, they work well with things that can be manipulated. In later grades, they need examples, models, and templates.

Example. Military training tends to be very concrete. This is fortunate, because most military enlisted personnel tend also to be concrete. The military does not typically present lectures on how to fire a weapon. Rather, soldiers are handed a weapon and walked through the steps required for firing it.

One of the few exceptions is the field of military intelligence, in which much is taught in the classroom, even though most soldiers in that branch are also concrete learners. As a junior officer in charge of a platoon of such soldiers during one field exercise, I realized that these soldiers were not performing as well on the job as they should because they had been introduced to indirect fire only as a concept, using pictures, explanations, and lectures. Calling for a time-out, I marched them out to the field artillery (FA) range, where the surprised FA officer was quite happy to let a group of soldiers from a different branch, who were supporting the same mission he was, fire the artillery pieces and assist the fire direction center in determining weapons' settings. After that, these soldiers' performance on related paper-based and communication tasks dramatically improved.

Abstract learners, on the other hand, prefer those pictures and explanations. They learn through lecture and concept. They accept theory well. They are, in essence, "book learners."

Example. Military intelligence officers are a mixed group of concrete and abstract learners. Military training for intelligence officers has alternated back and forth between concrete and abstract for a number of years. I was in the first group of mixed-gender officers, and our course was highly concrete, based on the history of training intelligence officers first in the combat arms, then in intelligence procedures. Being concrete, I found immediate use for the combat arms training, and as an accommodator (see description of this learning style below) had no end of ideas as to how it could be modified, implemented, and otherwise applied. My class, however, was composed mostly of abstract learners, and they definitely did not see any reason for writing operations plans, calling for fire, bumping around uneven terrain in low-ceilinged tanks, and a myriad of other concrete activities. Vociferous complaints were raised—"we are intelligence officers; lecture to us about preparing intelligence reports"—and an abstract course was developed for the next group of officers. (I have watched this approach swing back and forth for the past 25 years, first teaching the concrete subset of students, then when they complain, teaching the abstract subset of students, until the concrete students complain.)

Identification. Identification of concrete versus abstract learners can be made by how they react to new information. Concrete learners often ask for an example or think up an example. Abstract learners jot down notes (unless they are auditory, in which case they may just look at the teacher knowingly).

Student journals, which we have not mentioned so far, are an excellent way for teachers to find out the concrete and abstract needs (and other learning-style needs) of introverted students. They are among the techniques that I used in the highly introverted class that I taught at Middlebury College. What students won't say in class, they often write in a journal, especially if they realize that the journals are "no-holds barred" activities with no repercussions for what they write.

Feedback is another way that teachers can identify the difference between concrete and abstract learners. Certainly, the trainers in the military intelligence officer course described above received useful feedback on the learning styles of their students. Unfortunately, they were not attuned to learning-style difference, so they simply grasped onto the pendulum of change and let it swing them back and forth between two bipolar extremes. It would have been more efficacious for them to use the feedback to add elements of the missing style to whichever course iteration was under attack.

More information on concrete-abstract differences can be found in a number of sources. These include Gregorc (1982) and Huber and Prewardy (1990).

Sequential-Random Differences

Sequential and random learning, another learning-style dimension that can have very strong implications for successful classroom learning, differ depending on the source of organization. Another way of looking at the sequential and random difference is how each integrates information in task completion. A former colleague of mine, Dr. Allen Weinstein, refers to line integrators and point integrators. In essence, these are sequential and random learners, respectively.

Sequential learners, who are linear in approach, follow an externally-provided order of processing. A sequential learner "wants to learn step-by-step, following a logical order, usually that provided by the curriculum and the textbook" (Ehrman, 1996, p. 64). Weinstein gives the example of someone putting together a bicycle. The sequential learner (or line integrator) lays out all the pieces and the instructions, then proceeds to put the bicycle together piece by piece.

Sequential learners also usually want to do one thing at a time, becoming proficient in one skill or knowledgeable in one area, before moving on to a new topic. Those who are required to work in multi-tasking environments can sometimes feel "scattered" (D. Bolduc, personal communication, March 31, 1997).

For some learners, sequentiality includes the need to receive written information from left to right and from top to bottom. Any other order confuses them.

Example. Remember Eliza (Chapter 2)? Eliza was a sequential learner. She needed external organization. When none was forthcoming from her random psychology teacher, she began to flounder, even in a subject which she liked. She could not follow lecture notes that were written wherever a kinesthetic instructor ended up standing.

Random learners, on the other hand, are nonlinear or parallel in approach. They follow an internally-developed order of processing. Returning to Weinstein's bicycle example, the random learner (or point integrator), knowing what a bicycle looks like, simply puts the pieces together and retains any leftover parts, just in case there might be some need for them in the future.

Often, there is a mistaken assumption that random learners are disorganized or have no organization. This is simply not true. They organize in nonlinear ways, which might not be apparent to linear (sequential) organizers. The best explanation of random learning that I have seen comes from Ehrman (1996). She summarizes this approach in the following way:

> Random learners . . . tend to find their own learning sequence, and it may vary from time to time and subject to subject. In fact, most random processors are very systematic learners, but their systems are often idiosyncratic, and their approach seems "random" to the outsider. This is one of the reasons for this label; the other is that such learners treat the learning process much the way a computer finds data, through a process called "random access." This means that the data are stored in various places, and the computer can find them quickly, no matter in what order they are requested. A random learner does something very similar in finding information and making connections between new and old knowledge. Random learners tend to tolerate ambiguity relatively well and embrace surprises that might disrupt the learning of others. (p. 64)

Example. Madeline Ehrman (personal communication, March 26, 1997) describes her experience as a concrete random in classrooms oriented towards other learning styles: "I have to suppress my random learning in order not to interfere with other students. I know that my approach is idiosyncratic. It works splendidly for me, because it meets my immediate, stochastically determined needs, but it can come into conflict not only with curricula and lesson plans but also with other student's needs."

Identification. As with other cognitive styles, identification can be made through observation. Let's take Eliza as an example. Her sequentiality can be determined rather easily. A look at her notebook would have shown her teacher that everything was highly organized. Her subjects were compartmentalized; teachers' lecture notes were copied verbatim on the right-hand side of the notebook; and on the left-hand side were references to the textbook, student comments, or Eliza's own ideas. On the other hand, identifying a random learner is often a matter of identifying the student as "not sequential," because every random organization is unique and unpredictable.

Readers who wish more information might read Ehrman (1996) and Gregorc (1982). Ehrman focuses on foreign language education, and Gregorc includes the sequential and random learning-style attributes only as part of and inseparable from concrete-abstract attributes. However, readers can make any necessary interpolations to make the information pertinent to their own situations.

Information Acquisition Preferences

Gregorc (1982) suggests the existence of four different learning styles: abstract-random, abstract-sequential, concrete-sequential, and concrete-random. He calls these styles information acquisition preferences. In his system, these types are integral wholes; they cannot be further broken down. (I disagree with Gregorc. I think that looking at each axis independently provides additional insight into learning.)

Abstract-random learners are students who learn conceptually, often with or through relationships with others, and impose internal organization on information. This implies demonstration and small-group work.

Example. When Nellie first attended kindergarten, the teacher thought that she was overly diffident. As the other children played, Nellie stood outside the group and watched. When the teacher spoke with Nellie's mother, she learned that outside school, Nellie was very outgoing. So, she observed Nellie some more. What she discovered was that Nellie was an abstract random learner. She did not remain outside the group because she was shy. She remained outside the group because she needed to watch what was going on in order to understand it. Once she had the rules figured out, she became as actively involved as any of the other students.

Abstract-sequential learners are students who learn conceptually and expect external organization. This implies the use of lectures and textbooks. Every classroom has a certain percentage of abstract-sequential learners. These are the students who thrive in traditional classrooms. They are quietly working on assignments, answering questions when asked, and taking notes.

Example. James had always been expected to enlist in the Army because his father had spent his career in the Army. Unfortunately, James, an abstract-sequential learner, was not very much like his father, a concrete-sequential learner. Basic training was very difficult for him. He did well on written tests, such as identifying insignia and ranks, but he could not learn from field activities. He needed to be able to read about the field activities first, but, of course, reading materials were not available. To his family's disappointment, after repeating basic training unsuccessfully, James was discharged from the Army.

Concrete-sequential learners are students who learn through example and expect external organization. This implies field trips and hands-on implementation of principles. It also means the use of modeling.

Example. All Joseph wanted to do in his French class was to use the language. He wanted to write to a pen pal in France in French. His teacher, an abstract-sequential instructor, told him that it was too early for this; Joseph would need to learn more vocabulary and grammar first. Joseph brought in magazines sent by his pen pal, but the teacher told him that they were too advanced. At the end of the year, the French teacher recommended to Joseph's parents that he not continue into second-year French. That summer, Joseph's mother sent him to France. Joseph tried out his French in realistic environments and returned fluent enough to pass the entrance exam for third-year French (even though the test was translation-based).

Joseph's example is not unlike some others we have seen. Often, what the student asks for is what the student needs. *Sometimes, the teacher knows best; other times, the student knows best.* A style-aware teacher stays open to both possibilities. Joseph asked for hands-on, applied learning. He was told that this could come only after he had proved himself in cerebral activities. However, Joseph needed the hands-on activities to learn the content *before* he could become proficient at the required cerebral activities.

Concrete-random learners are students who learn through example and impose internal organization on information. This implies independent work and experimentation. Concrete random learners, unlike most learners, are flexible in organization and, when needed, can reorganize on the spot.

Example. "Don't flit," says the husband of one concrete-random learner. An abstract-sequential, computer specialist, he cannot teach her to use new computer programs (she does not want to "be taught," anyway) without threat of marital strife. She mostly relies on her concrete-random son for computer assistance.

Identification. If one breaks apart the four styles, in spite of Gregorc's objections, it becomes easier to identify these learning styles through observation. The same behaviors described above for isolating concrete-abstract and sequential-random differences can be used to determine the four learning style differences proposed by Gregorc. It then becomes a matter of combining the two axes. An example might be four students who are learning a new computer program. Because there are many ways to go about this, the astute teacher, through observing the choices made by the learners, can determine which of the Gregorc styles the students prefer. The chart below summarizes how this might be accomplished.

	Student A	Student B	Student C	Student D
Help Menu (HM)	ignores	uses but prefers CM	in conjunction with PT	uses when stuck
Programmed Training (PT)	ignores	after reading CM	starts with this	ignores
Computer Manual (CM)	reads when needed	starts with this	ignores	ignores
Demonstration	starts with this	accepts but prefers CM	ignores	ignores
Independent Practice	after demonstration	after PT	after PT	starts with this; ends with this

Student A is obviously an **abstract-random** learner. The programmed training is not attractive, but demonstration is essential. The use of the computer manual, when needed, underlines the abstract traits of the learner. The willingness to proceed straight to independent practice shows the lack of desire for external organization, signifying a more random approach to learning.

Student B is clearly an **abstract-sequential** learner. This student starts with the abstract, the manual, then proceeds step-by-step (sequential) to implement the information, with the assistance of the accompanying training program.

Student C is a **concrete-sequential**. This is clear from the emphasis on the hands-on opportunities for learning. This student ignores the abstract opportunities—manual and demonstration—and proceeds to the training program, which is concrete and sequential and does not undertake random activity (independent practice) until after the program has been learned.

Student D is clearly a **concrete-random** learner. These students are easy to pick out. Ignoring all external input, they proceed to figure out things for themselves in their own way, whether or not their conclusions and procedures match any one else's expectations or intentions.

For further reading on this learning-style dimension, the best source is Gregorc (1982) himself. His works are identified in the references.

Kolb's Learning-Styles Typology

Kolb divides learning styles into a four-stage cycle, based on two axes. Axis A plots the continuum between active experimentation and reflective observation. Axis B plots the continuum between abstract conceptualization and concrete experience. Kolb defines active experimentation as learning via experimentation or changing situations; students working in this stage want to get things done and display ingenuity. Reflective observation, on the other hand, requires objectivity, observation, and understanding through the exploration of differing points of view; students working in this stage do not usually take action. Abstract conceptualization involves logic and ideas; students working in this stage rely on theories and systems for problem resolution. At the opposite end of the continuum, concrete experience emphasizes personal involvement and emotional commitment; students working in this stage rely on open-mindedness and adaptability (Kolb 1985). The intersection of these axes produces four learning styles.

Divergers, or Type I learners, seek meaning. (As with other learning-styles terms we have seen, the term, *diverger*, as used by Kolb, does not have the same meaning as when used in lay terms; that is, it does not mean someone who departs from traditional ways of thinking.) Divergers ask, "Why should this be?" "Why should I do this?" They involve themselves in the process of learning, believing in their own experience and seeking a connection between study materials and their own life. They also are able to view an event from multiple points of view. They desire harmony, learn from demonstration or from observing peers, and tend to work more effectively with small groups or in class than in tutorial situations. Kolb says that they perceive information concretely and they process it reflectively (Kolb, 1984). Violand-Sanchez (personal communication, 1986), using the image of a flower, says that divergers, given a flower, will put the flower in a vase and enjoy its beauty. McCarthy (1997) calls these learners "imaginative."

Example. One second-grade teacher described to me her frustration with a diverger in her class. The students were learning to tell time using wall clocks. The diverger stated that she saw no reason to spend effort on this activity. Wall clocks were not of importance to her because she had a digital watch and all the family's clocks were digital. When the teacher explained that there were nondigital clocks in the world, the diverger calmly replied that she would wait for them to disappear and wear a digital watch in the interim. If this teacher wants the diverger to learn to tell time, she is going to have to find a way to connect the information with the diverger's real life.

Assimilators, or Type II learners, build theories and concepts. They learn through facts and the opinions of authority figures. They prefer ideas to people, thoroughly investigate information presented, and enjoy traditional classrooms. They ask, "What should we know?" "What should we study?" "What is this all about?" Kolb says that they perceive information abstractly and process it reflectively (Kolb, 1984). Violand-Sanchez (personal communication, 1986) says that assimilators, given a flower, will dissect it to determine "what" a flower really is. McCarthy (1997) calls these learners "analytic." (This is a different meaning of analytic than the term used for the synthetic-analytic construct.)

Example. Sam's mother complained to the teacher that Sam's "nose was always in a book." She could not get him to ride a bike, although he loved reading about motorcycles. She could not get him to participate in sports, although he liked reading action stories. As an assimilator, Sam was quite happy with vicarious experience. He felt no need to try things out for himself in order to understand them and enjoy them.

Convergers, or Type III learners, are located on the Kolb grid directly opposite divergers. (Note that the term, *converger*, does not have the lay meaning of conformity.) Convergers want to know "how" things work. They develop skills, seek hands-on experiences, and solve problems. Their tolerance of ambiguity is low. They apply ideas, believe in cause and effect, and want learning to bring results. Kolb (1984) says that they perceive information abstractly and process it actively. Given a flower, says Violand-Sanchez (personal communication, 1986), they want to know how to grow it. McCarthy (1997) calls these students "commonsense learners."

Example. Accommodating a converger turned one student from a capable student into a star. When teachers at the Foreign Service Institute selected a group of Russian students for a program in which capable students would work one-on-one with newly arrived Russian emigrants, putting their language skills into practice, the characteristics they looked for were strong proficiency and a learning style that would allow students to benefit from external programming. In essence, they found accommodators (see description of accommodators below), who relished the challenge of shaping their own learning, and convergers, who craved the opportunity for real-life application of their language skills. One converger, a military attache, was a marginal choice; his language skills were good but assimilator teachers thought he could benefit more from direct instruction. The student selected the external program. Two months later, his language proficiency was at the top of the class.

Accommodators, or Kolb Type IV learners, are located on the Kolb grid directly opposite the Type II (assimilator) learners. If assimilators are the ideal traditional school students, accommodators are the bane of teachers, and school is often torture for them. They don't particularly feel the need to be taught; in fact, they resent a teacher getting in the way of their learning. Often, they are inductive learners, and this increases the desire for self-instruction. It is no surprise that a large number of school dropouts into home study programs are accommodators. It is also no surprise that accommodators are among the best graduate students, if they last until this stage; graduate schools prize the innovation and unique perspectives of accommodators. Accommodators take both physical and mental risks; display comfort with people (although others sometimes claim that accommodators overwhelm them); relish and seek out change (creating it, if it is not forthcoming); and learn through trial and error. Their favorite question, "what if," can be an exciting one, full of risk—and it can sometimes strike terror in teacher or parent. Kolb (1984) says that accommodators perceive concretely and process actively. Violand-Sanchez (personal communication, 1986) says that, given a flower, accommodators will try to turn that one flower into two flowers or turn the flower into something that is not a flower. McCarthy (1997) calls these students "dynamic" learners.

Example. Parents of accommodator children who have raised these children to adulthood should consider themselves fortunate if they have survived to this age without disaster. My accommodator son, perfectly capable of independent care, nonetheless routinely wrought near-disaster by his experimental approaches to learning, especially as a young elementary school student. In one instance, he accidentally set the bathroom on fire by trying to determine whether two candles with the same amount of wax, one short and wide and the other tall and thin, would burn at the same rate. A few weeks later, I found a number of partially burned objects on the lawn. Questioning the universal application of the Newtonian principle that all objects fall at the same rate regardless of weight, he postulated that even identical objects, if one were on fire, would drop at different rates in the presence of thermal updraft. (I don't remember what he proved, other than that even accommodator parents of accommodator children draw the line somewhere!)

Identification. Teachers who listen to what students say, watch what they do, and examine where the performance excels and where it does not can pretty reliably determine the style of their students. Divergers in the elementary school years can be easily picked out at recess time; they are the students who are standing outside the group, waiting to join in an activity after they have fully understood what the activity really is. Assimilators often walk around with books in their hands. Convergers are doing things, often with their hands. Accommodators are climbing the tallest tree or finding a rule to break—whatever risk might be available to them to take. As with other styles, an interview with each student often serves to confirm the intuition and observations of the teacher.

For more information on this style dimension, the best source is Kolb (1984) himself, although others have also written on the topic. One of the more prolific to write on these styles is McCarthy (1987, 1996, 1997).

Cerebral Dominance as Learning Style

Hemisphericity, or cerebral dominance, has been researched for more than three decades. Recent interest in whole-brain learning is turning public attention back to this cognitive-style dimension. I have had much experience and much success with this area. It is the one with which I started my own research into cognitive styles. I do not use it as extensively any more, partly because other cognitive styles overlap with cerebral dominance and partly because of the infelicitous labeling of the concept. Hemisphericity has a physiologic aspect and a metaphoric aspect. When doctors talk about commissurectomies (the severing of the corpus collosum, the strip that connects the right and left hemispheres of the brain), hemispherectomies (the removal of one of the brain hemispheres), hemisphere preference for speech and handedness, or location of mental functions, they are talking about the physiological brain. For example, if a doctor says that someone is right-hemisphere preferent for speech, what he has in mind is that the speech center, normally located in the left hemisphere, is located in the right hemisphere in the patient he is treating.

In learning styles, when we talk about hemisphere preference *we are using a metaphor*. Obviously, both hemispheres are used in learning, and mental activity is usually accomplished in the hemisphere in which that function is normally located. If someone we have classified as a student displaying right-hemisphere preference is completing calculations or doing verbal processing in the classroom, that student is probably using his or her left hemisphere. What we mean by "hemisphere preference" as a learning style is the inclination for a specific kind of mental activity.

Hemisphericity as a cognitive style has been segmented differently by various researchers and theorists. Torrance (1980; Torrance, Reynolds, Riegel, & Ball, 1977) posits a tripartite system: right-hemisphere preference, left-hemisphere preference, and integrated preference. Hermann (1983) posits a quadripartite system: cerebral right, limbic right, cerebral left, limbic left. Although the multipartite systems impart more useful information, most commonly, hemisphere preference discussions differentiate between two dominances: right-hemisphere preference and left-hemisphere preference.

Right-hemisphere learners' interests focus on intonation and sound. They are fascinated by patterns and relationships and attracted to conceptualization and symbols or images.

Example: On the Russian final exam, a proficiency test, Gary, a Foreign Service Officer, confirmed his right-hemisphere preference. Part of the exam required him to listen to one instructor explain the 1986 accident at the Chernobyl nuclear plant in Russian, then renarrate the information in English. He was allowed to take notes. While the instructor spoke Russian, Gary seemed to understand fine, but what he renarrated had little to do with what had been said. He related facts that were not given and omitted details that were described. The instructors were baffled, because Gary's language skills had seemed very good in class. The problem was clarified, when they looked at Gary's notes. Gary had turned the information into drawings, then had narrated whatever the drawings had prompted. Gary was instructed to take verbal notes the next time and to report only the things that he had written down; his second score (on a different, but related topic) was much higher.

Left-hemisphere learners focus on verbal processes. They are fascinated by logic and rational argumentation and attracted to accuracy and words. Because schools are verbal and left-hemisphere-preferent organizations (Bogen, 1975; Springer, 1981), they have a strong impact on student learning, with many students developing more left-hemisphere traits over time but not increasing their right-hemisphere traits (Leaver, 1986). Left-hemisphere students rarely stand out as anything except good students, although they can be slow starters in foreign language classes until the verbal aspects of the language show up (Leaver, 1986). The few other courses that favor right-hemisphere students, such as art and music, can also be difficult for left-hemisphere students.

Example. One left-hemisphere-preferent eighth-grade student related how she never could seem to get any grade higher than a C in her art class, no matter how hard she tried. Finally, on one work, she received an A. She tried very hard to paint an accurate self-portrait, and the teacher very much liked the "caricature."

Identification. Observation techniques can assist in identifying hemisphere preference. In general, right-hemisphere-preferent students tend to have many of the characteristics of global learners and left-hemisphere-preferent students, of particular learners. In addition, right-hemisphere-preferent learners tend to have good pronunciation in foreign language classes, and left-hemisphere-preferent students tend to have good grammar (Leaver, 1986, 1988). In English classes, the writing of right-hemisphere-preferent students tends to be creative, and the writing of left-hemisphere-preferent students, articulate. In other classes, right-hemisphere-preferent students tend to focus on patterns, spatial elements, and relational aspects. Left-hemisphere-preferent students tend to focus on precision, verbal elements, and organizational aspects. Right-hemisphere-preferent students associate words with images, and their errors often show this kind of processing. One right-hemisphere-preferent student, in reading a children's story, misread "the old man and the old woman" as "the old man and the old lady." Error analysis provides clues to the hemisphere preference of a student.

Occasionally, claims are made for connections between subject matter and cerebral dominance. For example, the interests of right-hemisphere-preferent learners are said to focus on art and music and left-hemisphere-preferent learners on science and math. However, these distinctions are not without exception and cannot be used to differentiate between the two types without some other confirmation. Einstein, for example, appears to have been a right-hemisphere-preferent scientist, or a visual thinker, to use the designation given by West (1991). Perhaps that is why Einstein was able to propose such a nonsequential and unconventional theory as relativity by imagining himself riding on a beam of light.

There is much information available in the area of hemisphere preference and whole-brain learning. In addition to the works mentioned above, readers might consult the following specialists: Jarsonbeck (1984), Sinatra & Stahl-Gemake (1983), Williams (1983), Wolf and Koff (1978), and Young (1983). Related work in brain-based learning and the connection between physiology and cognitive processing is described by Pool (1997) and Sylwester (1995).

Multiple Intelligences

☞ *Inherent differing abilities and talents are sometimes considered to be learning styles.*

I diverge to include a discussion of the concept of multiple intelligences (Gardner, 1983, 1993) here because so many people associate multiple intelligences with learning styles, and probably rightly so. Because Gardner's construct makes a compote (apples and oranges and other fruit) of learning categories, we need to talk about these concepts separately from those learning styles discussed in the previous categories.

I am usually willing to accept and promote nearly any system of learning styles, because no matter how we slice the learning styles pie, the simple act of slicing it tells us something about its ingredients. In the case of multiple intelligences, however, I cannot defend the compote (the requirement to select among 1 modality preference, 4 cognitive styles, and 2 personality types, when students have a modality preference, several cognitive styles, *and* a personality type), the medicine (accommodation of learning styles) it replaces, or its claims to create a healthier individual and classroom life. *The concept of multiple intelligences is fraught with multiple problems*.

According to Gardner (1983, 1991, 1993), all human beings possess the potential to develop intelligence in seven areas: logico-mathematical, linguistic, musico-rhythmic, visuo-spatial, bodily-kinesthetic, and two areas of personal intelligence: interpersonal and intrapersonal. In simpler terms, this means that people can have several kinds of "smarts" (Gabala & Lange, 1997).

Type of Intelligence	Kind of " Smarts"
logico-mathematical	logic smarts
musico-rhythmic	music smarts
bodily-kinesthetic	body smart
visuo-spatial	picture smart
verbal-linguistic	word smart
interpersonal-social	people smart
intrapersonal-introspective	self smart

As a result of these various intelligences, we can expect to find different talents in the classroom. The logico-mathematical student excels at math and science, the musico-rhythmic at choral and instrumentation endeavors, the bodily-kinesthetic at sports and shop, the visuo-spatial at art and photography, the verbal-linguistic at writing and foreign language, the interpersonal-social in cooperative activities and social organization, and the intrapersonal-introspective in invention and independent activities.

Even though most people are more skilled in one area than another and more attracted to one area than another, the implication is that all intelligences can and should be developed. This may be a noble goal: to create the perfect human being, well-rounded and multitalented. I ask, however, Who are we as teachers to remake people in the image of perfection, if that is at all possible? I further submit that *instead of trying to remake people in the image of perfection, it is more helpful to understand and accept people in their imperfections and assist them in developing the skills they need to cope successfully with an external world that differs from their internal world.*

In fact, trying to develop seven intelligences each per student not only may be doomed to failure, as many teachers have found ("I tried it, and it didn't work" is a common complaint), but doing so also conceptually contradicts results of learning styles research. For example, playing background music is recommended for developing musico-rhythmic intelligence. However, we know that some students need silence in order to learn. Forcing introverted-thinking students to work on cooperative tasks may or may not develop their interpersonal-social intelligence. These students, in general, are more comfortable in mastery learning environments, where they can work independently and control their own learning (Block, 1971; Bloom, 1968, 1971; Morrison, 1926; Torshen, 1977; Washburne, 1922). In fact, the cooperative learning experience may have the opposite effect of making these students feel inferior to their extraverted-feeling peers. Multiple mischief can be created by trying to develop students' multiple intelligences.

LEARNER PROFILES

One problem with learning-styles systems is that they restrict us to a narrow range of traits. Learner profiles, on the other hand, are a composite of traits from a wide range of learning-styles systems. Learner profiles can include environmental preferences, sensory modalities, personality types, and cognitive styles. Using only the domains that I have presented in this book, there are over 400,000 possible profiles, and they differ from each other in some aspect.

The key to understanding these 400,000+ profiles is not to understand each individual profile, because none of us has the time to consider this large a number. The critical element is to understand how the traits work together, that is, how they interact to produce unique learning attributes. For example, global learners are usually very good foreign language learners. However, global-visual learners experience difficulties that parallel those of particular-visual learners.

Some students will have profiles that include "typical" combinations of styles. For example, a strong relationship exists among the styles within each column below. (Column 1 relates to what Ehrman and Leaver call "synoptic" and column 2 to what they call "ectenic.")

column #1	column #2
global	particular
synthetic	analytic
auditory	visual
inductive	deductive
concrete	abstract
random	sequential
extravert	introvert

However, any mix of these styles is possible. There are many visual-global learners in the world. There are random-analytic learners, sequential inductive learners, and so on. Where such atypical profiles exist, it is easy to be fooled by one trait, as in the case of Mark, the extraverted-reflective learner described earlier, whose extraversion made him appear impulsive. What "seems" is not always what "is." Determining learner profiles by observation requires looking below the surface.

MEMORY STAGES

One area that has not been explored in sufficient depth is the interplay between learning styles and kinds (or stages) of memory. To understand this relationship requires a short digression into memory research.

Contrary to popular thought that memory comes in two varieties—long-term and short-term—we now know that there are at least five kinds of memory: sentient, short-term, long-term, permanent, and activated/working memory. Each kind of memory plays a different role. New information on memory arrives daily from the operating rooms of neurosurgeons (e.g., Calvin & Ojemann, 1994) and from the laboratories of neuroscientists (e.g., Damasio, 1989; Damasio, Damasio, Tranel, & Brandt, 1990; Damasio & Tranel, 1993) and psychologists (e.g., Cooper, 1994; Reiser, 1991). Although our understanding of how memory operates remains under construction, there are some aspects of memory about which researchers know a lot but which have yet to inform most classroom practice.

Sentient Memory

Sentient memory refers to being aware of a phenomenon. It has a very limited capacity and lasts quite briefly. This type of memory involves processing mainly through the senses. The senses communicate together to form a picture of one's environment.

Items in sentient memory require attention if they are to transfer to short-term memory. If one sits on a chair and does not notice anything particular about it, it is unlikely that one will remember that chair later. For this reason, global learners are unable to answer detail-based questions on reading comprehension tests. They do not focus attention on details, and therefore, the details do not enter memory store.

Short-Term Memory

Transfer to short-term memory is mandatory if information is to reach permanent memory store. Short-term memory lasts up to a few minutes and is also capacity limited. Information not transferred to memory is lost.

Here specific sensory information obtained through sentient memory coalesces into a general package of information. For example, a person walking down the street may hear a loud crash, see two cars colliding, feel a chill, and smell burning rubber. Each of these sensations is handled as a separate input in sentient memory. This information becomes the overall scene of a car accident in short-term memory, fractured into a multitude of pieces, based on sound, color, texture, and so on, and stored in separate parts of the brain (Reiser, 1991).

Interpreting the pieces of information as a whole may be easier for synthetic learners and inductive learners; storing it in all its componential parts may be easier for analytic and deductive learners. When new information arrives for which students have no schemas, it may be essential to provide instruction to help them become aware of this new information (sentient memory), as well as the opportunity to do something with the information in order to keep it in short-term memory. Most instructional methods do well in assisting analytic and deductive learners in keeping information in short-term memory store but do not do well at assisting synthetic and inductive learners with the same.

Long-Term Memory

Entering of information into long-term memory requires active rehearsal or repetition by the individual of the information while it is in short-term memory. Mere repetition can assist in transferring information to long-term memory store. However, rehearsing the information is more effective for complex knowledge, such as the acquisition of meaning connected to morphologic structure in foreign language classes or in vocabulary expansion in language arts classes. If information is not transferred to long-term memory, it is lost. In a foreign language or ESL class, the understanding of a spoken sentence needs to be put together as a packet of information; phonemic distinctions, lexemes, morphologic structure, and syntax are some of the elements that are perceived separately and repackaged when "recalled." Levelers, in entering information into long-term memory are apt to look for commonalities between the elements, melding together information that they are not later able to "recall" because they did not store the information as received.

Long-term memory is also capacity limited. It stores information until it is entered into permanent memory. Neurosurgeons estimate it takes up to 3 years for information to enter permanent memory. This is why stroke patients can sometimes remember events that occurred many years ago but little that has happened in the last three years. Information held in long-term memory can be retrieved. However, little is known about how to retain information in memory.

Permanent Memory

Permanent memory is that memory that lasts for very long periods of time, including, sometimes, for a lifetime. Storage into permanent memory occurs in one of two ways: (a) an "aha" experience in which an association is so strong that storage is immediate, and (b) the result of frequent rehearsal, repetition, and reconstructive use of information in memory for approximately 3 years.

Permanent memory, contrary to its name, is not entirely permanent. One of the more recent discoveries by neurosurgeons and neuroscientists is that memory, like hard disk space on a computer, can be overwritten by new information (Calvin & Ojemann, 1994). This finding alone has immense implications for learning and teaching. The most famous of the studies on memory distortion involves asking accident witnesses to describe a scene in which there is a stop sign, then later asking the witnesses what they saw just beyond the yield sign. Very frequently, the witnesses will then recall having seen a yield sign, when they really did see a stop sign originally. Other sorts of events have similar "distortions" (Ross, Read, & Toglia, 1994; Whittlesea, Jacoby, & Girard, 1990). This overwriting of information is not restricted to events. When witnesses have been presented with additional contextualized information about people they have seen, the number of misidentifications increases; rehearsal of old information does not ensure accuracy in identification (Luus & Wells, 1991). To some extent, this explains the loss of old information when students learn new information. For example, students who are studying the present perfect tense forms in German may begin to make mistakes in the past tense forms, which they knew sufficiently well to prompt the teacher to move on to the present perfect forms. Arithmetic students, in learning to multiply, may forget how to carry.

Activated Memory

We are now fairly certain that "recall" as such does not happen. What happens is *reconstruction* of old information or *construction* of new information, using those pieces of information that have been stashed away in various parts of the brain. To do this, we rely on activated memory. Activated memory is more or less what we have referred to as working memory for years. It is memory in use. Activated memory seems to work in a very specific way, basically shifting information into and out of short-term memory, because short-term memory has a very small capacity. Activated memory involves applying memory and deciding how to respond. Information required at a given time is pulled from long-term or permanent memory. This information is then transferred to short-term memory, where the information is analyzed. When we ask students to complete a task, we are asking them to "load" their memory, that is, to start using their activated memory, pulling information to and from short-term memory and long-term/permanent storage (Leaver & Leaver, 1996).

We also are now fairly certain that some "lost memories" are actually due to retrieval dysfunction. In other words, the memories are there, but all the pieces are not moved into activated memory for some reason, and reconstruction cannot occur. This explains why students will know the answers to some questions yesterday and tomorrow, but not today. In some cases, retrieval dysfunction may be occurring because the retrieval task has been posed via a different learning style from the style in which the information was stored. For example, perhaps a global learner experienced the new information as part of a bigger picture (comprehension/sentient memory), filed it attached to some aspect of the whole (storage through short-term into long-term memory), and is now asked to reconstruct it unassociated with the original framework. For global learners, this may not be possible.

When subjects under study are unable to retrieve information, researchers often must attempt to decipher whether information loss is due to old information being discarded/overwritten or the inability to retrieve the stored item. How much information actually reaches permanent storage is an interesting question, given the length of time required. The distinction between long-term and permanent memory may explain, to some extent, the "marination factor" in learning, in which time alone seems to help in repackaging and remembering information.

In Summary

This chapter has summarized some of the more important (in my experience) learning-style differences. Where a style war erupts depends on the relative inflexibility in one domain or another of student and teacher. In most cases, some trial and error is needed to determine which learning-style difference is creating the difficulty. With time and experience, teachers identify the cause of style wars pretty quickly. However, teachers who are just starting out may wish to select one category of learning styles or one construct—whichever feels most comfortable. Over time, other categories and constructs can be added, including the concept of discontinuity in learning style. Elementary school teachers might want to start out with the sensory modalities; these seem to be already developed in young children. High school teachers might want to move on to personality issues, because changing physiology and a focus on relationships of many sorts give high school students a heightened awareness of themselves as individuals, and college professors might want to concentrate on the cognitive styles initially. These are only recommendations, and as a random learner, my approach would be to pick whatever "falls under my hand" and just start the research and application process with that.

Those who have been working in the learning-styles field a while may prefer to work with a more elaborate set of variables. They may also wish to research and explore the issue of memory and learning style further on their own.

PRACTICE EXERCISES

1. Look at the description of Shawn and Shane in Chapter 2. How many learning-style differences can you find between them? For each, draw up their learner profile.

2. Draw up the learner profile of someone you know very well: your spouse, a friend, a classmate (current or former). Then, check with that person to see how close you came.

3. Draw up your own learner profile.

4. The following are teacher observations of students from real classes. How would you assess their learning styles? In cases where information is insufficient, what other steps would you take (other than instrumentation) to assess the student's style?

    a. Student A routinely receives bad grades on quizzes, especially quizzes given shortly after the introduction of new material. However, grades on lesson tests are good.

    b. Student B is a law student. He studies for hours and hours, working hard to memorize all the case studies and accompanying rules. However, his grades are marginal across the board. Where he does excel is in proposing emendations of current laws that seem unfair or insufficient.

    c. Student C reads poorly. She can answer detailed questions but not generalized ones. She can explain the meaning of words, but not the meaning of discourse.

    d. Student D constantly asks nitpicking questions, to the point of driving the teacher and the rest of the students to distraction.

    e. Student E diligently copies everything from the board.

    f. Student F is a Spanish student. He wants films replayed over and over again and asks the teacher to stop the film periodically for explanation. This annoys many of the other students in the class.

    g. Student G is a Spanish student in the same class. She speaks very slowly and haltingly. However, her language is accurate.

    h. Student H is very quiet in class. This student almost never volunteers an answer, but if called upon, usually has an appropriate response.

NOTES

1. The Greek types are an interesting way of looking at temperament. I have chosen not to treat them here, but a number of teachers, especially in Europe, use these in much the same way that I am using the Keirsey temperaments to explain differences in student classroom behavior.

2. I have followed the following convention in spelling. I have spelled the word *extroversion* as it is spelled in the dictionary where referring to the lay use of the term and have spelled it as the term *extraversion* in keeping with the MBTI convention, where it refers to the use of the term by Myers-Briggs.

3. The treatment provided here is very synoptic. Each of the 16 types is very rich in characteristics. The reader is invited to read the literature on type by Jung, Myers-Briggs, and Keirsey (see the reference section), as well as many other psychologists and learning-styles practitioners who write on this topic.

4. There is a growing interest in the application of MBTI results to the workplace and classroom, as well as to family life. In most communities, public libraries have information the MBTI and on the Jungian system of typology. Most larger communities also have type talk groups. Although members of these groups come from a range of professions, their insights can be very useful to a teacher trying to teach in style by being aware of the Jungian types.

5. The newest construct about to emerge into the world is the Ehrman-Leaver distinction between synopsis and ectasis (Ehrman & Leaver, 1997). It addresses the issue of why global and analytic are not opposing learning styles but each are a piece of a larger construct. I do not use this construct in this book, because the theory and research are too recent to be confident of the initial, exploratory results from data collection. I do include in this book several, but not all, of its subscales and have identified those that are unique to this construct. Synopsis, a word derived from Greek, refers to a summary. Synopsis as a learning style refers to the "perception of phenomena as wholes" (Ehrman & Leaver, 1997), a summary, or sum total. Thus, synoptic learners approach learning and cognitive processing in a holistic or summative manner. Synoptic learners tend to be global, leveling, synthetic, field dependent, impulsive, and analog learners. Ectasis comes from the Greek word *ektasis* meaning expansion or extension. Ectasis as a learning style is the "perception of phenomena as composites" (Ehrman & Leaver, 1997). Ectenic learners (from the Greek adjective *ektenis*) approach learning and cognitive processing in an atomistic or expansive manner. Ectenic learners tend to be particular, sharpening, analytic, field independent, reflective, and digital learners. Ehrman thinks that "the ectenic process may make conscious what is done unconsciously by synoptics and may account in part for the observed tendency of synoptics to appear impulsive and for ectenics to appear reflective" (M. Ehrman, personal communication, 1996), whether they really are or not.

4

Failure to Learn:
Diagnosing the Causes

People are born to learn. It is a natural instinct. Students who fail to learn, like babies who fail to thrive, usually lack one or more essential nutrients. Unfortunately, some students do fail to thrive. Most school programs are designed in ways that nourish one group of learners while placing another group at risk of starvation. Specifically, there are four groups of learners who are typically at risk:

1. Any student whose learning style does not match the teacher's learning style, especially, if the teacher is inflexible in style or unaware of style differences
2. Any student whose learning style does not match the orientation of the curriculum
3. Any student who does not match the class profile (the set of predominant learning styles among any given group of students)
4. Any student who is misplaced in the educational system from a mismatch between the student's learning style and the learning style of the placement test

Although these conflicts in style might seem to be highly varied, in reality, most teaching styles, textbooks, and class profiles correspond to Western norms, or those styles which we in the West expect and encourage. Therefore, although there is a risk of failure any time there is a mismatch, the students most at risk are the ones whose learning styles deviate the most from these norms. It is no surprise, then, that students with non-Western learning styles are more highly represented among the gifted dropouts, underachievers, and special education students (Connor, 1976; Hamilton, Blumenfeld, Akoh, & Miura, 1989; Keogh & Donlan, 1972; Lester, 1974; Levin & Pressley, 1985; Long, 1977; Mangan, 1982; Morgan, 1981; Naigle & Thwaite, 1979; Scarr, 1981; Tsang, 1983; Yong & McIntyre, 1992).

NON-WESTERN APPROACHES

In their educational practices, Western approaches require specific kinds of perception and processing. These include the ability to analyze; solve problems (and to solve them quickly); follow and use linear sequencing; understand chronological organization, timelines, and deadlines; work in a social group; and use one's eyes and ears for most activities.

The Western world, with its emphasis on logic, order, and technology, places at an *a priori* disadvantage those students whose learner profiles contain a majority of the following traits: globality, leveling, synthesis, reflectivity, concreteness or abstraction (depending on grade level), randomness, induction, right-hemisphere preference, kinesthesia, and sensing-perceiving. Additionally, some intuitive-thinkers, who more often than not turn out to be scholars and find their way into college classrooms at some point and in some manner, may experience frustration, irritation, or annoyance with classroom activities and tests that fail to challenge their minds and may be suppressed; others may choose to leave school. Depending on the grade level, even visual learners and auditory learners can experience dissonance between learning approach and school expectation.

Osmond and colleagues (1974) describe the children's game, "Chin, Chin, Chin, Chinique," in which children make the symbol for paper, scissors, or stone behind their backs and on the word *chinique* all show the symbol they have selected. Depending on the combination, the winner will be the one whose object is not disabled by the objects chosen by the other players. In this game, stone blunts scissors, scissors cut paper, and paper wraps stone. In any given combination, any one of the instruments could be favored (paper prevails over stones, scissors over paper, and stone over scissors). In comparing this game to learning styles in the classroom, Osmond and colleagues contend that "there is no such thing as intrinsically successful or unsuccessful types, or intrinsically better or worse types; there are simply contexts favorable to one and unfavorable to the other" (p. 37).

Although there are not "good styles" and "bad styles" when it comes to the learning process itself, we as Western educators do tend to consider students with styles that match standard teaching practices to be "good" students and other students to be "bad" students, although both sets of students might be labeled just the opposite in other parts of the world. In reality, learning styles, or rather the strategies associated with those styles, are simply more or less effective, depending on the requirements of a given task.

As with the children's game, in the United States, Western standards for assigned tasks disable students with non-Western perception and information-processing styles. Often, these students do not understand their own needs and assume that they are slow or untalented learners, as do their teachers and administrators.

Students who have more than one nonstandard trait are at even greater risk. Noelle is one such example. Her work in mathematics was quite uneven. She performed fine on tests, and this raised her course grades. Her classwork, however, was usually very poor, which had the opposite effect. Whereas the other students began work immediately after receiving an explanation of the math principles and hearing the instructions, Noelle usually sat staring at her book, until the teacher tapped her on the shoulder to get her to start. At that point, Noelle would act confused and would need personalized reexplanation in most cases. Even then, she usually got the problems wrong. Homework was somewhat better, but in a few cases, such as in the computations requiring borrowing, Noelle was consistently incorrect. In these instances, her test grades were also lower.

An interview with Noelle indicated that she had trouble understanding what the teacher was talking about during class. She said that she tried to listen hard, but it made no sense. Sometimes, it began to make sense when she did the problems, especially if the teacher helped her. At night, she read the examples in the book and tried to do those for herself. She really liked doing the examples and seeing how many different ways she could do them and still get the same answer as in the book. She often did not read the explanation because she found it confusing, but she could follow the examples that were worked out, especially if she could compare them to her own way of doing the problems.

On several learning style dimensions, Noelle was not receiving the kinds of input she needed from her teacher. The teacher provided verbal explanations, and she preferred to see what was going on. Perhaps Noelle could have managed the modality conflict (visual-auditory) if that were the only conflict she had to manage.

Unfortunately, she had two other conflicts occurring simultaneously. One of these was a conflict in approach to information acquisition: inductive-deductive. She needed to learn new information through an inductive approach, where she could use examples to come up with the rule, but the teacher preferred to present explanations in advance, which then got in the way of Noelle's ability to later figure out things for herself. Noelle did use induction at home. However, there she had no way to confirm her hypotheses. That meant that she sometimes made wrong assumptions, then learned how to do her math in this incorrect way. Lack of hypothesis confirmation would explain some of her inconsistencies. An error analysis of her mistakes would tell her teacher right away whether or not she was completing her math assignments using an incorrect assumption or hypothesis: There would be a pattern of the same kind of error occurring repeatedly. This turned out to be the case. In subtraction, she had made an incorrect assumption: Error analysis showed that she did not borrow; rather, she always subtracted the smaller number from the larger number. These assumptions can be corrected with explanation and practice, but they first have to be ascertained.

The second cognitive disconnect occurred in the sequential-random dimension. Noelle had trouble, even when working on her own, in following the step-by-step instructions in the book. She needed a less-ordered presentation, so that she could put her own meaning to it and order or organize it in her own way. The organization imposed by the textbook author did not help Noelle; it confused her.

When style wars occur in one dimension, students can experience frustration and less success; they must often use coping strategies or expand their strategy use to manage the assignment in the modality or style necessary. Sometimes, they can use matches in other dimensions to compensate for the dimension in which the learning style conflict is occurring. However, multiple disconnects put students like Noelle at grave risk for failure, no matter how bright they are.

A look at the specific needs of each of these kinds of learners, as shown in the chart on the following page, demonstrates how many learning needs are just not met through standard teaching practices. These needs and conflicts are discussed throughout this chapter as single issues. However, some students may have unmet needs in many domains, compounding their problems. Such situations are discussed in more detail in Chapter 7.

Type of Learners	They Need	They Get
visual (elementary school)	written instructions	verbal instructions
auditory (high school)	aural support	written work
kinesthetic	movement	stationary work
sensing perceiver	rapid pace changes to make things	demand to concentrate listen and memorize
intuitive thinker	to control own learning	orders from others
global	general meaning	details
leveler	commonalities likenesses	contrast differences
synthetic	synthesis creation form new conepts	analysis disassembly explanation of old concepts
reflective	time to think	time restrictions
random	three dimensions holistic organization	two dimensions linear organization
concrete	to practice to try out things to touch field trips trial and error projects	reading explanations pictures films lectures reports
abstract-random	to observe others	tutorials
concrete-random	uncontrolled experiments internships dreams allowance for eccentricity	controlled experiments classrooms reality demands for conformity
concrete-sequential	hands-on activities	workbooks
inductive	rules in action principles in action whole processes	rules in isolation principles in theory sequential segmentation
right-hemisphere preferent	gestalt art background music image	details technology silence verbal input

STYLE WARS

Oxford, Ehrman, and Lavine (1991) suggest that conflicts in learning styles result in psychological battles (from whence they proposed their term, *style wars*) and that untrained students usually lose these battles. The focus of Oxford et al. is on teacher-student conflicts. I contend that the war is much more complex and the "enemy" more guerrilla in form than direct teacher-student conflicts. Style wars take place on four fronts. Students do battle with incomprehensible curricula, inscrutable teachers, incompatible peers, and inappropriate placements. These battles are not restricted to Western versus non-Western learning styles, although that is a common variant. Curricular styles, teaching styles, and class profile can deviate from norms, and in such cases, the students with learning styles favored by the most common approaches to teaching in general education in the United States may suddenly find themselves on the front lines. Any time there is a mismatch for whatever reason on any front, there may be a skirmish.

To the extent that embattled students can "westernize" their behavior, do as they are told, style-flex to accept mainstream learning styles or match the prevalent learning styles in their classroom, and develop secondary preferences to fill in behind their primary preferences, they will become successful students. However, they are still trying to learn out of style, and their success could be greater, if they were allowed to learn in style.

If students cannot adapt, no matter how bright they are, they fail—unless the teacher makes the accommodation to the student in the curriculum, classroom activities, and testing. Often such students are mislabeled and misplaced as learning disabled, fail out of programs, drop out, or are expelled for unacceptable conduct. Knowing which students are at risk and what their needs are helps teachers make the adjustments. It also helps teachers understand where there is a real learning problem and where there is an artificial one caused by style conflict.

Incomprehensible Curriculum

> ☞ *Battles occur where student learning styles do not match curricular styles.*

Typically, professors of subject matter areas are abstract-sequential, analytic, visual-verbal learners and INTJs (Lawrence, 1993). Not surprisingly, most textbooks reflect these characteristics, since most textbooks, even those for elementary school, are written by professors. These authors present information in a logical, sequenced format and in an abstract form. Students are left to make their own connections with the real world. Abstract-random and concrete-sequential students often can cope with such materials, using their abstraction and sequentiality, respectively, but usually only marginally so. Concrete-random students, however, quickly find themselves strangers in their own land. Teachers with concrete-random learning styles (rare) and teachers who can assess the risk that concrete-random students will encounter in working with abstract-sequential course materials supplement the textbook with real-world experiences to contribute to the confidence and success of concrete-random students. Students of teachers who do not make these kinds of accommodations either intuit how to make the necessary adaptations themselves or their success, if any, is less than it could be.

Teaching movements, which dictate the kinds of curricula available, often swing in pendulum-like fashion from one learning style preference to its opposite in an effort to find the perfect curriculum. *We are all too frequently victims of our own method madness.* Usually, changes in teaching movements are promoted by new statistics or some empirical research that appears to show that a hot new method can make a significant difference in learning success. (As an intuitive, I look at most of these statistics with a fair amount of skepticism. When the research methodology and population is explored in-depth, most of the "fantastic" results—empirically supported, of course—can be explained by the effects of conducting the experiment itself: halo effect, more time on task, greater individual attention, teacher buy-in.)

As the pendulum swings, one group of learners falls out of favor, and another group rises to the top. Thus, phonics approaches to teaching reading and grammar-translation approaches to foreign language instruction favored NT, particular, analytic, abstract-sequential, and left-hemisphere-preferent students. When the whole language approach to teaching appeared on the elementary school reading scene and the Natural Approach appeared in the foreign language education world, global students thrived, and particular students suffered. In audiolingual foreign language classes, auditory-impulsive learners flourished, whereas visual-reflective learners floundered. Inquiry method favors the inductives and leaves the deductives unsupported. Direct method favors the deductives and wraps inductives in a straitjacket. Cooperative learning favors the intuitive feelers, and independent study favors the intuitive thinkers. And the list goes on. *Whenever we select one method—whether our choice is prompted by an educational philosophy (itself dictated by the economic and political state of the country in which we are teaching at the time), personal preference (based on our own learner profile and experience), administrative mandate, or persuasion from empirical data or methodologists' claims—we favor some of the learners in the class and disadvantage others.*

Rarely do curricula take into account more than one learning style. Thus, it falls to the classroom teacher to assess the risk of each student vis-à-vis the orientation of the curriculum and to make the necessary accommodations and supplementation to ensure the success of every student.

Some subjects by nature, reinforced by the way they have traditionally been taught, favor one style or another. Algebra speaks to the left-hemisphere-preferent learner and to the abstract learner for whom symbols have meaning, whereas geometry speaks to the right-hemisphere-preferent learner and the concrete learners, for whom form has more meaning than symbols. It is not surprising, then (although math teachers are sometimes surprised), to see the good algebra student wither into a mediocre geometry student and the mediocre algebra student blossom into a good geometry student. Foreign languages with accessible cultures and linguistic systems that parallel English in many ways (e.g., Spanish and French) often appeal to right-hemisphere-preferent learners, whereas languages with complex morphological systems and cultures that are not readily accessible for travel and study by foreigners (e.g., Slavic languages) tend to attract more left-hemisphere-preferent students.[1] Spanish and French have long been taught as means of communication and Slavic languages as linguistic systems for parsing and analyzing. In recent days, professors of Slavic languages in increasing numbers have been teaching these languages as means of communication, with the result that they stylistically disadvantage those students who historically filled Slavic language classrooms, throwing these languages into competition for students with programs such as Spanish and French.

In addition to textbooks, classroom tasks and assignments also have a style orientation, unless the teacher is style-aware and is careful to include activities for a variety of learning styles. Style-aware teachers also remember that the learning disabled (LD) student may be, in fact, disabled or may simply be a victim of a style war. Because students more often than not rise (or fall) to expectations, such teachers give the benefit of a doubt. The specifics of the assignments, then, become very important, and being aware of the style of learning required by a particular assignment can be very useful.

It is often true that a good teacher can teach using any curriculum or textbook, whether or not the teacher believes that the curriculum or textbook has value, and that any teacher can teach a specific curriculum or textbook if that teacher believes in the value of the specific curriculum or textbook. Nonetheless, students learn more effectively and efficiently when teachers use materials that account for students' learning styles (Claxton &Murrell, 1987; Dunn, Beaudry, & Klavas, 1989). In fact, many teachers who can make any curriculum or textbook work are probably already intuitively adapting their approaches to different learning styles.

Inscrutable Teachers

> ☞ *Students with learning styles that differ from those of their teachers lose daily battles in the style wars.*

Teachers often bring expectations to the classroom based on their own teaching/learning preferences, or else they bring a style not their own in which they have been so thoroughly trained that they do not recognize it as alien. When these teaching styles do not match students' learning preferences, conflicts usually occur.

Conflicts in Modality

Conflicts in modality can take many forms. Regardless of the modality preference of teachers, student needs will not be addressed if the teacher teaches only according to his or her own learning style.

Visual teachers are quickly spotted. These teachers write all over the board, bring copious handouts, use overhead projectors and VCRs frequently, and expect students to want to take notes. These teachers reach the visual learners in the class. Auditory and motor learners do not need the kinds of support provided by visual teachers, often tune out, and don't take notes. Over time, they experience battle fatigue. In the classrooms of visual (and motor) teachers, auditory learners end up waiting to hear an explanation that never seems to come, and motor learners seek other outlets for their physical activity needs.

Although visual teachers provide the support that visual learners need, teachers with other modality preferences do not. The result is that visual learners are blinded in some classrooms. The risk that visual learners face changes as they progress through school, which becomes more and more visually oriented. Often, when a teacher points out a "late bloomer," it turns out to be a visual learner, who in the higher grades is beginning to be taught in accordance with his or her learning style.

In early years, visual learners need to "see" answers, which, if we believe the research in neurolinguistic programming, is best accomplished by looking up to access visual memory (Dilts, 1979). They are told to keep their eyes on their own paper, that the answer is not on the ceiling. Yet for many of them, the answer *is* on the ceiling. They need to read directions; they are given verbal instructions on tests. They need to see math problems in order to calculate answers; they must perform oral math in order to meet state requirements. Especially in foreign language and ESL classes, they need to see new vocabulary; in elementary school foreign language classes, they often encounter new words first through videotapes, audio recordings, demonstration, or discussion. Remember McCorkle's struggles (Chapter 2)? All he ever really needed was to see the assignment written on the board. Like McCorkle, visual learners in classes of auditory and motor teachers fail to receive the visual support they need. As a result, visual learners end up with notes that are often meaningless for them later. Without organizational assistance from the blackboard or handouts, visual-sequential learners fail to receive the external organization they need to be able to comprehend, store, and reconstruct lecture material. Visual-random learners fare somewhat better because they can put their own structure on the materials, but they still suffer from paucity of visual input.

Auditory teachers are a blessing for auditory learners and are also easily spotted. Classrooms are set up as round tables, with discussions and the formal presentation of opinions the forum for instruction. Classes tend to be lecture or discussion. Auditory teachers usually provide little visual support, and visual learners suffer in the ways described above. Auditory learners thrive in such classes.

On the other hand, in the classrooms of visual and motor teachers, auditory learners' needs often fall on deaf ears. Auditory learners' risk changes in just the opposite proportions and directions to that of the visual learners; as they progress through school, the amount of input students receive through auditory channels, with the exception of college lecture classes, all but disappears. Once they have learned to read well, they should be able to take in the information visually, the accepted wisdom might contend, but this is not true for auditory learners. Auditory learners need to hear stories and articles; they are told to read them in the book. They need verbal instructions; they get written instructions. In foreign language classes they need to hear the sound of words in order to remember them; they are given paired lists of printed vocabulary words at the beginning or end of textbook lessons. They need to access auditory memory through lateral eye movement; they are told to look at the teacher when talking. They need sound; they get silence.

Motor teachers keep kinesthetic and mechanical students physically involved. Motor teachers, especially kinesthetic ones, can be easily spotted—they are never in the same spot for more than a few moments. I once overheard teachers discussing my kinesthetic teaching style when I took on a group of kinesthetic learners who had fallen behind classmates: "Don't look for the dean in her office; she's probably somewhere in the woods with the students!" Had not all members of the class been kinesthetic, the students may have experienced the typical reaction of visual and auditory students in the classroom of a kinesthetic teacher. Not only do they not receive the learning support they need, they just get plumb tired!

As teachers, we are often as true to type as our students are as learners, even when we are style-aware. It is always an effort to keep the peace where style wars threaten. As I was teaching a class for faculty at a local college recently, I realized how much of my modality comes through in my own teaching, even where the class profile is a mixed modality. Before class started, one of the faculty members in the seminar approached me with a question that he thought related to a previous class but actually related to the content of the upcoming class. I began to brainstorm possibilities with him, and both of us began drawing pictures of the process in action on the blackboard, trying to get an intersection between concrete learning needs and an abstract topic. As other students came in, they were drawn to the activity at the board. After about 15 minutes, I noticed that we as a class had cov- ered a portion of the day's topic, all standing up, all drawing, or reading, or observ- ing, or moving up and away from the chalkboard to point things out, depending on our learning styles. Here we were, a group of well-aged adults, and no one was in a seat. The participants had conformed to my kinesthetic learning style, and any ad- ministrator looking through the door would have considered this gathering to be a nonclass. That portion of the topic covered and my consciousness of other modality needs reawakened (kinesthetic teachers can wear out visual and auditory learners very quickly), the visual and auditory learners went back to their seats and prepared to take notes or to listen, and the one kinesthetic learner found a lounging spot on the side of the classroom.

Kinesthetic learners in classes taught by visual and auditory teachers are often immobilized. These students need to move. They are told to sit still. They need to exercise between classes; they are given five minutes to walk from one room to another. They need to stand; they must sit. They need to touch; they are told to keep their hands to themselves. And far too often, instead of schools finding the right teaching "medicine" to accommodate these students' learning styles, the students are diagnosed as hyperactive and medicated into compliance with school needs (McGuinness, 1985).

Remember Rory's story (Chapter 2)? He did not need medication. He needed a program that would allow him to learn through movement. Of all the learning types, the students who suffer the most are the kinesthetic learners. Classrooms are not set up to include the amount of physical activity and sometimes even noise that they need, and holding still is nearly impossible for them. These students often find themselves face-to-face with truant officers as they find their own kinesthetic ac- tivities—long walks away from school. They simply do not have the patience or attention for the typical pen and paper activities that pervade most classrooms.

At a milder level are the students who express kinesthesia through fidgeting. They are so often told to sit still and pay attention that they waste energy in sup- pressing kinesthetic needs to move about, energy that could be used for learning. I have seen kinesthetic learners who have learned to direct their kinesthesia become voracious readers, boring through several pages a minute, completing research as- signments in half the expected time, and writing full computer programs within minutes. Unfortunately, most teachers, themselves visual or auditory, encourage kinesthetic students to suppress their energy rather than to focus it positively on activity completion.

Temperament Wars

Wars also erupt from differences in psychological type. Schoolhouses are filled principally with SJ and NF adults, although children come in all varieties. Approximately 56% of teachers are SJ types, along with most administrators, although only about 38% of students are SJs. Approximately 32% of the teaching staff types as NF, along with about 12% of the student body. This leaves only about 8% of the teaching staff, who are NT types, to work with a student body of approximately 12% NTs, and about 4% of the teaching staff, who are SP types, to work with a student body of approximately 38% SPs (Keirsey & Bates, 1988).[2] The chart to the left shows the spread of types across teaching and learning bodies more graphically.

% Students	Type	% Teachers
38%	(SJ) sensing-judging	56%
12%	(NF) intuitive-feeling	32%
12%	(NT) intuitive-thinking	8%
38%	(SP) sensing-perceiving	4%

Nearly any student can be at risk, depending on the personality types involved. However, given the spectrum of personality types typically found in schoolhouses, the most likely students to be at risk are the NTs and the SPs. Ironically, the risk factors change dramatically at the university level. There, the majority of professors are NTs. The NT students who felt repressed in SJ-flavored K-12 settings, or were behavior problems, blossom in these professors' classrooms. The SJs, who flourished in K-12 settings, often find themselves in unfamiliar and uncomfortable territory. The NT professors do not provide them with all the logistical details they want (logistics bore NTs), they don't tell them what the rules are (for NTs, most rules are a convention to be ignored), and they don't make explicit expectations (NTs expect everyone to work according to internally-derived expectations).

NTs, by nature, are scholars. In past years, based on a social climate that accepted limited choice in educational venue, these students usually performed well but harbored unpleasant memories of school situations in which they felt constantly thwarted and held back. In wealthier homes, parents placed these children in private schools, where sometimes there was more opportunity for scholarly work. Today, many of these children drop out of school. Some go into home schooling. Others leave education behind. In fact, in the populations I have encountered, the NTs represent the majority of gifted children who drop out of school programs; they cite "boredom," "restriction," and being able to "learn more on their own" as their reasons for leaving school. If the NT is also an introvert, then the dropout rate appears to be even higher.[3]

An NT student can be perceived as a threat to an SJ teacher. A clear example of this occurred a number of years ago when I was a student in a doctoral course in curriculum and instruction. Most of my classmates were local teachers and administrators preparing for certification as superintendents. The professor had opened the class with a question that seemed to be an innocuous icebreaker: "What is a good student?" For 45 minutes, sparring between the rest of the class (clearly solid SJs for the most part) and me (an irrepressible NT) continued along the following lines:

> NT: A good student is one who does what has been assigned, is polite to the teacher, treats other students with respect, completes assigned work on time, prepares for tests, and remembers what has been taught.

> SJ: A good student is one who challenges my assumptions; who sends me back to the drawing board or to the library; whose work takes me in directions I had not previously contemplated; and who changes my assignments to make them more complex, insightful, or useful.

Of course, the SJ teachers were appalled by my NT attitude. One stated, "I would not want a student who challenged me at every turn." As an NT, I live for such students. A good example of this is a recent conference at which papers are normally presented in an abstract-random format—largely read-through with a few questions (maybe) at the end. A colleague, who is also a concrete-random NT, and I presented very tentative results from very new research and theory. The interaction with the audience was intense, informed the direction and content of our presentation, and began almost immediately. One of the participants remarked at the end that he was surprised by the presentation because we probably had the most tentative information of anyone at the conference due to the recency of our work, yet, from the sessions he attended, we were the only presenters "confident enough" to conduct an interactive session. This is not a matter of confidence; it is a matter of style. Concrete-random NTs learn by theory and experimentation; they seek conflict in ideas in order to test hypotheses, to analyze (most are synthetic, so disagreement with analytics help them analyze more deeply), and to reshape their ideas (concrete-random NTs are always ready to rethink, reshape, and take input—on their own terms).

Now, imagine an NT student—who is looking for the goal, the purpose, the ability to reshape ideas—being not in an NT class but in an SJ class, taught by the kinds of teachers who were arguing with me over the definition of a good student; who focus on details, procedures, and tradition; and who want the NTs to learn how to transmit predetermined information and values. *Is it any wonder that many NTs let their teachers focus on transmission of tradition while they themselves focus on alternatives to that classroom?*

In short, NTs need to fly, but non-teachers clip their wings. NTs prefer to produce their own insights. They are met with the need to justify each insight through some form of empiricism. Intuition, as such, is usually neither taught nor allowed. This is true not just of today's schools; it has been true of schools for quite a long time. As early as the 1950s, Guilford (1956, 1959) noted the need to include insight and creativity in school programs. In the 1960s, Bruner (1963) complained that not only is intuition not allowed to operate in school curricula, but that students' intuitive approaches are discouraged. More than 30 years later, little progress has been made in allowing students to fly.

Intuitive thinkers need learning space and hands-off treatment; in other words, they need to learn to fly on their own, in their own way, at their own pace, and on their own time schedule. Unfortunately, SJ teachers usually want to teach them rather than to let them learn. Often, being taught results in boredom for these students. They do not tolerate boredom well nor do they recognize positional authority. *Schools usually provide boredom and authority in large doses and learning space and facilitative teaching in small doses.* The result is the loss of numbers of talented NTs either through dropping out or tuning out.

An NT 12-year-old who had spent most of his life in home study decided that he would give high school another try. After standing in line for more than 2 hours to register for classes the first day, he came home and announced that as long as the school had a paper-based registration system, he would not be standing in line. It wasted his time; he had more worthwhile things to do. Rather than take in a sick note (being an NT, he never feared authority figures nor hesitated to tell them the truth), he returned the next day and explained to the principal that he had cut school, that he would not stand in line for such nonsense as paper-based registration systems, but that he would, if desired, set up a computerized system for the school. (The principal must have been an NT, too, or a very unusual SJ, because he accepted the offer of help without punishment for the behavior!)

An NT in an NF classroom is usually not much happier. While the NF may focus on making the NT happy, the NT usually would prefer to be left alone with his or her books. I remember a college English teacher, obviously an NF type, who frightened me with her writing requirements. Until then, most of my English teachers had been Ts of some sort, or at least accepted me as a T. They were happy with the development of ideas on paper. This teacher, however, returned my papers, asking me to provide personal reactions to the ideas. I pointed out that I had stated my opinion pretty clearly. However, she did not want an opinion; she wanted an emotion. As an NT, I found this to be an intolerable requirement and would put myself into other mindsets so that I could describe an emotion; it was rarely my own emotion, but she never knew. Ultimately, over time, I learned the value of personalization in writing, but I did not learn it from this NF teacher. I resented her, and I loathed the course, even though I liked to write. Had she been aware of the burden that she was placing on the NTs in her classroom, I suspect that she would have found an alternative way to teach them to personalize. After all, NF teachers usually do want their students to be happy and to like them.

The likelihood of an NT falling into the hands of an SP is pretty rare, but in such cases, if the NT cannot have an NT teacher, then this is the second best. The classes may not be cerebral enough for the NT, but the NT will at least appreciate the freedom that SPs usually allow.

SPs fare even more poorly than NT students in most classrooms. They share their temperament with only about 4% of the teachers in the United States. That means that most SPs may never have an SP teacher as a role model, and teachers with other styles usually do not fill the void. Not surprisingly, SPs are overly represented among the population of school dropouts. *They simply retreat from the style wars and leave the battlefield.*

Sensing types live in the world of look, see, and touch, of statistics and raw data collection, of the here and now, and perceivers seek freedom and choice. Sensing types are not out of line with mainstream learning styles. However, the sensing-perceiving combination is. The artisans, to use Keirsey and Bates's (1988) term for this temperament, do often become artists, painters, and musicians. SP students want to sculpt; they may only look and not touch. In the classroom, they need hands-on work, rapid pace changes, and freedom to choose their activities and the means of accomplishing the activities. They may daydream as a way of learning. Their teachers tell them to concentrate. They get rules, regulations, and deadlines. They need to try things out; they are expected to listen and memorize and are penalized when they do not. Clearly, art, home economics, and shop classes should be areas where SPs excel, and often they do. As long as their need for choice and self-expression is respected, these are some classes where they can feel at home in school. They could also be comfortable in other classes, but they usually are not because of the multitude of restrictions placed on their behavior and activities, and even artisan-type classes, such as art, home economics, and shop, can become just as tedious as other classes when taught as a series of rules and their application. SP problems are not endemic just to American schools. An artistically talented, erudite, literate Russian SP I know managed to avoid close to 80% of classroom attendance even in the highly regimented Soviet Union.

SPs' focus on freedom and choice and on *may* and *can* is quickly quelled by SJ teachers' focus on requirements and on *should* and *ought*. Is it any wonder that SPs, who fill elementary school classrooms in large numbers, are reduced to small numbers in college and to only 4% of the teaching body? Who volunteers to remain in prison or to return to prison as a guard?

SPs fare somewhat better in NT classrooms because these teachers are usually open to unusual activities if they enhance learning. After all, the natural focus of the NT is on learning, and many NT teachers will intuitively create the climate necessary for learning, often without understanding why. However, SPs may find NT classrooms too cerebral with insufficient scope for action, especially if the SP is extraverted and the NT is introverted and visual or auditory.

SP students who are Fs may also enjoy an NF classroom. In this case, at least one aspect of their personality needs is being met. If the SP is a T, however, he or she may feel smothered by an NF teacher who offers too little freedom and too much relationship.

SPs, of course, fare best in SP classrooms. Surprisingly, so do many other students. SP teachers can sometimes appear "larger than life" to students of other temperaments. Although they make up a small percentage of the teaching force, most of the SP teachers I have known have been very talented. (Perhaps it comes from all the style flexing that they had to do to succeed in a hostile educational system.) I know a wonderful ISFP foreign language teacher in a regimented government school. The combination works well for the students. The SPs get the hands-on work and freedom that they need. The teacher's focus on freedom allows the NTs to fly. The NFs receive the personal interaction they need, because the teacher is an F. The SJs thrive, because the U. S. government imposes such strict regulations that SJ students do not have to rely on the teacher for external structure;

they meet it the minute they walk through the door. The person who suffers the most in this arrangement is the teacher, who may not be comfortable with the extent of external structure imposed on the classroom and who has few SP colleagues.

NFs in classrooms of NTs, SPs, and SJs, unless the SPs and SJs are also Fs, may find school a cold place. NFs in general display strong flexibility and can usually suffer classrooms of teachers with other styles well from the teacher's point of view. Although many NFs crave an unrealized opportunity to learn synthetically (they may call it "creative"), the greatest difficulty, probably unexpressed, is that the affective needs of the NF students may not be met, so that the overall feeling is one of dissatisfaction. In this case, the learning styles of peers become important, as well as the relationships with them. (Chapter 5 provides suggestions to T teachers on ways to meet the F needs of NF students that extend beyond these teachers' own comfort range in interpersonal relations.) Fortunately, NFs, of all the personality types, tend to be the most flexible in the classroom, and many adapt to any instructor, albeit with some occasional emotional scarring.

SJs who find themselves in the classroom of SJs (there is a high probability of this happening frequently) know that all is well with the world. However, SJs in the classroom of teachers with other learning styles have different reactions. They may find themselves shocked by NT irreverence, smothered by NF warmth, and lost in SP freedom. However, being SJs, they try to follow whatever "new rules" appear on their horizon. The problem is that NTs and SPs are likely to give them few rules, and the NFs are likely to give them rules that are too personal for comfort.

Perhaps Machiavelli was a relative of mine, or perhaps NTs have a sadistic underside. Whatever the reason, in teaching methods courses and seminars for practicing teachers, I like to arrange conditions not only so that participants understand teacher-student learning-style differences but feel them acutely. This usually means deliberately placing opposing styles together in a small-group and giving them a time-sensitive task requiring consensus. In one such activity, conducted in Ukraine, an NF university dean, working with a group of SJ teachers, broke away from the group, came to me trembling, and begged, "Please make them stop being so dogmatic!" In another instance, an SJ school principal, working with a group of SP psychologists from Novosibirsk and Tomsk, Russia, stood up, stated, "I'll return when you all come to your senses," and strode out of the room, slamming the door. (I'm not totally sadistic; following this exercise I include some other activity that reunites the participants.) The point is that if teachers, who are becoming style-aware, experience intensely negative emotions when required to complete a joint assignment in collaboration with colleagues of different learning styles, it is likely that these same emotions will be felt (and even more intensely) by students studying with teachers whose personality types differ from theirs.

Cognitive Variances

Similarly, conflicts in the cognitive domains can occur on any of several planes. While it is more typical to find a student with a non-Western learning style in conflict with a teacher with a Western learning style, other possibilities occur more frequently than we think.

Particular-global conflicts, especially the negative influence of the particular teacher on global students, are readily visible. Global students often become bored, even when they are being presented with new information. Global learners are not interested in all the details that fascinate particular teachers; they focus on the big picture. In other words, they see the forest. Most schools, programs, and tests emphasize details; they expect all students to see the trees. As a result, *students who see the forest usually test and feel inferior to their peers who see all kinds of trees.* In foreign language classrooms, for example, particular teachers tend to fully explore a listening text in detail with global students. Global students almost always unconsciously pick up the general meaning, which is good enough for them; they don't really care to go into the details but want to move on. Global learners thrive on authentic language, and communicative approaches to teaching foreign languages attract them. Multiple choice tests and the decontextualized language of traditional textbooks are just as difficult for global learners as authentic materials for particular learners. Global NTs may consider the particular teacher incompetent; after all, he or she cannot see beyond the details.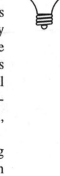

Even humanities courses can have a particular bent, which may cause learning difficulties for global students. An example of this is the experience of Susan in eighth-grade English class. She failed an English test which required her to find 10 grammar errors in a list of 20 sentences. This was not unusual; she almost never was able to pass this section of the unit tests for English. Susan was a global learner. Her teacher had given her a test that was more appropriate for students who are particular learners. Susan was not flexible enough to change her learning style to accommodate the particular requirements of the test. If students are global learners, they tend to miss such details as the wrong tense or a dangling modifier, even though they may be excellent writers, because their global style causes them to "see" the sentences through their underlying meaning, as they fit into a global picture, not as they are presented on the page before them. Susan's ability to recognize incorrect grammar declined even further when the sentences appeared in any kind of context at all, such as a paragraph. This should have been another indication that Susan was a global learner, not a poor writer. Proofreading is the forte of the particular learner, not of the global learner. As matters turned out in reality, Susan proved herself not only a good writer but an excellent writer when the terms of the test did not require her to work in a nonpreferred learning style.

Although the combination of particular students with global teachers is rarer, as is the use of global assignments in classrooms, when the tables are turned and particular students are paired with global teachers, particular students quickly become demotivated. What has worked for them before—memorizing all the details— is no longer esteemed. Particular NT students may also write off the teacher as incompetent—after all, any teacher who cannot see and remember all those details cannot be very smart. In foreign language classrooms, to return to the example above, particular students prefer tradition. They find the use of authentic language and authentic materials difficult, especially if they are not allowed to use dictionaries. As a reaction to teaching aimed at real communication in the field of foreign language education, based on an extensive use of authentic materials in the classroom, some textbook publishers are now asking for fewer authentic materials in foreign language textbooks. They claim that these materials are too difficult for teachers and students. It is very likely that these textbook publishers or the teachers or the students (or all three) are particular learners.

Sharpening teachers, as already shown, can unconsciously create difficulties in learning for **leveling** students. Levelers seek the patterns, the commonalities, the likenesses. Levelers experience trouble placing items in a category (e.g., phyla in biology), solving analogies, and noticing morphologic differences in foreign language classes because they do not focus on characteristics that differentiate items. In English class, they may be asked to write a composition contrasting two items, concentrating on their differences. Although this may seem like a small detail, an assignment that requires the application of a nonpreferred learning style in providing content for a writing assignment can effectively disengage an otherwise industrious student. Before levelers can be graded on their ability to *write* about differences, they often need help to *see* those differences, or the assignment needs to be changed to allow them to write about likenesses. Before they can put information into categories, they need to acquire the strategy of categorization. Before they can remember to apply appropriate grammar in communicating in English or foreign languages, that grammar must have some significance for them.

Leveling teachers can create as much trauma for sharpening students as sharpening teachers for leveling students. They expect sharpeners to find the relationships between seemingly disparate items (e.g., squares, triangles, and circles) readily; sharpeners do not. Foreign language teachers expect sharpeners to gloss over details and begin to read or listen at a native speaker tempo in order to develop fluency; they usually cannot. Leveling mathematics teachers expect sharpeners not to get mired in calculations but to use the calculations to understand theory; they often cannot. Social sciences teachers want sharpeners to put aside their fascination with empiricism and dates and concentrate on trends and superordinate characteristics; frequently, they cannot. (Chapter 6 provides some suggestions on strategy training to help levelers begin to see differences and sharpeners to begin to see relationships.)

Analytic teachers, as we have seen, can be the bane of **synthetic** students. This is a very typical style war in American schools, as well as in a number of European schools. Synthetic students need to form their own worlds. They are told to explain someone else's world. In most school programs, analysis, not synthesis, tends to be encouraged, perhaps because it is easier to grade the accuracy of the disassembly of a thing than the value of the creation of a thing.

Some gifted programs use synthesis and synthetic tasks in teaching math, such as allowing students to apply math knowledge, including developing new math concepts, for solving social problems. Regular education students, who are synthetic learners, could also benefit from such activities. However, they rarely receive them because they are considered too difficult for the average math student by analytic writers of math textbooks.

Math is perhaps the strongest example of subjects taught nearly exclusively by analysis. However, it is not the only example. Rarely before upper undergraduate university levels does synthesis become a requirement for learners. Where it appears earlier, it is usually in isolated art, music, foreign language, and ESL classes.

In English classes, typical writing activities include textual analysis, reporting, retelling, and emulating a specific style of writing. Combining three kinds of writing styles to create a new genre would be considered beyond the capacity of high school students, as would most synthetic activities. Yet for synthetic learners, these activities are easier than the conscious unraveling of matter that characterizes the analytic approach.

When I was in high school, I wrote an autobiographical essay using stream-of-consciousness style and much synthesis, combining experiential themes into a unique theory of existence. The essay was intended as a dry run for college applications, and the teacher definitely did *not* like it. She was not a bad teacher, and she did point out important coping strategies for getting into college and succeeding in an analytic world. On the other hand, the message, like many others I received in K-12 days, was that synthesis was unwelcome in the classroom.

Synthetic teachers, however, do appear in classrooms, and for analytic students, they are frightening enigmas. They expect instantaneous appearance of product and process, and they usually do not feel any need to elucidate or elaborate on the thinking process needed to get the product. In these instances, analytic students who may have been stellar performers find themselves clueless as to how the teacher has arrived at a specific conclusion and without strategies for completing synthetic assignments. (For these students, teaching synthetic learning strategies, as described in Chapter 6, can be very helpful.)

Reflective learners sense grave risks in the classrooms of **impulsive** teachers—risks that they are reluctant to take. Reflective learners need time to think in class before responding, but they often are not allowed this. They are told to hurry up and answer, not to be "poky." They need Socratic dialogue; they get comprehension checks that ask a simple question and require a quick response. They need to be the last to answer; they get called on first. They need time to ponder test answers, but their exams are taken from them just as they are getting started. This is perhaps more true for the United States than for other cultures, but to some extent, it occurs wherever impulsives and reflectives meet.

A faculty member in one of my seminars aptly described the reaction of a reflective learner to interaction with an impulsive learner. Recounting a telephone conversation that she, a reflective learner, had with her impulsive son, she mentioned that she had advice and ideas to share with him, but before she could formulate these, the conversation was over. "It was," she said, "like trying to drink from a fire hose." Or, to use a different analogy, impulsive teachers often psychologically trample their reflective learners.

In discussing reflective learners, the case of one fifth-grader comes to mind. Frank was an enigma to his teachers. He seemed somewhat shy, particularly withdrawn, and, at times, especially obtuse. When called upon for an answer in class, he often hesitated. Sometimes, he did not respond at all. Occasionally, when pushed, he would respond, but in these cases, his answers were usually incorrect. However, he did do well on tests, especially power (untimed) tests, in spite of taking longer than other students to finish. Because he did not leap forward with answers, Frank was initially labeled socially insecure by his teacher.[4] This can be a very unfair label for students who simply need to think before responding, rather than responding while thinking. In fact, Frank was quiet by nature, but he was far from shy. When it was important for him to speak up, he would do so. His teacher was an impulsive learner, and possibly the vast majority of students in the classroom were impulsive. The teacher expected immediate responses, and the students were eager to give them. But Frank needed time to think and analyze what was being presented, to fit new information into information he already knew, and to consider how to phrase his response before answering. Sometimes he needed to be able to observe other students interacting with the same information in order for that information to be "learnable" for him. Frank's in-class participation and his test performance, especially his performance on power tests, indicate that Frank was the victim of a style war, not a poor learner.

To make matters worse, impulsive learners often experience much frustration when many reflective learners are in the same classroom. They don't want to "wait" for them. At a faculty development seminar I conducted with a colleague, we deliberately gave an involved questionnaire to the participants. The impulsives, not anxious to invest much psychological energy in a questionnaire, finished rapidly, then complained about having to wait for their reflective peers. "Just give them a time limit, and they'll meet it," they urged us.

Impulsive students in a reflective classroom, a much rarer combination, encounter a different set of troubles. Impulsives often move on without really completing their first task. They are quickly bored with routine and impatient with waiting for responses. Impulsive students with a reflective teacher, especially if the student is global-synthetic and the teacher particular-analytic, rarely want to put the time and effort into thinking that the reflective teacher expects. The result is often a tug-of-war, with the student trying to move the class along and the teacher trying to explore the topic more thoroughly. If there are a number of impulsive students in the classroom, reflective teachers may feel beleaguered. If there are a few impulsive students in the classroom, the teacher may consider the impulsives learning disabled or think that they suffer from attention deficit disorder and request an evaluation for special education placement. According to Keogh and Donlan (1972) and Naigle and Thwaite (1979), surveys of special education classrooms indicate that the majority of students in these classrooms are impulsive learners. Ironically, impulsives are risk takers, a good characteristic for learning, but in this war, the risk taking put them at such risk that they lost the battle. (And if their special education teachers, or if the resource teachers in an inclusion program, are also reflective, they may lose the war.)

Inductive learners need to teach themselves, but instead they frequently get taught by **deductive** teachers. They learn by discovery, by seeing examples, and by observing how things work in a larger setting. They understand without conscious explanation, and they make hypotheses that they need to test out. Teachers routinely try to "teach" these students through step-by-step procedures and explanations, which more often than not simply confuse inductive learners and preempt them from making hypotheses. Deductive teachers want to go from the whole to the part; inductive learners want to see multiple parts so that they can understand the whole. Inductive learners can attempt to memorize rules, but they usually ultimately fail to do so. Even if they memorize the rule, they can rarely subsequently apply it. To cope, many inductive learners tune out during class and do their studying in study hall or at home. Other times, as teachers begin deductive explanations, inductive students quickly figure out what is going on, yet they have to sit through long, boring, detailed explanations, anyway. *Sometimes teachers are too busy teaching to realize that students have already learned!* As a result, the inductive learners become frustrated, stop listening, doodle, working on other projects, write letters, pass notes, and otherwise involve themselves in activities that teachers generally do not appreciate.

Especially difficult for inductive learners are traditional mathematics classes, where the rules are explained, then calculations based on the rules are completed. By presenting the conscious processing of rule explication, teachers deprive inductive learners of developing their own (usually unconscious) hypotheses.

One gifted 10-year-old, an inductive learner, asked his high school algebra teacher please not to teach during class because it interfered with his learning. (He won no brownie points. The teacher had not wanted a student whose "feet did not touch the floor" in her class. Now she found him impertinent as well as short, and he ended up studying his algebra in the guidance office, which actually worked out quite well.)

Contrary to popular thinking, inductive learners can be found in special education classes. Unfortunately, the typical special education approach of presenting an overview (in many classrooms even this does not happen), followed by very deductive and atomized explanations, then limited and highly controlled practice, further handicaps inductive LD and special education students. The teacher does all the thinking for the student; the student just has to remember the predigested material. In the case of inductive students, this does not make the learning easier; it makes it harder!

This reality became quite clear to me recently. The AGSI serves as a work site for multiple-handicapped teenagers. One day everyone was more than fully occupied when the folding machine being used by the teenager with the most severe learning disabilities broke. No one had time to assist him, and having seen evidence that this student was an inductive learner, I told him simply to "fix it." He looked at me as if I were crazy. This may have been the first time that anyone had put such a requirement on him—or given him permission to use his inductive skills. Given the latitude to experiment and make mistakes, if necessary, he took the machine apart and fixed it.

On the other hand, **deductive** learners live for rules and love to receive explanations from their teachers. However, the exceptions to the rules that the inductive learners take in stride, deductive learners labor over and demand logical explanations for. They rarely receive them from inductive teachers. The teacher is more likely to suggest that the students just accept the exception on faith. The concept in foreign language classes of giving students materials that are just slightly above their current level of knowledge in order to develop foreign language processing strategies for authentic materials (Krashen, 1982) is taxing to deductive learners. They usually want to remain at their current level, where everything can be explained. With deductive teachers, deductive students can usually force the explanation, but inductive teachers are usually less moved by such pleas.

Concrete-abstract battles change character depending on grade level. Elementary school classrooms often provide concrete learning experiences. However, by the time students reach high school and college, they are being told "hands off," even though they need to try things out, to practice, and to touch. They are given a book with pictures and explanations. They need field trips; they get films. They need trial and error; they get lectures. They need to work on projects; they are asked to write reports.

When concrete students do end up with a concrete teacher, they feel a great sense of peace and satisfaction. However, the abstract students, who have been advantaged, start to feel besieged. They love textbooks and lectures and dislike field trips. On field trips, abstract learners tire easily and remember little; they often do not take in the information to begin with.

The miscommunication between abstract learners and concrete teachers can occur at any level and seemingly even in cases where both parties are aware of learning-style differences. In 1994, I participated as one of several guest lecturers in a 2-week seminar for foreign language teachers from all over Siberia. The leaders of the seminar, mostly university professors, were abstract learners; the teachers were almost exclusively concrete learners. The ultimate task of the seminar, the culmination of a 2-year project to redefine foreign language education in the region, was to produce templates for new courses. At the final session, the teachers presented their sample lessons with pride, only to be berated by the seminar leaders for failing their country's hope in them by not producing "proper" templates. One of the teachers looked at me, with tears forming, and said, "Help us!" Asking for the floor, I pointed out that, although we had talked in some depth about abstract-concrete differences in the seminar, hoping to avoid future conflict, we had nevertheless just encountered such a style war in practice. The abstract leaders had assumed that a template would be a theoretical, symbolic model that could serve as a mold for new lessons and new textbooks. The concrete teachers had assumed that a template would be a real-life example that could be emulated for new lessons and new textbooks. Before the abstract leaders berated the teachers, they should have berated themselves for not providing these concrete teachers with concrete models (i.e., examples) of the theoretical, symbolic templates that they wanted.

Random students crave freedom; **sequential** students crave order. If the conditions are reversed, neither type of student learns effectively.

Amorphous random learners are boxed into a square world. They need to organize in three dimensions. They are told to use two. When they write essays, they organize them holistically. They are told that they are disorganized because their presentations are not organized, yet they know that they did organize them. The classwork and homework of random students usually garner comments such as "messy" or "disorganized" from the sequential teacher. My stream-of-consciousness autobiographical high school essay is an example of random organization. Because the teacher was likely a sequential learner, my organizing device (not a legitimate form of organization at all to her) gave her yet another reason for disliking this synthetic, random product. On the other hand, the ordered approach required by sequential teachers will probably always seem overly restrictive to the random leaner.

Sequential students who find themselves in the classes of random teachers feel lost without external organization, established procedures, and a step-by-step process. (Actually, random students also need order, but they provide it internally on their own, whereas sequential students follow an externally-provided order.)

The sequential student may find the random teacher's explanations to be "rambling" and "disorganized." On student critiques of teachers, I have commonly found such comments from sequential students who write about very capable random teachers. Some frustrated sequential students go as far as to say, "teacher does not prepare for class." At the same time, random students' comments on these same capable teachers include "brilliant explanations" and "intuitively understands what is needed for us to learn." As a supervisor, I long ago learned to read student critiques from the point of view of learner-teacher cognitive style (in)compatibility and to visit classes regularly to determine for myself the quality of teaching and the locus of any style conflicts.

As a random teacher frequently teaching sequential learners, I have encountered a minor learning-styles skirmishes when I have listed right-hemisphere traits on the left-hand side of the chalkboard and left-hemisphere traits on the right-hand side of the chalkboard. To me, there is a clear sequence (my own, of course: The right-hemisphere traits, which tend to be the ones at the center of discussion because they are the ones that tend to create conflict in the classroom, were put on the board first, that is, on the left). To accommodate sequential learners, I have frequently had to erase the lists and rewrite them in a more traditional order.

Kolb type differences between teachers and students can have a serious negative impact on the ability to establish rapport. They can also cause learning difficulties.

Accommodator teachers were self-learners as students: They learned from trial and error and independent effort. They often practice facilitative instruction because they themselves learn best when left to their own devices, supported by limited, targeted external assistance. Accommodators fare well in the classes of accommodator teachers, but the lesson may not appear to be a "real" lesson to students, teachers, and administrators of other types. Accommodators may have been the original survivors of the human race, if one views the history of education from the viewpoint of Borgen and Rudner (1981): "In the beginning, there was no education. No deliberate teaching or learning. Experience was the teacher. Learning took place, literally, by mistake. Learning was correcting a mistake, and, if one survived, trying not to make it again" (p. vii). Facilitative learning, when practiced by accommodators with accommodators, may well look like "learning by mistake." Accommodators, both teachers and students, love mistakes. These students are high risk takers; they realize that a mistake is not world-ending, but world-opening, a glimpse into something new, a step in another direction, or the opportunity to back up and start over. Accommodator teachers are fascinated by errors and error analysis; they enjoy looking for the reasons behind the errors that students make because these errors tell them so much about student thought processes.

Accommodator students often seek out accommodator teachers. In higher education, they do not hesitate to drop a class taught by a nonaccommodator professor if they can find a class taught by an accommodator. Thus, accommodators sometimes elect a subject not for its content but because they have ascertained that the teacher is one who will let them experiment and learn independently.

I had one such instructor in a college English class. Clearly an accommodator, he quickly intuited the presence of an accommodator student. "You don't need this class," he told me. "Make up your own assignments." Of course, I needed the class, and of course, I needed feedback on my writing. What he meant was that an accommodator does not need the deliberate instruction, rules, and outlines, followed by careful implementation, that he was providing to the nonaccommodator students in the class. He left me alone, and I turned in easily three times the total written pages required by the course. I learned a lot that semester and did a lot that semester, and I did not even consider it work. Other accommodators report similar experiences. Especially high on their list of favorite academic approaches is contract learning; they often report doing more learning than they contract to do and contracting to do more learning than the typical student would do in a traditional course.

Accommodator students do not seek out nonaccommodator teachers because these teachers won't leave accommodators alone. Accommodator students need independence in learning. They are placed in cooperative group activities, are given lists to memorize, and are punished if they do not act like everyone else. They need internships; they are given classrooms. They need to dream; they are washed in reality. Today's emphasis on team teaching and cooperative learning across disciplines assists the social learners, who were previously ignored, but disadvantaged a new group of students: those who learn independently (especially the accommodators and assimilators)—and doubly so if they are also introverts and intuitive thinkers. Accommodators, whether in gifted, regular, or special education, need to be able to make up their own activities. Few accommodators, given a choice, elect subjects such as home economics and shop, because all too frequently these subjects are taught as the proper following of a recipe or blueprint (of course, they do not have to be taught this way—there can be much creativity allowed in both).

Even considering that some special education students might be accommodators flies in the face of most contemporary education theory and practice. These students are not learning in regular education classes, the conventional wisdom goes, so they need more assistance, not less. Few special education teachers have the courage or insight to allow their students independence in learning.

Accommodator students who are paired with assimilator teachers may never show up for class. However, they may do very well on tests and somehow learn all by themselves. The teacher often is superfluous in traditional teaching roles. Furthermore, the assimilator teacher may find the accommodator student unruly. The accommodator student usually finds the assimilator teacher restrictive. These reactions may set the scene for a serious battle between accommodator students and assimilator teachers. I once observed a special education class in which the teacher wanted students to learn the value of money, shopping skills, and simple arithmetic in a seemingly integrated activity. The teacher clipped pictures of food items from the paper, along with their prices. The students were to write down the name of the item on one line and its price on the next. While this activity appears to be concrete, it was giving the students, most of whom appeared to be concrete-random learners, a hard time. They needed an activity that would allow them to organize in their own way and to do it in a meaningful environment. I suggested to the teacher that she consider handing the students a set amount of money and a newspaper, letting them determine what they wanted to buy and if they had enough money for it. The teacher, an assimilator, was shocked. To her, my exercise appeared much more difficult than the one that the students could not do. For her, it would have been: It represented a nonpreferred learning style for her. For her students, though, it might have been more manageable than her request for them to work out of style. *Teachers do not dream of asking all the right-handed students in the class to complete a task with their left hands and the left-handed students to work with their right hands, yet they are willing to ask students to work against their natural brain organization when it comes to cognitive, rather than motor, applications.*

In converger classrooms, accommodator students feel restricted. They are trial and error learners. Making mistakes is actually a very effective way for them to learn. However, many school programs are set up to reward only "correct" answers (and often "correct" is defined within very narrow parameters—these parameters can often be incredibly narrow if students are being taught via computer-based instruction). Mistakes are punished overtly and when not overtly, then subtly. In science classes, accommodators are handed manuals to follow. These frustrate them; they feel "tied in place." Manuals answer the questions "What?" and "How?" but the question that most accommodators want to answer is "What if?" — and they want to answer that themselves.

Accommodator students in diverger classrooms fare a little better. At least the divergers will let them put their own structure on learning. Their frustration usually comes from the amount of group work assigned and what they consider to be the waiting time (while brainstorming, watching filmstrips and demonstrations, etc.) before the "real work" begins.

Assimilator students work well with assimilator teachers. This is the happy coincidence that marks Western approaches to teaching. However, there are a number of instances when assimilator students end up in classrooms of teachers with other learning styles.

Assimilator students in the classroom of convergers complain of too much hands-on work. In the classroom of divergers, they complain of too much talk. They label both a waste of time.

Assimilator students in an accommodator's classroom may always feel like they are skating on thin ice: They never know what is underneath or when they will break through. The rules are usually not clear enough for them, and the amount of risk taking expected of them is just plain frightening.

Accommodator teachers may become frustrated with assimilator students' need for details, information, and deductive explanations and may label them slow. (An assimilator teacher would label the same student competent.) Accommodator teachers tend not to provide the sequence and step-by-step direct instruction often desired by convergers or the preactivity work (demonstration, discussion) and small-group interaction needed by divergers. When they must do so, they may feel annoyed.

Divergers in distress, whether in accommodator classrooms or the classrooms of a teacher with another learning style, are sometimes isolated in lonely waters. They need to experience subject matter and observe other students at work. They often learn more by watching than by doing, and frequently they must watch before they do. In some programs, when they encounter difficulty in learning, they are isolated in tutorials.

I made this same mistake myself as an administrator. A student in a Russian program I supervised was beginning to flounder. Because I happened to be flush with staff at the time (a rare occurrence), I thought myself quite generous and ingenious to place this student in a tutorial for a major part of the day. I felt less complacent when his grades immediately and sharply fell. Analyzing the situation, I became acutely aware that I had unintentionally deprived him of the only thing that was helping him—his classmates. This mistake, I am sure, is frequently made by other administrators. The subject matter being taught does not matter; divergers are consistent in their need to learn from others and from the use of demonstration and audiovisual presentation, that is, to watch before doing.

Diverger students in a converger's classroom find themselves pushed into activities for which they have little interest. They do not need hands-on activities; "a picture is worth a thousand words." They do not want someone else's order imposed upon them. They want to create their own order, and they want it to be accepted.

Divergers in the classrooms of assimilators are equally bored. They want to see and to organize, not to listen and to memorize.

Diverger teachers, on the hand, provide too much "show and tell" to keep assimilators, convergers, and accommodators happy. Assimilators and convergers often complain that divergers are "disorganized." They look for external structure, and it is not there.

Convergers need answers to the question "How?" and they require hands-on practice. They are told to memorize answers to the question "What?" and to learn through reading, listening, and memorization. They are asked to memorize rules in math classes, formulae in physics and chemistry classes, phyla in biology classes, dates in history classes, declensions and conjugations in foreign language classes, and vocabulary words in ESL classes. Teachers in elementary school are frequently convergers, so some of these problems tend not to show up until later. In the populations with which I have worked, very few of the college professor crowd have been convergers. The assumption I make, then, is that the changing methods of instruction weed out convergers somewhere between high school and graduate school.

Converger students become lost in the classrooms of diverger teachers. They look for sequence; they find none. They look for example; they find none. They look for application; they find none.

In the classrooms of assimilators, convergers get the structure they need. However, they do not get the practice they need.

In the classrooms of accommodators, they are frightened. They do not know where or how to begin self-instructed learning.

Right-hemisphere-preferent students need imagery. When they end up in the clutches of **left-hemisphere-preferent** teachers, they get verbal input. Our western civilization places value on verbal skills and downplays the importance of image. This places right-hemisphere-preferent learners, who prefer to learn non-verbally through image, at risk. Right hemisphere students remember faces; they are expected to remember names. They need gestalt; they get details. They focus on art; they are thrown into technology-based classrooms. They often want music in the background; they are expected to work in silence (which they find distracting).

In some courses, right-hemisphere-preferent students fare better than others. For example, they fare well in foreign language classes at the beginning of study, where the focus is on phonetics and intonation, although once words and grammar become the focus, their comfort disappears. They do occasionally run into language-learning problems, especially with left-hemisphere-preferent teachers, who are concerned with accuracy. To expect right-hemisphere-preferent students to monitor their foreign language speech output for accuracy is unrealistic; they do not monitor their speech output in their own language, and it is frequently inaccurate. Activities and tests which rely on monitoring are largely unsuccessful with these students. Equally unsuccessful is the attempt to get these students to acquire new information through didactic explanations or presentations of rules. At best they are bored, at worst confused.

When thrown into left-hemisphere style math and science classes, right-hemisphere-preferent students slip and slide. They search for the gestalt, which could be there, but they usually only get details—explanations and calculations. This is especially true for students from non-European immigrant families (e.g., Hispanic students, Afro-American students, and Native American students, most of whom tend to be right-hemisphere-preferent) in a class of descendants of European immigrants, who tend to be left-hemisphere-preferent (Bogen, 1975; Lennon, 1988; Melton, 1990; Scales, 1987; Springer, 1981).

The reason that right-hemisphere-preferent math and science students fare poorly is often not attributable to the nature of those subjects but to the way Western civilization has decided to teach them. Research into Native American populations, who tend to be more right-hemisphere-preferent, shows that mainstream public education does not value these traits, placing these students at risk in mainstream classrooms (Huber & Prewardy, 1990). Too often, the blame for failure in mainstream American schools is placed on the culture group as a whole ("They don't value education" is one of the more common complaints), rather than on the actual cause, the incompatibility between learning style of individual students and the orientation of the school program.

Left-hemisphere-preferent students fare little better in the clutches of right-hemisphere-preferent teachers. A clear example comes from foreign language class-rooms. Unlike their right-hemisphere-preferent peers who become "awfully flu-ent" in foreign languages, left-hemisphere-preferent students over. Attempts to draw them into free conversation, especially in the early stages of foreign language ac-quisition, are rarely successful. They want to wait until they have finished analyz-ing or memorizing the language! Listening skills develop very slowly in left-hemi-sphere-preferent students; therefore, to expect these students to learn through lis-tening, a typical expectation of right-hemisphere-preferent teachers, is unreason-able.

A number of years ago, one left-hemisphere preferent student in the 10-month, intensive Russian program at the Foreign Service Institute, studying with mainly right-hemisphere-preferent teachers, struggled throughout the course. Regardless of the impact on her grades, she steadfastly refused to speak a word until she had mastered the grammatical system and had acquired a sizable vocabulary. The teachers fretted over her seeming lack of progress, until 1 month before the end of the course. At that point in the course, students usually made presentations in Russian at a public conference on topics of current interest to the academic community. At this conference, the "mute" student spoke for the first time, delivering a well-organized, thoughtful presentation of 20 minutes' duration, then confidently fielding questions from the audience. She went on to graduate near the top of the class in proficiency level. She had done exactly what she had insisted on doing—not speaking any Russian until she could talk as eruditely in Russian as she could in English.

Incompatible Peers

☞ *When students do not match the class average,*
they wage war alone.

Interestingly, teachers often intuitively teach to the class profile (the set of domi-nant learning styles in a given class). Sometimes, this is done purely instinctively. Other times, this is done knowingly on some cognitive level. In 1994, I taught a graduate teaching methods course in which I encountered a class of near-clones, even though students came from across the United States and from as far away as Europe. This could have made for easy teaching, but the class profile differed from my own learning-style profile on every dimension imaginable. The students were particular; I am global. They were visual; I am kinesthetic. They were introverted; I am extraverted. They were reflective; I am impulsive. They were deductive; I am inductive. They were analytic; I am synthetic. There were sequential; I am random. Teaching that class required extraordinary adjustment on my part. My teaching on the first day, based on no known information about the students, reflected my own learning style. During that first hour, however, I determined the class profile through observation of student behavior and their reaction to my teaching style, and in sub-sequent lessons for the remainder of the semester, I adjusted the instruction not to match my comfort level but to accommodate the comfort level of the students. The students noticed this, and my accommodations taught them how they could accom-modate the learning styles of their own students.

As the teacher changes to accommodate these needs, the student whose learning style does not match the majority becomes at risk (even if the student has a "mainstream," or Western, learning style). In the teaching methods course described above, the one concrete-global in the class (who did match my learning styles in those dimensions) became at risk because of his deviation from the class profile, and I had to alter his assignments, both in class and for homework (as well as my concept of "deadline" because he was also a perceiving type versus my judging type), to match his learning needs in order to give him an equal chance for success, based on an equal, not greater, effort.

A teacher I know related the following situation in which accommodation to the class profile occurred sharply in the middle of a philosophy course that she was taking. The first half of the course, an admitted "experiment," was taught in the style of the philosophers being studied. That teacher was doing well and enjoying the course but was almost alone in that experience. As a result of the other students' difficulties, the professor changed the instructional format to a lecture and text approach, and the teacher nearly failed. That professor, in accommodating "the many," forgot to accommodate also "the one" (see Chapter 7 for a more detailed discussion on accommodating all students).

For students who do not match the class profile, their preferred learning style, which may have been favored in previous classes, is now in disfavor, and they are forced to take in new information in nonpreferred ways. By comparison with their classmates, who are using their preferred styles, the performance of these new minority students, who are using their nonpreferred styles, is often inferior.

As we have seen before, "what seems" is far more important than "what is." This is very true when we examine what happens to students who find themselves in a class with a profile that significantly differs from their own learner profile and learning styles. For example, the reflective learner in a group of reflective learners will blend in with the group. That same reflective learner in a group of impulsive learners will appear to be slow. The impulsive learner in a group of impulsive learners will blend in with the group. That same impulsive learner in a group of reflective learners will appear aggressive or sloppy and careless. The random learner in a group of random learners will blend in with the group. The random learner in a group of sequential learners will appear to be disorganized. The sequential learner in a group of sequential learners will blend in with the group. That same sequential learner in a group of random learners will appear to be uncreative or a limited thinker.

In classes that have a highly global class profile, no matter what the teacher's learning preference or the persuasion of the curricular materials, the global majority is apt to turn almost any activity, and especially small-group work, into a global activity, and especially if the global majority is also extraverted and impulsive, a typical combination. In this case, the mainstream particular learner becomes at risk. In highly particular classes, the global learners drown in details, especially if the teacher is also particular and the curriculum abstract-sequential. Similar analogies can be made for any learning-style dimension. Whatever the student-teacher conflict, it is highly exacerbated when the individual learner's profile does not match the class profile.

Inappropriate Placements

> ☞ *Students who are inappropriately placed find*
> *themselves fighting on the wrong battlefield.*

We place students into programs through a variety of testing instruments. Roughly, these fall into several categories: intelligence or ability tests, achievement tests, and disabilities tests.

Defining and Measuring Intelligence

Most people seem to agree that inherent intelligence, something psychologists call *g*, for general intelligence, exists (Spearman, 1927). We are not yet very skilled at defining it. Because we can't define it, we have to question any of the means we use to test it. Binet did not intend for his tests (which ultimately evolved into the Stanford-Binet test) to be used for labeling and placement but rather to determine who was at risk for the schools of his time (Binet, 1980). Terman's kids, the brightest of the bright according to the Stanford-Binet test, did not all rise to the top of their professions. In fact, only 70% completed college, whereas peers with lower IQ scores became more successful on a number of criteria (Terman & Oden, 1947).[5]

Is there a style issue involved in how we are computing basic intelligence? I think so. Guilford and Hoepfner (1971), who discount the existence of *g*, imply that they think so. Carroll disagrees, citing irregularities in the studies of Guilford and Hoepfner (Carroll, 1993). Gould (1981), in arguing that some cultures and subcultures are mismeasured by IQ tests, thinks so. Feuerstein (1972) and others who have found ways to "teach IQ," or train students to get higher scores on IQ tests, think so (Sharron, 1987). The majority of school psychologists continue to use ability tests, the implication being that they provide some kind of useful information. So, the argument would seem to linger.

Let's take a look at the nature of **ability tests**. IQ tests are timed. This provides an advantage to impulsive learners. IQ tests assess sequencing skills. This favors sequential learners. IQ tests require decontextualized work; this favors learners who readily work out of context. (This skill is related to a learning style known as field dependence and field independence, which has not been discussed in this volume. The notes to Chapter 3 provide references for readings on this topic and a short description of the style.) Analogies, used on some, but not all, intelligence tests, depend on sharpening skills. This favors sharpeners. Carroll (1993) describes the dozens of factors used on tests for abilities in a number of areas. Readers are encouraged to analyze Carroll's analysis. When I did so, I found that over and over again, the factors that indicate intelligence on most of these tests are closely related to Western, or mainstream, learning styles. Interestingly, Carroll dismisses cognitive styles as too complex to include in intelligence testing but admits that they could have an influence on the results.

Nearly 20 years ago, a nonplussed psychologist who tested my 7-year-old daughter for a gifted and talented education placement told me that she had been unable to score the test. One section of the test required the examinee to provide verbal definitions for a list of vocabulary words. My daughter had explained very politely to the psychologist that words out of context defy definition, because the surrounding context supplies the real meaning. Therefore, because she was provided no context at all, she elected not to answer at all.

Until IQ tests become style sensitive, they will remain approximate instruments. Perhaps a time will come when ability tests are structured differently. As early as 1975, Witkin predicted, "it is not farfetched to imagine that test batteries emerging from cognitive style research may in time replace intelligence tests" (p. 306).

Sternberg (1985, 1989, 1990, 1997) has looked at the issue of intelligence not from the point of view of a single entity but as a multifaceted concept and suggests the existence of a "triarchic mind," in which we can consider that three kinds of intelligence exist: analytic, creative, practical. IQ tests typically only test analytic intelligence. As such, these scores best predict performance in American schools. "The problems that one society might consider as important bases for distinguishing the intelligent from the unintelligent might be viewed as trivial bases for the distinction in another society" (Sternberg, 1986, p. 145).

The bottom line is that we must use IQ scores cautiously or not at all. We all know the myriad of students who could be classified as overachievers or underachievers based on IQ test scores. Reynolds and Birch (1977) suggest that the more accurate labels are undertested and overtested. Teachers who are sensitive to learning-styles variables do not need a test to tell if a student is a good learner, capable of completing a specific assignment, or ready to undertake certain kinds of study. (Even those not sensitive to learning-style variables but who understand Vygotsky's Zone of Proximal Development [Vygotsky, 1982] or Piaget's stages of readiness for specific cognitive activities [Piaget, 1967, 1974; Piaget and Inhelder, 1959, 1973] can at least plan appropriate next learning steps for their students.)

For placement purposes, we frequently use **achievement tests** for specific subjects. Many, if not most, of these tests are very biased toward learning styles preferred in Western classrooms. The Scholastic Achievement Test (SAT), for example, often weeds out reflective learners by its restrictions on time. It also favors the learner who can handle decontextualization; the sharpener, who can handle analogies; and the particular learner, who can quickly find details.

We also use evaluative batteries for placement into restrictive environments. As mentioned earlier, these instruments, which can be considered a form of **disabilities test**, tend to be biased against students with non-Western learning styles. Inappropriate placement effected by biased testing instruments only exacerbate the learning problems of these students.

OF POISON AND MEDICINE—AND TRIAGE

All students at one time or another are likely to meet with a teaching style, classroom profile, or textbook that conflicts with their own. This happens even if their dominant styles are Western in general. In such cases, even students with Western learning styles can become quickly disabled.

Teachers can avoid disabling their students if they keep in mind one important axiom: *What is one student's medicine is another student's poison.* Many activities intended to assist students in learning have the opposite effect. Many test results give a false picture of what a student knows or can do. The activities listed in Chapter 5 are enabling activities for each of the learning styles listed. If the columns in each table were to be reversed, however, the activities would either make learning more difficult for students or give an unfairly low and false impression to the teacher of their knowledge and abilities.

In Summary

Contemporary teaching methods are not going to remedy the situation in which there are competing learning-style needs in a classroom, nor will the teaching methods of tomorrow, no matter how prestigious the university that will unveil them. There is no dearth of such magic pills for the classroom. The problem is that a methodological approach to teaching the whole class absolves the teacher from having to think about how each one of the students learns, allowing the teacher to think of the class as an aggregate student body. Even with systems based on multiple styles, there is a finite set of molds into which students are expected to fit. In actuality, each student has his or her own unique mold (learner profile), and that mold gets broken before any other students come along to match it. The reward for the teacher (and the great fun of being a teacher) is that when we see through the eyes of all these different students, we discover the world and its myriad representations again and again and again, and each time it is new.

Accommodating each student's learner profile is the challenge for the teacher who wants to improve the results of his or her teaching. Reaching each learner requires understanding each of the styles and the relationship between them. In an ideal world, it requires accommodating the learner profile. In a less-than-ideal, real world it requires empowering students to make the adaptations themselves.

Practice Exercises

1. Draw a family tree for your family. Enter personality types or temperaments for each member. Where should the conflicts occur, based on your family tree? Is that where they do occur?

2. Do the same exercise for the sensory preferences and again for the cognitive styles.

3. The following statements were taken from interviews with real students in actual classes who were experiencing some form of style wars. These were adult students in a foreign language classroom. However, most of their experiences and their conflicts parallel those that can be found in the classrooms of teachers of any subject matter. The course materials were traditional ones, mostly grammar-translation work or multiple-choice activities and dependent on visual memorization. To some extent, the teacher supplemented the traditional materials with authentic newspapers and television broadcasts. The teacher was an ISTJ, visual, particular, analytic, deductive, sequential, left-hemisphere-preferent, mildly abstract learner. What do their comments tell you about their learning styles? Keep in mind environmental preferences, sensory modalities, personality types, and cognitive styles, and note

that where a conflict is in full swing, affective variables (motivation, relationships, emotions) often come into play. Where do you think the conflict has occurred? How would you help the student, if you were teaching a class in which the class profile did not fit the student's learner profile. If it did? (Don't worry yet about helping the class as a whole; we will discuss how to do that in Chapter 7.)

a. "I expected the whole course would be memorization, and it is. And in a way, I am lucky because I am good at memorization. If I can see the word written in my mind, then I can remember it. Some of the exercises are not very natural. I wish I could listen to two instructors talking to each other, I would understand better. I study in 15-minute stretches. I go over the words just before going to bed and then early in the morning. Staying motivated is no problem. If I don't succeed, my family is going to be homeless.

b. I had heard that the biggest problem in the course was to keep motivated, so I keep reminding myself of the money and college credits I am going to get. I want to learn to think in German. I don't want to translate from English. I write letters to my friends in German. I write poetry in German to my girlfriend. I learned Spanish through Total Physical Response, and I thought it was great.

c. I can keep myself motivated through discipline. The way I learn best is by being called upon to perform individually. I want to be put on the spot. I don't want to do reading aloud in groups. I do not learn by repeating in a group. I don't want to do anything childish. I expect to get a 100% all the time and to be perfect. This type of classroom instruction is different from the one I received when I was studying electronics.

d. I knew I was going to suffer from information overload, and I am. I get confused and totally lost. I do not know what is expected of me in the classroom. I feel more comfortable if I have studied the lesson before I come to class, but I have a very hard time studying. I stare at these words, and I cannot remember them. I do not like reading newspaper articles. I want to read real stories with emotional appeal.

e. I expected it to be very hard and very intense, and I was told I would be stressed out. I am. I am scared that I am going to be overwhelmed by the course, and I won't be able to keep up. I have had bad experiences with trying to learn a foreign language. My family really wants me to do this, and I have a goal. I want to work overseas. I was very good in philosophy and psychology, where there is not only one right answer. In class there seems to be only one right answer. In order to keep myself motivated, I will have to accomplish something. This is why I will buy myself a children's book in German. I love it when we use German for something real, like going outside and giving directions.

f. We spend a lot of time and effort practicing sentences that make no sense. Why do you ask me where I am when I am sitting right in front of you? I was expecting the class to be a lot harder than it is. It seems to be very straightforward. If I don't have outside problems, things are not too hard for me. I study by writing down the words and practicing over and over. It does not seem as difficult as French, Spanish, or Russian. But when I saw all those verb endings, I got scared. I keep myself motivated because I am staying in California, and this is what I want.

4. Take any one student in your class. How does his or her style differ from yours? from the general trend of styles among his or her classmates?

NOTES

1. This statement is based on a survey I did of foreign language students at the University of Pittsburgh in 1983.

2. These figures have been questioned by a number of psychologists and type researchers. I use them, although given the symmetry of the figures, it is unlikely that these figures are very precise. They are, however, the only figures I have seen for the distribution of personality type in the United States. I should also note that these figures refer to K-12 teachers only. There is some indication that a majority of teachers in higher education have a very different profile: INTJ being the dominant psychological type among college professors. The distribution of students will also be different in higher education, since a relatively higher number of NTs continue their education, whereas large numbers of SPs do not.

3. This information is based on informal research I did in 1995, looking at populations in Salinas, California, as well as whatever data I could gather through Internet resources. This was not a rigorous study, and figures (not given) would be skewed by the fact that responses were voluntary and contacts were made through parent groups. Therefore, I did not have the full population of gifted dropouts with which to work. I suspect that the patterns will hold, and hopefully, someone will undertake such a study.

4. Another sign of the times is the interest in social maturity, emotional IQ, and dysfunctional families. Although these phenomena are legitimate social concerns and certainly can have an impact on student success, too often they are used as an excuse to avoid the more thorny cognitive issues of working with students, rather than an explanation of how to work with them best. As with hyperactivity, often the symptom is mistaken for the cause, with the result that only the symptom is treated.

5. Admittedly, there are some difficulties with this study (e.g., at that time, it was more difficult for girls to reach the same levels of success as boys), and the results have been called into question by some researchers. However, these are some of the few statistics available on this phenomenon.

5

In an Ideal World:
Accommodating Students

I once had a teacher tell me, "I am the king in my classroom." This is akin to the attitude of those who conceive of the teacher's role as actor. The focus in all these cases is on the teacher, but the teacher is not the most important person in the classroom. The student is. The teacher is not doing the learning. The student is. "If teaching were merely a matter of communicating the content of a course to a student without worrying too much about what happens at the student end, then the taught lesson or lecture might be considered to be an ideal and efficient way of doing this" (Hill, 1986, p. 13). We know, though, that *good teaching is more about what happens to students than about teacher performance.* To move the focus from teacher to student requires understanding learners and learner differences, i.e., how and why learning does or does not take place.

The ideal teacher in the ideal world uses learner differences to advantage. Instead of thinking of differences as an impediment, as do the teachers described by Frumin (Chapter 1), ideal teachers in an ideal world look upon differences as liberating, interesting, challenging, and a source of learning for themselves.

I frequently team-teach with a colleague who is my opposite (and not only in gender: male vs. female; coloration: blond vs. brunette; and height: six-foot-plus vs. five-foot-minus). We have different sensory preferences, personality types, and cognitive styles. He is analytic; I am synthetic. He is reflective; I am impulsive. He is abstract; I am concrete. He is sequential; I am random. He is visual; I am kinesthetic. He is introverted; I am extraverted. In spite of these differences, we really enjoy teaching with each other. Students can tell; our rapport devolves onto the class. We are both NTs (our only shared style), and that provides a powerful fulcrum with which to balance our differences. We have learned how to accommodate each other's learning styles, and in so doing, we have found our differences to be liberating and a source of learning for ourselves and for those who fall into our hands. In like fashion, we are able to accommodate our students' learning styles.

Why should teachers accommodate students and not vice versa? Because "learning styles are not lightly held" (Dunn, Beaudry, & Klavas, 1989, p. 56). Because research indicates that the closer the match between teaching and learning styles, the higher the level of achievement (Cafferty, 1980). Because empirical research has demonstrated that when teaching styles match student learning styles, student performance is better (Pask & Scott, 1975). Because classroom failure leads to low self-esteem with all its attendant problems (Mruk, 1995). Because all our students have a right to equal opportunity for school success.

Knowledgeable teachers can modify tasks associated with texts, textbook activities, and handouts to accommodate the learning styles present in the classroom, whether or not these styles are mainstream learning styles and whether or not they match the teacher's own learning style. When this happens, as Dunn, Beaudry, and Klavas (1989) have found, failure rates dramatically decrease and competency dramatically increases, resulting in higher test and attitude scores. *Students who might have failed or who might have been counseled to drop the course become "fascinating challenges" and learning opportunities for the teachers involved in teaching the whole class.*

In an ideal world, not only is instruction accessible to all students, but also testing is fair. If more than one type of test is needed, it is provided. If teachers need to interpret test results in different ways for different students, they do so. The emphasis is on allowing students to show what they *do* know and what they *can* do, and not what they don't and can't.

In an ideal world, teachers create balance in the classroom. They do this by treating all students equally, not by treating them the same. Our national existence was born of the belief in every citizen's right to equality, as stated in our Declaration of Independence: "We hold these truths to be self-evident, that all men are created equal." Our collective subconscious treats these words as sacred; they serve as arbiters of our laws and actions. At the end of the 20th century, as America strives toward implementation of this concept a full two centuries later, educational administrators and even members of the general public who insist on "equality" without understanding the meaning of the term have created a situation in which all students are treated the same:

1. Teaching focuses on a nonexistent "average" student.
2. Students are encouraged to become clones of this nonexistent "average" student (an egregious result being the "dummying down" of requirements placed on gifted students).
3. Testing is standardized and objective (which favors students with some learning styles and handicaps others).
4. All subcultures, regardless of the differences in specific needs, abilities, and cultural values of racial and ethnic minorities, are taught and tested the same way.

I would point out that the Declaration of Independence does not say that "all men are created the same." Treating all students the same is not the equivalent of treating all students equally because students have very different needs. Treating all students the same means that some will have their needs met but others will not. As Gary and Glover (1976) note:

... the nature of humanity is so diverse (and is so with good cause—that of survival) that it is absurd to attempt to force all people into a single, evaluative model, to respond to all individuals by one procedure or process, or to hold up the "holy mean" as the only standard by which to consider the worth of our fellowmen. (p. vii)

The result of that "absurdity" is a frenetic search for a uniform teaching method and a uniform measuring instrument—absurd because the goal of treating all students the same (and therefore, presumably, equally) cannot be reached in this way. For example, Levy (1973) contends that "any program based upon one single concept for the correction of the reading difficulties of all children is doomed to failure" (p. 133). Whatever the program—remedial reading programs, gifted science and mathematics programs, or the range of regular education courses—the only guarantee that can be made, if uniformity in teaching is the rule, is that some students will, indeed, fail. An approach that meets all learning needs in fair and uniquely necessary ways comes much closer to the concept of having been created equal and has a better chance for success.

This chapter discusses how to treat students equally, and it provides some examples for doing so. It also presents a system for knowing when to expect students to show style flexibility. Both approaches, accommodating student learning styles to make learning more accessible and empowering students to become more flexible in choice of learning style, are important. Where one or the other is used is situational but not interchangeable. (Chapter 6 provides more detailed information on *how* to develop flexibility.)

TEACH-REVIEW-TEST

Although students learn best through their preferred learning styles, there is also value in helping them increase their flexibility in responding to input that comes in a nonpreferred learning style, especially because not all instructors they encounter will be able to adjust the instruction to their liking. The teacher with knowledge in learning styles can use the Teach-Review-Test (TRT) approach, developed by the American Global Studies Institute, in helping students to become more flexible in learning preferences. The TRT approach recommends that "T" be associated with a strength or preferred learning style and "R" with a weakness or nonpreferred learning style. That is, TRT teachers teach students via their preferred learning styles, review the material via their nonpreferred learning styles, and test them through their preferred learning styles. In this way, students do not feel out of control—they are pushed to be flexible in learning style only after they have mastered the subject matter. Moreover, tests are fair and provide equal opportunity for all students to show what they know or have mastered.

TEACHING AND REVIEWING IN STYLE

In the TRT system, teaching (i.e., the time when students first encounter new information) is done in accordance with preferred learning styles. The charts that are provided throughout this section identify activities that work for teaching in style. To review out of style in order to help students increase their style flexibility, the content in the columns can simply be rotated. Some students may have to be explicitly taught the accompanying strategies. (Chapter 6 explains how to do this.)

Sensory Modalities

Most classrooms are filled with students who represent all the modalities. Ideal teachers who wish to reach all students will need to bear this in mind when planning lessons. The chart below provides ways in which teachers can accommodate all the modalities in one classroom. For review sessions, teachers can rotate the columns and work on getting students to style flex.

	Visual	Auditory	Motor
Language Arts/English	read a book spelling bees	recitations tell a story	drama write a story
Mathematics	written problems picture problems	oral problems	calculations manipulatives
Science	read a textbook	watch a film	do experiments
Social Sciences	read a historical novel	oral reports watch a film	make maps reproduce artifacts
Foreign Language/ESL	read the board read an article	listen to a story broadcasts role plays	role plays Total Physical Response games

Visual learners in language arts classes are not given reading activities in vain. Most are excellent readers (many even embark on careers that depend on reading skill), and they learn through reading. Good readers also tend to be good spellers, and there is some evidence (not without dispute) that most spelling bee champions are visual learners (Jacobson, 1983). Reading as an activity in any classroom is beneficial for visual-verbal learners, and audiovisual support is beneficial for visual-imagist learners. This means that flashcards, now considered taboo in many foreign language classes, especially those that are proficiency oriented, are a useful, if not necessary, tool for verbalists. They are a useless tool for imagists.

Auditory learners prefer the "audio" portions of audiovisual support. In language arts classrooms, they find discussions and narration more interesting than reading. In nearly any subject matter class, they are more naturally drawn to oral reports (if they have acquired public speaking skills at some point in their educational experience), films, verbal interaction of any sort, and, if they are assimilators, lectures. Language classes, taught with contemporary techniques (role plays, authentic broadcasts) can be great havens for auditory learners (but, of course, the visual learners may experience difficulty with these kinds of activities). The expansion of book publishers into books on tape has opened up an excellent source of learning for auditory learners.

Motor learners need to find ways to use their fine and gross motor skills. Writing and copying activities are fine in nearly any subject for mechanical learners. Game tables are an excellent language arts activity for kinesthetic learners. So is drama, both theatre for older students and acting out information for younger students. As an example, a colleague recently shared the following experience with me:

> I was subbing in a Grade 3-4 special ed class the other day. We had a reading selection about wolves. Imagine a fairly large kid (for his age) standing up and acting the answer to the question "How do the other wolves in the pack greet the pups the first time they come out of the den?" Answer: "They wag their tails, they sniff 'em and they lick 'em." (E. Franke, personal communication, March 5, 1997)

Most subjects do lend themselves to kinesthetic teaching, although teachers, being more often of the auditory and visual variety, tend not to include them. The activities described above are just the tip of the iceberg in terms of what can be done kinesthetically—including in university classes. For more examples of modality-sensitive lessons for elementary school children, look at the suggestions made by Dunn (1993, 1996).

Giving a little work in each modality to every student during class is one way to reach all students, but it is inefficient. With this approach, at any given time, two thirds of the students will be working in a nonpreferred style. Having students work in their preferred style most of the time is more efficient and effective.

Work in cooperative groups and on collaborative projects can allow most students to work in their preferred style most of the time. Homogenous or heterogeneous groups can be formed. In the latter, the motor learners in the group can organize the group physically and keep the records. (This activity will no doubt also appeal to the SJ sequentials.)

Giving in-class choices of activities on tasks is another means of allowing most students to work in their preferred style most of the time. If students are given a task which they can accomplish in several ways, based on a) reading something, b) discussing or listening to something, and c) doing something, most students will select according to their own modality. Students with bifurcated and trifurcated styles can be easily handled in the same manner: They can use the activities in each of their preferred styles, depending on whether they are acquiring, storing, or reconstructing information. Homework assignments can be devised in the same way— allowing choice by style in each requirement made of students.

Interestingly, the two populations which are usually the most "set" in their ways tend to fall into the clutches of teachers who are also "set" in their ways: learning disabled (LD) students and gifted students. The LD population tends to be set in its ways because these students lack a sufficiently wide range of strategies for the tasks presented or the skill to determine which of the strategies to apply in a given learning situation, and some empirical results have suggested (results of other studies disagree) that certain learning styles predominate in LD classrooms (in terms of modality, specifically the kinesthetic preference; Kempwirth & MacKenzie, 1989; Languis & Miller, 1988; Naigle & Thwaite, 1979; Woo & Hoosair, 1994).

The gifted population is used to learning quickly and, therefore, gifted students usually have experienced the luxury of selecting their own mode of instruction.

Because often they are quite confident in their own ability to learn, when they encounter teachers with opposing modality preferences, they may dismiss the teacher as "incompetent," and that can be the end of much of their in-class learning during that school year. Perhaps part of what is involved in being a gifted learner is that one has worked out effective strategies that match one's style, and efforts to impose what works for the teacher or even most other students can just get in the way of the gifted, already metacognitively and cognitively prepared learner.

Personality Types

Teachers meet a wide range of personality types in class. Often, the type differences mean that there is no natural rapport between some students and their teacher or among the students themselves. In faculty development groups where conversations have become very frank and revealing, a question that has been asked of me more than once is: How can any teacher reach all students (i.e., all personality types) when that teacher does not like them all and they don't all like each other?

We often hold teachers to unnatural and unrealizable ideals. Teachers are human; they tend to establish rapport with people, including students, of like personality type but less commonly seek out opposite personality types. In fact, of all the variables I have examined, coincidence of temperament type appears to be the most essential for establishment of naturally occurring rapport, acting as a fulcrum to leverage like and unlike styles.

Most people would be shocked by the following statement: "Teachers don't have to like all their students." For me, as an NT, the concept that a teacher has to like everyone is incomprehensible. The teacher's purpose is to create learning in students, not to develop lifelong friendships. The teacher's responsibility is to treat all students equally, whether or not they like them all, and to maximize learning and learning opportunities for all students. (In saying this, I add one caveat: Students, especially NF students, should never be aware that the teacher does not like them. This is not always easy; NFs often quickly intuit the true feelings, expressed or not, of the people around them. A suggestion made by one teacher I know is to pretend that a student with whom a teacher has minimal rapport is especially likable. Sometimes, reality turns out to match the pretension.)

Students don't have to like each other, but they do have to respect each other. Teaching them about their own personality differences is one way in which they can begin to talk about the irritations they experience with each other without labeling each other "bad." The same kind of training will help them to understand that perhaps they are different from their teacher, but neither the teacher nor they are "bad." When we don't have impersonal labels for traits, we tend to associate values with them. Thus, traits, which in and of themselves have no particular value, become labeled simply "good," meaning "like me," and "bad," meaning "not like me." This is as true of differences in personality traits as it is of differences in race, gender, or culture.

The chart on the next page provides some activities that should be appealing to each of the temperaments. Other, similar sorts of activities can be added by the teacher who is guided by the temperaments of the students in the class.

	NF Intuitive-Feeler	NT Intuitive-Thinker	SJ Sensing-Judger	SP Sensing-Perceiver
Language Arts/English	discuss a story in a group play-act a story write story in style of own choosing	write original story in author's style analyze story	memorize a poem narrate story contents	draw scene for story
Mathematics	work with a group on a real-life application	solve problems	make calculations	go outside and take measurements
Science	apply science to human welfare project	develop own experiments	implement lab manual experiments	take a nature walk and make a collection
Social Sciences	group projects on various countries	independent exploration of social documents	work with chronology and time lines	map work
Foreign Language/ESL	interactions with native speakers	linguistic theory etymology	grammar and vocabulary work	study of the art and music of the culture field trips

NF (intuitive-feeling) students, as mentioned earlier, generally fare well with cooperative learning and small group work. More of that is becoming available in elementary schools and high schools, as well as in some community colleges and foreign language classes of universities, as cooperative learning becomes the method of the day (Golub, 1988; Hamm & Adams, 1992; Johnson, Johnson, & Smith, 1991; Morgan & Foot, 1990; Slavin, 1985). In general, though, the situation in today's universities has not significantly changed from the situation in 1976, when Lesser (1976) complained of the lack of opportunity for cooperative learning in higher education: "Small-group and individualized instruction in higher education have been revealed to be pitifully inadequate" (p. 155). The problem is a matter of implementation, rather than opportunity, because there are many classroom situations in higher education, including at the graduate school level, where cooperative learning can be used effectively (Bruffee, 1993).

Nearly any subject matter can be taught through group work. Some examples are given above, but nearly any information that can be taught by lecture or independent work can be accomplished in a group setting, including group writing (Spear, 1993). Blackburn (1976) provides examples of individualized activities and group activities that would work well with NFs, and readers who want some additional ideas for cooperative learning tasks might wish to obtain a copy of Blackburn's book.

NFs need to feel rapport with a teacher in order to learn. Teachers do not have to be NFs or to like NF students to establish such rapport artificially. Understanding the personality type needs of each student and meeting those needs provides the support needed for learning. Although extraverted NF teachers tend to have an advantage over other personality types in establishing rapport and can unconsciously create learning in many students through the warmth they exude, teachers with other personality types who understand learning styles theory can create even more effective learning environments consciously.

When taught by teachers of other styles, NF students, especially extraverted ones, may appear to be "needy." Knowing the NF need to "relate," the teacher can set up small groups with other NFs (transferring the means of satisfying the need). The teacher can take the time to make a comment on each NF homework assignment, noting effort even if the effort did *not* result in a spectacular product (e.g., "I really appreciate the time you took to write this, and I have made some comments on how you can improve it")—but please note that this could be an *inappropriate* comment for an NT paper and misinterpreted by an NT as patronizing. Depending on the program, the teacher can motivate the NF with an occasional touch, although the only programs left where it is still considered safe to touch a student are adult programs where teachers and students are considered equals (I have seen touch work remarkably well in such programs). In today's litigation-happy, hands-off environment, NF students often have to grow up before they have their childhood needs met. Where physical touch is unwise, the equivalent in words, especially noticing and expressing appreciation for effort or an occasional personal interest question or comment, can go a long way toward establishing rapport.

NT (intuitive-thinking) students sometimes disconcert teachers of other types. "How can I establish rapport with an NT student?" is a question typically asked by teachers who are not NTs. They are often disconcerted and occasionally intimidated by the NT students in class. For NT students to listen to, take the advice of, or develop respect for a teacher, the NT must have a reason to consider the teacher competent—and simply holding the position of teacher does not count. Rapport between any teacher and an NT student comes from a positive assessment of the teacher's competence by the student. NT students do not necessarily attach personal emotion to the concept of teacher-student rapport. They do not feel a particular need to personally like a teacher (or to be liked by that teacher) in order to respect the teacher, learn from the teacher, and develop rapport with the teacher. The young NT likes to work without assistance (or, in NT terms, "interference") and to be praised for his or her product once it is completed (but not before). In interaction with teachers, young NTs, who have not yet learned about the kinds of feelings and reactions others may have, are apt to be very factual, for example, "That green dress really looks ugly on you," "You have bad penmanship," and "You're not very good at that" (R. Stilgenbauer, 1995). This personality trait can disconcert non-NTs, who attach more implied meaning and emotion to the observation than the NT ever meant. These students are not intentionally trying to insult the teacher; they are just sharing an opinion. Student-teacher exchanges do not even have to be personalized. Older NTs enjoy written repartee—as long as they have a forum for comeback. Watch an NT student and an NT teacher with well-established rapport in action. Those who are not NTs would be hard pressed to understand that rapport exists. The exchange of comments are likely to be critical, to the point, questioning, exploring—and both are enjoying them. Rapport is displayed by animated intellectual exchange. The greatest compliment that an NT student gives a teacher is not "I liked that teacher" or "that teacher was very good or very nice or my favorite," but "I learned a lot from that teacher" or "that teacher made a difference in my thinking." NF teachers, who feel a need to be liked, and SJ teachers, who feel that authority should be respected, will likely experience discomfort in establishing such a relationship, but for motivating NTs (or any type that does not match one's own), putting aside the sources of one's own motivation is imperative.

NTs are motivated by content itself. Therefore, any kind of independent work, as long as it is content focused, works well for them. They are concerned with their own competence and usually do not mind competition, whereas some other types struggle with and often try to avoid competition (Kagan, Zahn, Widaman, Schwarzwald, & Tyrrell, 1985). They tend to shy away from collaboration (especially in younger years), feeling that individual contributions should be judged individually, so cooperative learning environments can be difficult for them. A parent recently commented to me that given schools' current emphasis on cooperative learning, she is encountering difficulty in finding an appropriate junior high school for her NT daughter, who needs more independence and even competition in learning than cooperative classrooms permit. The kinds of work described above—independent projects, reading, writing, development of one's own ideas—are generally enjoyed by NT students and serve as bases for their learning. (One must usually keep in mind that many NTs learn what *they* want to learn, not what teachers think they should learn so, if teachers want them to learn something specific, activities need to be cleverly organized so that the NT can do this on his or her own.)

NTs' confidence in their own knowledge can be both a positive and negative quality. On the positive side, a school principal related to me the story of one highly gifted mathematics student, an INTJ. A fourth grader, he was already studying algebra. Because the teacher was unable to incorporate him into a classroom—in an hour he would complete 30 to 40 pages of calculations and new concepts—the principal took him to work in her office. He completed so much so quickly that she did not have time to look at the problems herself but used an answer book and told the student to make the corrections. From time to time, the student would approach her and indicate that the answer book was wrong, and the two of them put together a correction sheet that they sent to the publisher. (Under similar circumstances, students with a different temperament would have been more likely to be confused and try to find some way to make their answers respond to those of the answer book.) On the negative side, when INTJ students think they are right, only an intuitive approach that helps them to discover their own error by themselves is likely to disabuse them of their *idées fixes*. Most teachers have met this attitude firsthand.

SJ (sensing-judging) students can appear easy to teach because they are usually willing to listen and to take input in traditional ways. Because the majority of their teachers are also SJs, there is instinctive rapport in many cases. The most significant area of instruction adaptation relates to whether the SJ students are abstract or concrete, because they differ in their needs. The cerebral activities of listening to lectures and explanations, watching films strips and videotapes, and reading appeal to the abstract SJs, and the applied activities of making timelines and conducting experiments appeal to the concrete SJs. Foreign languages can be difficult for those SJ students who did not grow up in a mixed-language community. They expect languages to follow clear rules without exceptions, and languages don't. To teach an SJ student, teachers of any temperament need to remember that these students want detail, instructions, direction, and deadlines. Whereas these come naturally to the majority of K-12 teachers, who are SJs, they do not come naturally to the NT and NF, let alone the SP, teachers. On the college scene, where the majority of professors are NTs, SJ students who performed well in high school often find themselves with lack of sufficient guidance in what and when to study. However, they will put in seat time for even the most grueling of courses, whereas the NTs and SPs, each for differing reasons, will cut classes that they do not find to their liking.

Even if an SJ does not like an activity, he or she is likely to do it because it has been assigned. Two examples come to mind that clearly contrast the NT and SJ student response to the "oughts" and "shoulds" of the classroom. Example 1 is an INTJ who returned his homework assignment to his third-grade teacher with the words "No, thank you," explaining that he already knew the concepts in the assignment but that he would be willing to do something more complex for homework, should she care to assign it. An SJ, she complained to his mother about the student's sauciness. The mother suggested that perhaps the student had identified a problem, to which the teacher replied that he obviously got his sauciness from his mother. Example 2 is a second-grade boy, an ISTJ, in a classroom of about 40 years ago, when desks had hinges. His teacher had told him not to put his fingers in the hinged part of the desk, but he found himself doing that without thinking. At one point, when he had his fingers over the hinges, the teacher, a very heavy-set lady, selected his desk to sit on while explaining something to the class. He refused to say anything because he was "not supposed to have his fingers in the hinges" and gritted his teeth until she moved on to the next desk. A student with a different temperament would have spoken up immediately—or cried out in pain.

SP (sensing-perceiving) students, of all the temperaments, may well be the most difficult to teach for people of other styles, but it is important to determine how to do so because there are so many of them, particularly at the K-12 level. Because of their great need for hands-on application and out-of-classroom experience, they often appear to be hyperactive when they are not. Their bodies cannot sit still when their minds are unchallenged. Field trips, use of manual arts, experiments, and out-of-classroom activities work best with them. They can work well in groups, if their interest is piqued, and they can carry out some of the more active, applied, artistic tasks that are assigned to a group project. SPs can be unusually creative, especially if the creation is concrete and practical. Fostering an environment where their kind of creativity is appreciated can draw them into completing tasks that they would otherwise find uninviting.

The greatest difficulty in an ideal world in teaching students of other personality types is accepting a certain amount of discomfort as teachers. Because personality differences entail value differences, it is often difficult to "let go" of our own style. Instinctive, pressured, and surprised reactions to unanticipated behavior will undoubtedly always reflect the teacher's own personality type (and teachers should forgive themselves when this happens). On a deliberate and controlled level, however, it is possible to go beyond instinct in order to teach the whole class.

Cognitive Styles

Although modality differences and personality types certainly do have a strong impact on classroom performance and must be considered whenever one does an analysis of failure to learn, cognitive styles, in my experience, have an even greater influence on ultimate academic success.

Teachers can handle cognitive-style differences in the same way that they can handle modality and personality differences: by giving choice in assignments, by making assignments with multiple ways to carry out tasks, by using small group and independent work to advantage, and by developing style flexibility during review sessions. Each of the cognitive styles that was presented in Chapters 3 and 4 is discussed below from the point of view of accommodating that style in the classroom. To develop style flexibility during review sessions, teachers can reverse the columns and teach the attendant learning strategies.

Global-particular differences are among the most salient cognitive style constructs in both child and adult learners. The chart below makes some suggestions for including work for both kinds of learners in various classroom environments.

	Global	Particular
Language Arts/English	create stories word creation	word attack analyze stories
Mathematics	word problems develop a theorem	calculations prove a theorem
Science	brainstorm significances predict results	conduct experiment and determine results
Social Studies	group cultures	map cultures
Foreign Language/ESL	vocabulary via "islands" developing a monitor	vocabulary study: roots letting go of the monitor

Global learners do better when the focus moves from the part to the whole. For them, creating stories is easier than answering comprehension questions, and looking for patterns and significances are fun.

In mathematics classes, they are likely to make mistakes (as opposed to errors) on the simplest of materials. Asked to check their work, they are apt not to find their own mistakes, although this is a skill they need to build. Although it may frustrate them, returning papers to be redone and redone, until they are accurate, is one way to build the skill. Initially, some hint may need to be given as to location of the mistake.

In social studies classes, they might group cultures by some salient attribute: political system, geographic location, demographics, religion. Teachers may need to return reports and maps to them to rewrite or to include additional details. It is more effective to return work for rewrite than to mark the mistakes—global learners often overlook all the marks.

In foreign language, they learn more effortlessly through such techniques as building "islands" (memorized discourse that they can use as models).[1] Where they run into difficulty is in monitoring their own speech. The monitors of the global learners appear to have been turned off. To turn on their monitors requires some practice. To assist global students in turning on their monitors, teachers can record extended discourse by the global students and let them take their recording home and find their own mistakes. (Note: Students cannot find their errors because errors are only made when students do not know what the rules are. If they know the rules and do not apply them, then they make mistakes.) After this, the teacher can point out any mistakes that were overlooked, as well as any errors that occurred. Once the mistakes and errors have been reviewed, the same presentation (or discussion) is made and taped again. The process repeats itself as many times as needed until the speech is nearly mistake free.[2]

Particular students need to be able to focus on the pieces. Typical language arts and English activities that include comprehension questions, requests for information, word analysis, and similar exercises take care of this need. In mathematics class, traditional practice in calculation does also. Activities that carry out some application, such as proving a theorem or conducting an experiment, generally work well, as does word study in foreign language and ESL classes. In social studies class, while the global learners are grouping cultures, the particular students might plot those groups on a map or on some other kind of chart. Unlike their global counterparts, they do not need help building a monitor; they need help getting past the monitor. This can be accomplished by the development of "islands," so that they have some pieces of discourse which they feel comfortable uttering without labored thinking. They can also be encouraged to do extensive out-of-class reading in the foreign language; often, as chunks of language become lodged in the memory banks of particular learners, they do begin to monitor their speech less rigidly.

Leveling-sharpening differences can present a dilemma at times because some subject matter by its very nature appears to require sharpening skills. The chart below provides ideas on incorporating both kinds of activities into the classroom.

	Levelers	Sharpeners
Language Arts/English	model paragraphs vocabulary similarities style commonalities	contrastive essays analogies style differences
Mathematics	theory	word problems
Science	categorization (find relationships)	assignment to phyla (find factors)
Social Studies	compare constitutions for similarities	compare constitutions for differences
Foreign Language/ESL	gisting paraphrase activities language comparison	vocabulary exercises language contrast style differences

Most textbooks center their activities around the learning approach of sharpeners: calculations, analogies, and finding differences. Therefore, teachers need to help the levelers. In language arts classes, sharpeners can be expected to find smaller words within larger words; levelers can be expected to take a group of words and determine what they have in common. In English classes, in comparing the works of two authors, sharpeners can be expected to find stylistic differences and levelers to find stylistic similarities; defining the style of each can be a joint task. In similar ways, sharpening students in science classes can be expected to identify differences among objects in order to assign them to specific subhierarchies, and leveling students can find similarities among objects in order to classify them as members of the same group. This same search for similarities versus search for differences can be used to guide activities in social studies and foreign language/ESL classes. In foreign language classes, gisting (where the aim is to determine the general meaning of a passage) is likely to be congenial to levelers. Retelling or other activities that require paraphrase give them the opportunity to use strategies that they already possess. They are more likely than sharpeners to feel and notice similarities between their native language and the foreign language. Sharpeners are more apt to focus on the differences. The outcome, whether students focus on similarities or on differences, should be the same: a better understanding of the information.

Leveling students in math classes usually require strategy training to develop sharpening skills (see Chapter 6). Although a teacher can find some activities, usually related to math theory, where levelers can excel, math is by nature a sharpening subject. In this case, the ideal approach is not to accommodate but to assist students in the development of style flexibility. Bookkeeping and accounting are other subjects that require the acquisition of sharpening strategies by levelers.

Synthetic versus **analytic** approaches to learning can also create "unequal" situations in the classroom. The chart below gives some suggestions on providing equal opportunity for all learners.

	Analytic Learners	Synthetic Learners
Language Arts/English	find the meaning in a story	write an ending to a story
Mathematics	interpret a graph do complex calculations	make a graph find a new/alternative way to calculate
Science	determine the significance of the result of an experiment	devise an application for the result of an experiment
Social Studies	determine the principles upon which a foreign government is based	given a set of principles, devise a new government
Foreign Language/ESL	assess a schedule of events for a visitor, using newspaper information	make a schedule of activities, using events from a newspaper

Tasks that use the words *make*, *devise*, or *create* are more apt to attract synthetic students. Tasks that use the words *evaluate*, *assess*, or *determine* are more apt to attract analytic students. Most subject matter lends itself readily to either kind of activity. Teachers may want to put students in same-style groups for some of these tasks in order to assign the appropriate kinds of tasks to students with each of these learning styles.

Making and creating in English class is easy; it is called creative writing. Another kind of writing, critical writing, falls into the category of evaluative tasks. Mathematics also lends itself readily to both kinds of tasks: making a graph (synthetic work) versus interpreting a graph (analytic work). Proofs can be handled in similar ways. So can theorems and algebraic formulas (devising them versus implementing them). The concept of devising versus implementing can be used to guide activities in science classes. In social studies, world history, and government classes, synthetic learners can devise new ways to organize traditional sociopolitical structures. Analytic learners might be happier determining the effectiveness of current organizations. In working with time schedules and advertisements of upcoming events in a foreign language class, the teacher could ask the synthetic students to combine the information and come up with a schedule for themselves. At the same time, the teacher could give the analytic students a ready-made schedule and ask if the schedule makes sense vis-à-vis the local weather broadcasts, the distances between places (which they will have to check on a map), and their own interests.

As generic activities, case studies and investigations work well with analytic students. Group investigations can be used with extraverted-analytic students. Synthetic learners generally like gaming and simulations. Role plays are sometimes more appealing to analytic students; they have some way to control what they will be doing. Improvisation is often more appealing to synthetic students. Any of these activities can be applied to any subject matter at any level of instruction.

Impulsive students typically intimidate, or at least preempt, the **reflective** students in the class. Teachers need to watch for this. It is very easy to let impulsive learners receive more time on task than reflective learners.

	Impulsives	**Reflectives**
Language Arts/English	read and retell spelling bees	read and journalize tutor
Mathematics	mathalons	written problems
Science	in-class experiments	science fairs
Social Studies	Q&A sessions review relay races	brainstorming projects
Foreign Language/ESL	brainstorm rapid response activities role plays in-class checks	small-group work delayed response activities journals post-class checks

Teachers can comfortably and with a fair amount of assurance check on impulsive students' ability to comprehend and produce in a foreign language classroom during the class time. Nearly any activity that is short in duration and requires a rapid response pleases impulsive students. Science teachers can expect impulsives to complete their lab work on time. (While dissecting a frog, for example, impulsive learners may have the whole brain out of the frog's body well ahead of their reflective peers, but teachers would be well-advised to check to ensure that all parts are intact, e.g., missing frontal lobes—impulsive learners, who are often also global learners, have been known to miss these kinds of small details.) Mathematics teachers can expect impulsive-deductives to complete calculations quickly. Social science teachers can expect impulsive students to have a ready answer (and often a facile one that would benefit from further reflection).

Reflective teachers can be wonderful influences on impulsive learners. Because impulsive learners process and respond almost simultaneously, they rarely take time to think about issues in the depth that reflective learners do. I owe much of my critical thinking skill to a reflective teacher who questioned facile, impulsive answers.

Reflective learners take time to think through their responses, whether the time is granted or not. For them, immediate checks of knowledge occur too soon. It is often better to allow them the time to assimilate the information and check on them after class, through homework, during small group activities, or even via a seemingly casual conversation. Giving reflective learners time includes time to read, to write, and to observe both teachers and peers. They often perform well on written work, especially projects. Science fairs are an ideal learning tool for them, as is keeping journals.

A wonderfully empowering technique that I observed in one classroom is the use of colored cards: green, yellow, red. The teacher was using them for two purposes: (a) to determine how much of the presented material students had learned, and (b) to give students a sense of comfort in the classroom. The teacher would ask a question. Students who knew the answer and wanted to be called on would raise a green card, those who weren't sure would raise a yellow card, and those who did not want to be called on (presumably because they did not know the answer) would raise a red card. The teacher received colorful feedback on how much the class knew and how much each individual student knew—something that one student answering one question could never reveal. I especially like this technique because it gives students control even beyond the teacher's purpose. Introverts and reflective learners can "shield" themselves until ready to answer. When ready, they do not have to compete with impulsives. The playing field is even; they just have to raise a green card.

Inductive-deductive differences are easily accommodated in a whole class environment. Yet such accommodation often does not take place. The chart on the next page provides some ideas in how to go about making instruction accessible to both kinds of learners. In principal, the difference lies in which students are directly instructed and in what order hands-on work and explanations are arranged.

	Deductives	Inductives
Language Arts/English	etymological explanation	etymological discovery
Mathematics	explanation and practice	examples and hypothesis
Science	experiments using lab manuals	inquiry and hypothesis testing
Social Studies	explanation of how terrain affects economy	hypothesize terrain-economy relationship
Foreign Language/ESL	textbooks grammar rules	newspapers grammar in context

In an ideal world, inductive learners are allowed to use examples, read, interview, or use whatever other means may be at their disposal to figure out new information for themselves. Hints and inductive reasoning are provided to them. The inquiry method of instruction, popular about 20 years ago, provided relief for inductive learners (Joyce & Weil, 1972). In this method, students observed phenomena, established a hypothesis, developed a procedure to test the hypothesis, then tested the hypothesis. This method created happiness and success for the inductive students in the class but created frustration and failure for the deductive learners in the classroom. In an ideal class, the inductive learners will receive some time in advance of deductive presentation to work things out for themselves (in essence doing their learning *before* any formal presentation), whereas the deductive learners will receive an in-class explanation and assistance and have time to practice things for themselves in class and for homework (in essence doing their learning *after* any formal presentation). In an ideal class, then, timing and order of activities is important.

The inductive-deductive approaches to teaching and learning have been taking turns holding sway for a number of years. The pendulum is now speeding towards inductive learning; hence, the emphasis on whole language in language arts programs, the return of inquiry method approaches, especially in gifted and talented education (GATE) science and math classes (Joyce & Weil, 1972), and the growing acceptance of the Natural Approach in foreign language programs (Krashen, 1982). When the pendulum reaches its apex, the deductive learners will be as fully disadvantaged as inductive learners are in many contemporary programs. In inductive foreign language classrooms, deductive learners look for the explanations and the rules. Often, the (new) textbooks do not have them, and the teachers won't supply them. Lacking information about the pieces of the linguistic system of the language and being unable to induce the system, deductive students flounder, making errors and having no tools for remedying them.

Whether students needs deduction or induction, teachers concerned about teaching the whole class will find a way to assist the student whose learning style does not match the materials. About 10 years ago in one Pennsylvania private elementary school where arithmetic was taught deductively, a third-grade student was inductive to the point of being hopelessly confused by classroom explanations. The teacher worked out inductive learning opportunities for the student. However, when the teacher was absent, substitutes did not know what to do. After some thought, the teacher prepared a folder for substitutes with the student's work in it and the instructions: "Give the student this folder which contains three examples of the mathematics principles you will be teaching, put her in a corner, and she will figure out what she needs to do on her own."

Twenty to 25 years ago a curriculum, emanating from Texas and known as Accelerated Christian Education, was popular in a number of Christian elementary and high schools. This curriculum, which allowed self-instruction, was ideal for inductive learners. About 10 years ago, most of these schools dropped this curriculum in favor of a more traditional, explanatory curriculum because the majority of their students, deductive learners, could not handle the inductive approach. Unfortunately, now the inductive learners are working at a disadvantage.

Abstract-concrete differences in learning lie along a continuum that changes, depending on the level of education. Concrete activities in the elementary school tend to be routine, but by high school less common, and at the university level, abstraction dominates. Rising stars whose lights dim by high school days may well be concrete learners who are now expected to accomplish abstract tasks; late bloomers, as in the case of several other style dimensions, may simply be students who have acquired enough knowledge along the way in spite of working out of style that, once taught in accordance with style, can soar. The chart below provides some suggestions on how to help learners of both persuasions.

	Abstract Learners	**Concrete Learners**
Language Arts/English	etymology analyze a drama	write a story enact a drama
Mathematics	theory explanation	manipulatives application
Science	theory	application
Social Sciences	learn about cultures study history	visit cultures reenact history
Foreign Language/ESL	language system exercises	role plays projects

In any subject area, concrete students fare better when they can produce something, touch something, or do something; abstract learners prefer the cerebral version of information acquisition. In English classes, this may mean having one group of students (the concrete learners) rehearse and act a play and another group (the abstract learners) write a critical analysis of the play. Depending on their other learning styles, some abstract learners, together with some concrete learners, might like to write a play, which other concrete learners enact. The same approach applies in history classes for learning about history through reading and lecture versus learning about history through participation in historical reenactment. Field trips, which are often "ho-hum" affairs at best for abstract learners, can be powerful learning tools for concrete learners (with the exception that sensing-perceiving and concrete-random learners do *not* enjoy following someone else's itinerary). Concrete learners can be given the go-ahead to apply the abstract information presented in the classroom to personalized situations. For example, algebra is very useful in estimating future utility bills. As a rule of thumb, personalization of activities is often a "way-in" to concretizing the activities. Personalization of activities is also attractive to intuitive-feelers, regardless of cognitive style, so this approach can be used as a form of implicit strategy training (described more fully in Chapter 6).

In a few instances, some activities may be both concrete and abstract. For example, diagramming sentences, which occurs rarely (unfortunately) in today's English classes, uses both concrete and abstract strategies. Employing diagrams to explain relationships in math and science also uses both concrete and abstract strategies. Projects of nearly any type, although seemingly concrete in nature because they usually produce a product, can be used successfully with abstract learners; their "product" may be a written or oral report. Some other cognitive style domains occasionally permit the use of one activity that incorporates aspects of more than one learning style. Such activities are invaluable and efficient.

Sequential-random differences can be a major source of irritation in the classroom if not handled in a whole-class, ideal-world way. The chart below provides some suggestions.

	Randoms	Sequentials
Language Arts/English	reading discussion groups	outlining organizing essays
Mathematics	projects	proofs
Science	hypothesis and application description and rules end product	lab manuals
Social Sciences	trends	timelines
Foreign Language/ESL	authentic materials computer applications	textbooks computer training

The difference between being random and being sequential has more to do with how one organizes thought than with how one processes thought. Therefore, knowing what other cognitive styles are present will have an impact on the activities selected for these learning style differences. For example, providing a description and rules is more appropriate for random-deductive learners, and providing a vision of the end product is more appropriate for random-inductive learners. In general, random learners tend to prefer "open country," a metaphor used by Ehrman (1996) to indicate foreign language learners who prefer to self-guide their own learning (minimal external guidance and maximum internal control). Sequential learners, depending on their other cognitive preferences, prefer more externally guided learning, which Ehrman (1996) divides into three types, depending on the proportion of external guidance to internal control: "railroads," which provide maximum external guidance and minimal internal control; "major highway systems," which provide moderate external guidance and moderate internal control; and "trails," which provide moderate external guidance and extensive internal control.

Random learners, then, prefer to develop their own tasks, use materials in their own ways, and organize information according to internally developed frameworks. For this reason, in any subject area they tend to enjoy reading, participating in discussion groups, completing projects of any sort (as long as they have a fair amount of autonomy of the procedures associated with the projects), using authentic materials (as long as they can use the materials in the way in which they desire), and computer applications. An example of the latter is a computer program for Czech students at the Defense Language Institute. Accommodating a number of learning styles, the program presented information in Czech about the Czech Republic. Topics included history, geography, demographics, and culture. A minimal amount of information was originally entered into the computer. Sequential students could work their way through a prescribed sequence of activities; random students could proceed through the program in any manner desired. Projects assigned to students included the selection of one of the topic areas, about which the student interviewed a native speaker (in Czech) for additional information not already available in the computer program; wrote up the information (in Czech, corrected for accuracy by a native speaker) for addition to the program; and with the help of a computer programmer (if needed), entered the new information into the program. With each class, the program became more and more extensive, and a wide range of learning styles beyond random-sequential differences were accommodated through one activity: intuitive-feelers and extraverts (enjoyed the interviews), sensing-perceivers (liked adding graphics and using the computers), levelers and global learners (added information about generalities), sharpeners and particular learners (added details to the levelers' work), abstracts (liked selecting new subtopics), and concretes (liked obtaining the new information and adding it to the program).

Hemisphere preferences also have an impact on classroom work. The chart on the next page provides some thoughts on how to organize instruction to accommodate both kinds of learners in the classroom. In this section, I am treating this domain as bipolar, although in actuality, like the other domains, it is a continuum, and it has the additional feature that some students display integrated dominance. This latter attribute usually means that these students will learn from activities in either column. It has also been found to enhance learning and style flexibility in foreign language acquisition (Leaver, 1986).

	Left-Hemisphere Preference	Right-Hemisphere Preference
Language Arts/English	word-level work	discourse-level work
Mathematics	verbal textbook explanations	diagrams and illustrations
Science	text without distractions	illustrated text
Social Studies	dates and timelines	trends and patterns
Foreign Language/ESL	morphology syntax	phonology semantics

In an ideal world, a teacher would be able to provide right-hemisphere-preferent students with textbooks that use images for teaching and left-hemisphere-preferent learners with textbooks that use verbal descriptions. In an ideal world, textbooks would contain both. In an ideal world, mathematics textbooks would ensure that all word problems had accompanying diagrams or other graphics support and would present picture problems for right-hemisphere-preferent learners and word problems for left-hemisphere-preferent learners. Teachers of history, government, and the social sciences would begin with trends, moving to dates and/or timelines, for right-hemisphere-preferent learners and begin with dates, moving to trends, for left-hemisphere-preferent learners.

There is an implicit (and sometimes, explicit) understanding that right-hemisphere-preferent students tend to be better at music, art, nonempirical social sciences, geometry, and the nonverbal humanities, and that left-hemisphere-preferent students tend to be better at math, algebra, science, empirical social sciences, and verbal humanities (Torrance et al., 1977). Although there may be some underlying biases (as yet unproved empirically), much still depends on how the subject is taught. In programs where subject matter is taught in very traditional ways, right-hemisphere-preferent students comprise the largest portion of the talented students in a GATE program, and left-hemisphere-preferent students comprise the largest portion of the gifted. Although this is the trend, it is not always the actuality. As a nearly exclusively right-hemisphere-preferent learner, I was "turned off" to music for many years by an inept college music professor and "turned on" to algebra by a skilled high school mathematics teacher.

In recent days, more interest in the academic community is being focused on whole brain learning. In some ways, the whole brain movement has fallacies similar to the multiple intelligences movement, giving everyone a little bit of everything but not much of anything. The greatest disservice here is the implication that teachers are not able to determine for themselves the learning profiles of the students of a particular class and how to meet those needs. Nevertheless, a little bit of everything definitely works better than excluding right-hemisphere-preferent students entirely.

Kolb types are so different in their learning needs that I use this particular domain to demonstrate how students can all be good learners but suffer in the hands of a teacher of another type if that teacher is not style-aware. The exercise I use can be tried by any teacher on his or her own or as an in-service activity. Once types are identified through self-diagnosis or through instrumentation, I group teachers into like styles and ask them to produce a lesson plan for the opposite style: divergers for convergers, assimilators for accommodators, convergers for divergers, and accommodators for assimilators. After a typical 90-minute struggle, most teachers tell me that this is the most difficult task they have ever been assigned. I know it is. Even for style-aware teachers, there is little intuition about how specific activities might work with their opposite styles. Usually, when these lesson plans are shared, the response from the group of the opposite learning style is, "I wouldn't want to be in that class." The suggestions below provide a starting point for preparing lessons for the four Kolb types.

	Divergers	Assimilators	Convergers	Accomodators
Language Arts/English	discussions	readings	writing enactment	self-intiated projects
Mathematics	observation	explanations	practice	experiment
Science	demonstrations	lectures	application	hypothesis
Social Sciences	videos with a story line	textbook	field trips	constrct hypothetical systems
Foreign Language/ESL	movies	grammar work	language lab	interaction with native speakers

Some types complement each other and, at least on one axis, can reach students with congruent types:

1. Divergers share their abstraction with assimilators and their randomness with accommodators.
2. Assimilators share their abstraction with divergers and their sequentiality with convergers.
3. Convergers share their concreteness with accommodators and their sequentiality with assimilators.
4. Accommodators share their concreteness with convergers and their randomness with divergers.

In the case of Kolb style differences, much depends on the mode of instruction, as opposed to the activities *per se*. The chart above, then, emphasizes modes. For each mode there are many activities which can be designed. Moreover, some teachers design classes that contain multiple modes of instruction, in order to accommodate groups comprised of differing Kolb styles (McCarthy, 1997).

Divergers benefit from group instruction and from facilitative teaching. Letting them watch movies in foreign language classes or demonstrations in science class is a means of helping them to acquire new information and enough context to motivate their learning. They usually learn well through reading assignments in any subject area.

In teaching assimilators, one teaching method that works well is the direct instruction method that I have criticized roundly for its application in special education environments. Ironically, far more assimilators are found in regular education classrooms than in special education classrooms. However, direct instruction is found far more frequently in special education classrooms, where it can be less beneficial than in regular education classrooms. In directly instructing assimilators, teachers might present the overall concept (abstract presentations work well for this learning style), followed by the components and rules that make up this concept, giving students practice in rule application (Englemann & Bruner, 1968; Stephens, 1970). There is no limit to the submolecular level to which teachers can feel free to break down the information, because assimilators naturally atomize; in fact, most assimilators are also particular and analytic. Mastery learning is another method that works well with assimilators (and with accommodators).[3]

Teaching convergers usually requires action. Field trips represent excellent learning tools for them; so do applications of any type in any subject area. Working in the language lab, enacting plays, and conducting an experiment are excellent activities for convergers. (Many convergers are also kinesthetic, so these activities work doubly well.) Some recent programs for students in the upper elementary grades and junior high level, in which students carry out tasks on site (e.g., at a farm or at a store) attract convergers. In the classroom, they need the opportunity to practice (often physically) what they have learned. This can mean writing, enacting, reenacting, or most any other form of "doing."

Teaching accommodators requires risk taking on the part of instructors. Accommodators learn best and are most comfortable when instructors "let go," and of course, letting go is hard to do. Having students design their own learning programs is one way to let go and still maintain control. Using learning contracts, in which the student agrees to learn specified material, complete specified tasks, and turn in specified projects by an agreed-upon date and in an agreed-upon manner, is another way; however, with learning contracts accommodators may want to change some of the conditions after the onset of the contract period because new information that they are learning is reshaping their thinking and interests. In science classes, these students might be allowed to develop their own hypotheses, then design and carry out their own experiment to test them. (This may take a lot of courage and a little guidance on the part of the teacher.) In social sciences, these students may be allowed to construct new forms of cultures and civilizations as a means of understanding current ones. The seventh-grade social studies class at Universe School described in Chapter 1 was doing just that. In foreign language classrooms, they may need to leave the protection of the classroom and complete an assigned task (or internship) with a native speaker of the language they are studying.

When in doubt about classroom activities planned for specific learning styles, experienced style-aware teachers confer with colleagues with different styles to determine how close they have come to "hitting the mark." There are also resources available that can help with specific students. For diverger students, readers might try any of the whole language resources available (Newman, 1985). For assimilator students, nearly any traditional textbook should be appropriate. For converger students, readers might try Blackburn (1976) or Dallman (1971). For accommodator students, Kaplan, Kaplan, Madsen, and Taylor (1973) provide innovative concrete-random and kinesthetic activities for elementary school students. Some of the ideas can be adapted for higher grades. Although the specific topics in these books may be outdated, the activities presented there can serve as models for activities that can be used with contemporary topics.

Gregorc types have much in common with some learning styles previously discussed. For teaching abstract-random learners, teachers can follow the practices suggested for abstract learners, random learners, and divergers. For teaching abstract-sequential students, teachers can follow the practices suggested for abstract learners, sequential learners, and assimilators. For teaching concrete-sequential students, teachers can follow the practices suggested for concrete learners, sequential learners, and convergers. For teaching concrete-random students, teachers can follow the practices suggested for concrete, random, and accommodator students.

TESTING IN STYLE

Classroom tests are the area in which teachers who accommodate learner profiles can provide fair tests for all students. Too frequently, all students are examined in the same way with the same test with the same format. This means that only a portion of the students will be able to display their full knowledge. *The overemphasis on standardized testing in recent years has done much to ensure the equal failure of large numbers of students.* It is unfortunate that multiple-choice, machine-scorable tests are called "objective tests." They are anything but objective measurements of student learning because they favor students with Western learning styles and disadvantage the rest of the population. Too often, national, standardized tests of this type not only influence the construction of classroom tests but also the conduct of class.

Style	Testing Format
visual	written test
auditory	oral test
motor	performance test
impulsive	speed test
reflective	power test
synthetic	open-ended test
analytic	multiple-choice test

Written tests provide for more accurate assessment of visual and mechanical students; oral tests of auditory learners; and performance tests, which are harder but not impossible to design, of kinesthetic learners.

As already mentioned several times, speed (timed) tests are tolerable to impulsives but are problematic for reflectives. Reflective learners fare better with power (untimed) tests.

Open-ended tests (which are also good for random learners) allow synthetic students to be creative and to use their abilities to synthesize. Synthetic students perform better when they are working within a context and accomplishing a task that allows them to synthesize and apply. Most open-ended tests do this. On grammar tests, synthetic students work better when they are asked to use the grammar to accomplish some purpose. Remember Susan (Chapter 4)? She was not a poor writer, but she was a global-synthetic learner and experienced difficulty demonstrating her knowledge of grammar, when given a particular-analytic (i.e., detail-oriented) test. Conversely, problem-solving tests allow analytic students to use their abilities to analyze. Analytic students do best when they are asked to disassemble and identify.

The U.S. government has a special system for testing its foreign language speakers. Although there is an agreement among the various agencies that use foreign language speakers to consider the proficiency test results of government agencies to be equal, both research and practical experience has shown results are not equal. The Department of Defense, because of its large numbers, uses a written, standardized ("objective") test to determine students' proficiency levels in listening and reading. The Department of State, being considerably smaller and in general having foreign service officers whose proficiency levels range from minimal to levels significantly higher than those found among most military foreign language students, uses an interactive form of testing. Although the State Department test is seemingly more "subjective," having worked extensively with both soldiers and diplomats, I have often found it to be more accurate, mainly because the format allows style-aware examiners to adapt on the spot to examinees' learning styles. The test consists of three kinds of oral performance: conversation, interview, and briefing (oral report). Either concrete examples or abstract ideas can guide the conversation and interview portions of the test. The briefing portion provides written information in English that sequential learners can follow in preparing an oral statement; randoms can put their own structure on the information. Other styles may also be accommodated, given the relative flexibility in content and depending on the style awareness of the examiners.

The former U.S.S.R. used a similar system for many years for testing its students. Seemingly highly subjective because of its oral format and one-on-one conduct, these tests allowed teachers to explore students' knowledge in depth. Adjustments were not typically made for learning styles, but they could have been. The new Russia, in looking to the West for guidance in education, as well as politics and economics, is introducing standardized, multiple-choice, "objective" testing into its schools and general testing programs. My question, formally put to Russian educators on many occasions, is Why do they want to replace a sturdy but plain vehicle with a flashy, unreliable one (Leaver, 1997)?

There is another kind of testing that takes place in classrooms: informal testing. Activities that simply ask students to provide information that they have memorized, been taught, or have read are not learning activities at all. They are testing activities. It is sometimes possible to observe a half-hour of class where all the activity is nothing but testing in another form. This changes the nature of the classroom. Instead of being a place where students learn, home becomes the learning place and the classroom the place where students are tested. *Moving beyond a testing approach to teaching is essential if students of all styles are to be accommodated and if learning is to be facilitated for all members of the class.*

RENDERING SUBJECT MATTER IN STYLE: SOME SPECIFIC QUESTIONS

The following are actual questions which have been asked of me by teachers of various subject areas (organized alphabetically) from elementary school through graduate school. The questions were asked by real teachers, trying to make a more ideal classroom environment for their students. Although the list is not exhaustive either of the questions that have been asked or of the possibilities, perhaps the responses given will serve as models to answer other questions not presented here.

The suggestions that follow represent *some* ways that teachers can work with a range of profiles. The concept behind these suggestions is that not all students have to be doing the same thing at the same time in order to learn the same information equally well. In fact, *if all students are doing the same thing in the same way at the same time, they are most likely not learning the information equally well, and some students may not be learning the information at all.* Whole class teaching is unlike imposed systems where all students do a little of everything. In whole-class environments, many students never do most of the activities. Rather, most students do the few activities that are effective for the way in which they learn.

A whole class at work looks very different from a traditional classroom at work. In whole classes that are learning, students may be placed in various size groups, at work on different tasks. Some students may not even be in the classroom. Certainly, a whole class learning rarely pictures a teacher lecturing in front of the class— although that may occasionally occur and there may be subsets of the class to which the teacher routinely lectures. An observer can usually tell if a whole class is learning simply by walking through the door: Students are engaged in tasks (some in groups, others independently, and yet others off-site), and the teacher is assisting, helping, observing, or keeping hands off as the situation may require with each group of students or individual student. The teachers are creating the conditions for learning, then letting the students learn. Whole-class teachers even have time to talk to observers and explain what is going on!

The suggested activities can be mixed and matched, and new parallel activities devised, so that extraverted synthetic learners will have different activities from introverted synthetic learners. The activities provided for each style are simply representative of what can be done. By following the rationale and model behind each suggestion, teachers can adapt the suggestions to each unique student in their own classrooms. Sometimes, a given activity will be useful for more than one type of learner. In such cases, teachers can achieve economy of effort. Seeking out such cases is well-worth the investment.

◆ English
Why can't my student write descriptive essays?

This community college teacher was surprised when one student turned in an assignment to describe a place of her choosing, and, instead, described an event that occurred in the place. The teacher returned the assignment to be rewritten, and the student returned it with more event information.

An analysis of the student's writing—the words used (and not used), the kinds of verbs and sentence structure employed, and the specific information included—revealed that this student was a kinesthetic learner. Places in her mind were fully associated with activities that took place in them. Obviously, this student needed to develop strategies related to description.

One recommendation to the teacher included peer work with visual learners in producing a visual product (a videotape, a written report with pictures). This should help the kinesthetic learner observe the strategies that visual peers used. This works well with kinesthetic learners who are also right-hemisphere-preferent, accommodators, or synthetics.

A second recommendation was to have the student participate in a brainstorm session that focused on developing the contents of the paragraph before the paragraph was written. Such a session could be done in either a small group or a full-class environment. The purpose would be to have students sharing items of visual information that would then become part of the essay. This works well for kinesthetic learners who are also sharpeners or divergers.

A third recommendation was to provide the student with model paragraphs about a place. The assignment to the student would be to use the model and its contents, simply changing specific information, to write about another location of her choosing. This works well for kinesthetic learners who are also convergers.

A fourth recommendation was to have the student read descriptive essays about places and outline them. This would graphically demonstrate to the student the internal components of a descriptive essay. Based on these components, the student could then prepare an essay on her own. This works well for kinesthetic learners who are also analytics.

◆ Foreign Language
Why did my particular student not learn strategies from his global peers, when I put them in the same classroom?

This question came to me from a very effective, state-of-the-art English as a Foreign Language (EFL) program in Central Asia, where teachers and administrators teach the whole class routinely. The student, a 40-something national government official working in the field of economic justice, spent his nonclassroom time being responsible for legal and financial matters; this meant that accuracy, a trait common to particular students, was rewarded in his work. It is only reasonable that his natural style would carry over into language learning. However, that style was not rewarded here. Without other strategies, he set about memorizing English through the help of the dictionary, ensuring that he had an equivalent meaning in his native language for each word he read, and avoiding risk taking opportunities. His aim was for accuracy in language learning.

The teachers and administrators in this program first tried to teach him global strategies in a tutorial environment. They finally convinced him to shelve the dictionary for periods of time and to use context to determine meaning (they had to teach him how to use context), but they still had difficulty weaning him from making word lists, memorizing grammar rules, and restricting his communications to only those he was certain were accurate. Because he was studying alone, they reasoned that being in the classroom under the teacher's protection allowed him to avoid using the global strategies that they were teaching him. Furthermore, these teachers knew that strategy sharing during task completion by students of differing learning styles can often develop learning strategies more effectively than can direct instruction of those strategies.

Another group of students, studying in the same program, had a class profile of global learning. These students had developed English language proficiency quite rapidly. The administrators reasoned that if they were to put the particular student with these global peers, who were using the same curricular materials in the classroom, he would learn global learning strategies from interaction with peers. This is a reasonable assumption, but in practice, the particular student's performance actually deteriorated. Why?

In this case, the answer has little to do with cognitive style, the area on which the administrators had focused. It has to do with personality type and with self-esteem. The student was an INTJ, a scholar by nature. Language learning is more of an extraverted activity. Often, it is an NF activity—a yearning to establish rapport with another culture. By nature, then, this student would be looking at language, at best, as a communication system, and the development of an understanding of that system would be important to him. Not understanding the system, or not being able to devise a system of his own for the language (we call this "Interlanguage"), he would be left without communicative devices, which is what had happened.

As has been discussed earlier, another dimension of the personality issue is the need for NTs to feel competent; this is strongly related to an affective variable in learning—self-esteem. By putting this reflective and particular INTJ into a classroom of impulsive and global extraverts, whose linguistic skills were already superior to his even though all the students had started the program at the same time, he felt anything but competent! Instead of increasing his willingness to take risks, the experience damaged his self-esteem and caused him to withdraw further.

Ideally, this approach could have worked if it had been handled slightly differently. If there were global students with lower proficiency, the particular student could have been grouped with them. In this case, this option did not exist, so the only remaining option, if the administrators and teachers want the student to benefit from a sharing of learning strategies by his global peers, is to make sure that he can hold his own in the classroom. They can do this by preparing him in advance for each class. The tutorial sessions, then, become preparation for the group sessions, and the group sessions, as far as content is concerned, become review sessions. Thus, the student can be taught in accordance with his style, and he can review out-of-style. Once such a full TRT program is in effect, there is a chance that this student will develop some global strategies over time.

A very important lesson can be learned here, one that we have seen before in learning-styles assessment: "seems" is not always "is." It is important to look at the trees (the details of the student's learning approach) to determine learning style. The administrator in this case did so adequately. It is also important to look at the forest (the overall situation) to see how these styles work together with all other aspects of the program and with any proposed changes. The administrator forgot to do this, hence, the disappointment with the result. *Accommodating students is often a trial-and-error process.* For teachers who are not risk takers, this can be disconcerting. In such cases, I always keep in mind that teaching is a lot like parenting. Students, like offspring, don't come with instructional manuals, so the instructions have to be intuited or ascertained through trial, error, practice, and feedback. Fortunately, students, like children, can survive error on the part of well-intentioned teachers and parents. Over time, if an effort is made, both teachers and parents learn to "get it right."

◆ Foreign Language: Grammar
How can I teach grammar effectively to all my foreign language students, regardless of modality preference?

Visual learners tend to be best at grammar in its written form and auditory learners at grammar in its spoken form. Visual learners, in general, tend to have a small edge over auditory learners because they usually read more, and therefore get more exposure, usually at the sentient stage of memory, than do their auditory counterparts, who may be listening intently but listening for general meaning rather than for specific structure. Teaching grammar to visual learners, then, is a matter of giving them reading materials with many examples of the structure in it and written-out paradigms. Visuals generally have well-developed reading strategies (Hicks, 1980; Kempwirth & MacKenzie, 1989).

More appropriate for auditory learners are role plays that use the structure desired. These role plays can be seeded with the grammatical forms to be acquired. For more advanced students, oral reports, brainstorming and discussions, interviews, and the making of video- or audiotapes might be in order. Where these activities are content-based, processing, retention, and reconstruction of grammar may be learned more effectively and efficiently (Stryker & Leaver, 1997).

More appropriate for motor students are motor applications. For example, kinesthetic students might play (or lead) "Simon Says" (grammatical forms can be manipulated to reflect the ones needed) or BINGO (using grammatical features rather than numbers in the boxes). Total Physical Response works well for learning the imperative form and verbs of motion (Asher, 1988).

Mechanical learners can learn much structure simply by writing out drills or, preferably, meaningful essays where grammar can be controlled, as in copying paragraphs and structure but changing the topic and content (e.g., an essay on "my cat" becomes an essay on "my dog" or "my snake").

These activities can be conducted concurrently through the use of small groups. Four-handed instruction (team teaching, in which two teachers share students in the same classroom for the duration of the class hour) is another way to assist accommodation of a range of learning styles (Goroshko & Slutsky, 1993).

◆ *Foreign Language: Pronunciation*
How can I teach good Italian pronunciation to motor learners?

Kinesthetic and mechanical learners need to feel the sound before they can make it. For them, language laboratory work becomes essential, but the actual conduct of the lab work needs to differ significantly from that used with auditory and visual learners. They need to be shown how to make the sounds (the placement of the tongue, etc.). Looking at pictures of how sounds are made is only marginally helpful for them. They need to feel the sound with their own oral apparatuses. Trial and error, following explanation, is usually the most helpful for them. Although these folks seem like a hard group to teach, once they feel the sound, they need far less repetition and review than do other kinds of learners. They are only difficult because we are not used to teaching pronunciation in the way in which they need to receive it.

◆ *Gifted Education: Science*
Maryko, a new student in the gifted science program, is not keeping up with the class. She wants to return to her regular classroom, where she was bored. Should she?

Answering this question took a little exploration into who Maryko was and why she was not learning. Maryko's background was typical for students who were placed into this particular science program. She was a delight for any teacher. She learned quickly and easily. Some even thought she might have an eidetic memory.

The class into which Maryko was placed presented advanced science concepts to sixth-grade students. Maryko diligently listened to the lectures and scribbled away, taking notes as rapidly as she could during the high-intensity lectures. She took home the cassette tapes that had been prepared to accompany the lectures in order to assist students with review, and she listened to them every night.

An analysis of Maryko's notes indicated that they were disorganized and difficult to read. They contained many misspellings. (This was surprising; Maryko won last year's spelling bee.)

An interview with Maryko indicated that she perceived that she was having difficulty keeping up with the class. She said that she could not understand the lectures; they seemed too "advanced" for her. Maybe she was not as good as her peers. She wanted to return to her old science class, where she was getting good grades, even though she found the book and the course boring.

As it turned out, Maryko was a visual learner. In her first program, where she succeeded, most of the work was visual in nature. When she entered the advanced program, the work turned to an auditory mode, but Maryko kept reacting as if she were in a visually oriented classroom. As a result, the strategies (visual ones) that worked for her earlier failed her in the new setting.

There are several ways for Maryko to succeed in the new setting. The teacher can adapt the instruction to give Maryko opportunities to use visual strategies. Reading ahead on the lecture topic is one way. Handouts are another way. Providing a written summary of the lecture or having Maryko study with or borrow notes from an auditory learner who has a secondary visual learning preference will also help.

Maryko could also help herself. She could develop some auditory strategies. To facilitate the development of such strategies, she could take notes on the tapes that have been provided and then compare those notes with the ones she took in class. She could also compare her notes with the notes of other students. Given extra practice with note-taking skills and the analysis of where her classroom notes are deficient, she could learn to take better notes from lectures. Because Maryko has attributes of an assimilator, she might also benefit from direct skills training in note taking.

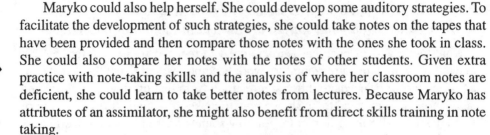

◆ *International Affairs*
How about an example of how to prepare a whole-class lesson,
for example, for a class on comparative political systems?

The first step in putting together a whole-class lesson is to determine who is in the class. Even if the topic and the background reading or textbook are the same for two classes, the lesson plans for these classes will differ, based on the background knowledge, individual students' learner profiles, and class profile (learning style of the majority of the students)—the process for making these determinations and teaching decisions based on them is described in detail in Chapter 7. Some of the activities suggested below would not be used if there were no one in the class with that particular learning style. The suggestions can be expanded upon, modified, used as models, or otherwise manipulated as needed to make them more appropriate to the individual classroom situation.

In accommodating differences in sensory modalities, teachers might assign a textbook reading on the foreign country political system for visual learners. Auditory learners might watch a movie on the same topic (if introverted) or conduct an interview with an expert (if extraverted). Mechanical learners might draw up a comparison chart of the American and foreign country political systems. Kinesthetic learners might participate in the interview process and, rather than taking notes, make a videotape or put together slides on the subject. All the learners can work together if the work is assigned as a group project. Each brings to the process information from various forms of research. The end product can be a videotape, supported by written materials, or an oral presentation, depending on the class profile.

If the teacher prefers to base whole-class work on cognitive differences in lieu of or in addition to modality preferences, other opportunities for learning present themselves. In making the videotape or the report, analytic students can address areas of deficiencies and advantages in the foreign political system versus the American political system, and synthetic students could propose a new experimental system to handle the deficiencies and retain the advantages. (Working together to accomplish this, the synthetic students would learn strategies for disassembling wholes—the current political system—in order to understand them better, and analytic students would learn strategies for assembling new wholes from available information—the foreign political system and the American political system—to achieve the same purpose.) Impulsives might want to conduct an extemporaneous debate on the "new system," which becomes a focus of the videotape; reflectives might prefer to prepare the script for the videotape.

Activities can be added or the suggestions modified to account for other cognitive styles or to incorporate personality types. The process is one in which, having determined the class profile and the learning needs of individual students, teachers can select or devise appropriate activities that will achieve the specific purpose desired: (a) development of knowledge, (b) development of skill, (c) repetition and review in order to facilitate mental storage, (d) a specific product or achievement, or (e) whatever other goal the instructor has.

◆ Mathematics: Algebra
How can I get students to understand that $(a+b)^2 = a^2 + 2ab + b^2$?

I've told them a hundred times that the answer is not $a^2 + b^2$. I've threatened them with a failing grade if they leave out the 2ab. Nothing works. They still do it. Perhaps they are not auditory and don't understand what I say; perhaps they are not visual and don't see this. This teacher was becoming versed in learning-style differences. However, the issue here was not a modality, but a cognitive style.

Mathematics is a language of symbols. As such, it tends to be more accessible to abstract learners. It is no surprise to me that the majority of mathematicians I meet, regardless of personality type or modality, are abstract-sequential in their cognitive-style preferences. Unfortunately, not all students of mathematics are abstract-sequential. The explanation given for the formula above omitted the concrete learners from the teaching process. Those flexible enough to follow an abstract explanation or with a strong ability to rote memorize ("put in the 2ab") without necessarily needing to understand theory could adapt to this kind of presentation. However, concrete students who are inflexible in learning style need concrete instruction. One way to handle this formula concretely is with manipulatives or drawings. For deductive-concrete students, make a square, using for each side a long segment, *a*, and a short segment, *b*. Connect the lines from the segments inside the square, and instantly, concrete students can see that there is a square *a*, a square *b*, and two leftover rectangles with a side *a* and a side *b* (2ab). For inductive-concrete students, replace the letters a and b with allegorical representations. The letter *a* could be the color blue, and *b* the color green. The result is a blue square, a green square, and two blue-green squares. From this, the inductive learners can induce the formula.

◆ Reading Comprehension
I know this student, a leveler, can read, but test scores don't show it.

Much depends on how the test is constructed and on what it focuses. The typical multiple-choice test focuses on details. The global learner, especially one who is also a leveler, does not. Using a multiple-choice test format as a reading comprehension check for levelers usually results in test scores lower than the reading comprehension level actually is. To test the reading comprehension of global learners, a more open-ended test that asks them to predict outcomes or next steps is fairer and more accurate. Asking them to write a similar story in the same style as the author, one with a parallel meaning or "punch line" to the story is equally fair.

◆ *Reading Instruction*
How can I teach reading to synthetic learners?

To assist both synthetic and analytic students in reading successfully, the teacher might include both word study exercises for analytic students and tasks that ask synthetic students to ascertain something from context, predict an outcome, or complete a task. For example, rather than asking the meaning of a list of words, the teacher could give the synthetic student the words in a story and ask the student to use the words to create a new story. In working with food, the foreign language or ESL teacher can ask the synthetic students to interview their classmates and put together a menu; at the same time, they can give the analytic students two menus and ask them to determine to which place they will take their parents and why.

◆ *Reading Readiness*
How can I determine if global learners are ready to read?

Reading readiness tests for global readers who already read often produce erroneous scores. One child who began reading at age 2 attended a kindergarten where reading was taught at age 4. Enrolled in a new school district at age 5 and already reading books and novels, she failed that school's reading readiness test. (Fortunately, it took her teacher less than a day to determine that the test score was quite wrong.) Why had this happened? The test was both difficult and inaccurate for a global learner, because global learners focus on meaning and the reading readiness test was about meaningless details: matching nonsense syllables. Nonsense syllables are much more appropriate for nonreaders—and for particular learners. Global learners and readers search for meaning in written symbols and are confused when they find no meaning in what they are trying to read. All that the score really signified was that a global learner could not handle a particular test.

The best way to check the reading readiness of global learners is to let them try to read and observe what they do. I realize that this seems like more work—one-on-one and individualized. But is it more work than assessing incorrectly, making incorrect placements, and reassessing? And what about the negative emotional reactions involved when assessment and placement are clearly incorrect?

◆ *Science*
How do I keep two average students, who are synthetic learners, from being bored in science lab?

The question is, What is going on in the science lab now? Why are these two students bored? Ask them! These two students have probably ended up in an analytic learning environment. Analytic students benefit from activities that allow them to see details, to analyze, and to draw conclusions, but synthetic students do not and quickly become bored with such activities. In science, synthetic students benefit from activities that allow them to create something new, to synthesize, and to predict. For synthetic students, looking at the relationship between two scientific principles, comparing the results of similar experiments, and creating an experiment to test their own hypothesis are exciting activities. Turning over the science lab to their imagination should go a long way in igniting their enthusiasm for lab class.

◆ Science: Biology
How can I get students to memorize a list of things well, such as a list of the bones in the body?

This question was put by an assimilator teacher. Learning via memorization of lists is a natural activity for her. However, she does not really want students to know the list. She wants them to know the bones in the body. ***The first step in determining how to get students to accomplish a task is to determine the underlying goal of that task.*** (The same is true of lists in other subjects. English teachers do not want students to know the list of new vocabulary words; they want them to be able to use the words in their reading and writing. Spelling teachers do not want students to know the list of spelling words; they want them to be able to spell these words accurately whenever they need to use them. Foreign language and ESL teachers do not want students to know the list of grammar rules; they want students to write and speak accurately.)

The underlying goal for which the list was prepared will often reveal other tasks that could reach the same objective. These other tasks may be more achievable for nonassimilator students. This question underscores what has been said before: ***No matter how we try not to, we tend to teach very much in keeping with our own learning styles.***

To remember bones in the body, concrete-sequential learners could reconstruct skeletons, using the bones. Abstract-randoms could watch movies and learn jingles. Concrete-randoms could reconfigure the bones to build an alien skeleton. If the teacher really wants to give that list, then she might hand it to the assimilators in the class, who won't mind memorizing it all.

◆ Special Education: Reading
I have broken down the reading system into small phonics units and shown my special education students how to build words, yet they still cannot read. Why?

A phonics approach assumes that students have mainstream learning styles. Often, special education students end up in LD classrooms only because they do *not* have mainstream learning styles. Levy (1973) found that 60% of dyslexic students were visual learners. For them, phonics is not the answer.

As has been pointed out earlier and with other subjects, atomizing the lessons into smaller pieces and using analytic approaches (giving the big picture, then instructing the small pieces) require synthetic, global, and leveling students, who comprise the student body of the majority of special education classrooms, to work out of style, making learning even more difficult for them (Keogh & Donlan, 1972; Naigle & Thwaite, 1979).

Special education programs have a nationwide reputation for not being able to teach students to read. In the case of the typical special education student, the requirement to work out of style may be a very important reason. What these students need in order to learn to read is the same approach that all synthetic-global-visual students need: whole language, creation of new ideas, and testing through prediction. If they are experiencing difficulties in doing this, they need assistance with polishing their synthetic skills—which are already latently available to them—not with developing brand-new and uncomfortable analytic skills. Although the teaching of analytic strategies *should* be accomplished, this is better accomplished during periods of review, when the information is already known and reading skill is stronger. Of course, if these students are to return to the mainstream, where analysis dominates and where most first began to experience difficulty, they will need both accommodation and empowerment, just like every other student.

If the teacher is required to use a specific, districtwide approach in the special education classroom, then the teacher faces the same dilemma and challenge as other teachers whose textbooks are selected for them. They will need to find, make, and create the opportunities and materials to provide students with the kinds of learning materials that are more appropriate for them. *In centuries of teaching, the nature of learning has not changed: the quality of students' learning experience depends on the teacher and how the teacher shapes the learning opportunities.*

◆ Spelling
How can I get auditory students to be good spellers?

Spelling aloud helps to some small extent. However, English words come from such a wide variety of linguistic sources that the common advice to "sound it out," which would help students with spelling words in languages such as Spanish, where the grapheme-phoneme correspondence is high, is inappropriate for students of English, whether or not English is their native language.

Teaching visualization strategies, a strategy that is not commonly possessed by auditory learners (or by kinesthetic ones) but one which will stand them in good stead in spelling and many other subject areas, is more likely to be effective than trying to work with auditory strategies. In this case, the best deed a teacher can do is to empower the student to deal with a curriculum-style/learning-styles conflict, adapting the instruction only until the student has been empowered.

Most students can learn visualization strategies. One suggestion is to have students practice "seeing" the words on the ceiling or in their minds with closed eyes. Students then "read" the letters in the word as they see them. Sometimes, using colored letters helps with developing visualization strategies in the very beginning of strategy training. (Chapter 6 describes one such visualization strategy using graph models.)

METHOD IN THE IDEAL WORLD

In the ideal world, teaching method is secondary to student learning need. All methods can work; all methods can fail. The teacher, striving to create an ideal learning environment, selects those methods which accommodate the learning styles of the learner profiles present in each classroom. Each class taught in an ideal world, even if the subject and topic are the same, will not look the same to the observer. *Methods should not be straitjackets for either teachers or students; pedagogic demagoguery has no place in a free country.* Methods, and the techniques that comprise them, should be part of each teacher's arsenal in the struggle to win the style wars.

PRACTICE EXERCISES

1. Which Kolb type are you? Write a lesson plan in your subject matter area for a student of the opposite type. (If you are a diverger, write a lesson plan for a converger, an assimilator for an accommodator, a converger for a diverger, and an accommodator for an assimilator.) Find a colleague who has the same learning style for which you have written the lesson and ask for feedback.

2. Now write a lesson plan for a Kolb type with which you have one axis in common: convergers for accommodators or assimilators, accommodators for convergers or divergers, divergers for accommodators or assimilators, and assimilators for convergers or divergers. (This should be a little easier than exercise 1.) As in the previous exercise, find a colleague who has the same learning style for which you have written the lesson and ask for feedback.

3. Repeat this activity for any learning style dimension with which you wish to work.

4. Take one learning-style dimension and plot the probable distribution of students in any one of your classes. (Use the information in Chapter 3 or the observation checklists in Resource B to make a style determination for each.) Based on this distribution, how might you group your students? Would you group them? What kinds of tasks might you assign to the groups?

5. Apply the concepts in this chapter to one student (any student). Choose a lesson with which you will be working soon. What do you think are the sensory modalities, personality type, and cognitive styles (i.e., the learner profile) of this student? (The checklists in Resource B might help you make some of these determinations.) How will you adjust the lesson to accommodate these styles? Try out your ideas, noting successes and difficulties. Analyze where you did not "hit the mark." Was your assessment off, or did the activities not quite match the need? Talk to the student about what he thought about the activities and about how he felt about the activities. Better yet, do a class debriefing on the lesson. (Student styles will start to reveal themselves in the comments.) Find out what the students liked and did not like and what they would liked to have done that they did not have the opportunity to do.

NOTES

1. A term introduced to the foreign language education community by Boris Shekhtmann (Russian Language Training Center, Rockville, MD) and Natalia Lord (Howard University), this term refers to chunks of memorized speech (like islands in the middle of river of speech) that students know so well that they can use them as a "resting place" as they are swimming in a river of little-known language. There are several ways that students can use islands. They can be used verbatim as fillers, giving the student time to think of what he or she wants to say next. They can be used as models, in which students change some of the key words and phrases in

order to talk about something new. (An example would be a memorized paragraph on the history of Russian-American relations. When the student is talking to someone else about a related topic, Sino-Russian topics, he or she can simply change the necessary words and details; the grammar and structure are already there and do not require cognitive energy on the part of the student in this communicative situation.)

2. A mistake is a slip of the tongue. Students know what they should say, but somehow the wrong expression slips out. An error occurs when students do not know the proper construction and just make something up.

3. Mastery learning (Bloom 1968, 1971) is a self-paced approach to learning in which students continue to work on materials until they have mastered the content (usually 80% is used as the criterion). In mastery learning programs, some students move quickly through materials; others move more slowly through materials. Mastery learning was the teaching method upon which Accelerated Christian Education was based. Mastery learning is still used in some programs today.

6

In the Real World: Empowering Students

Not all teachers and students live in an ideal world. In the real world, large classes task teachers' ability to individualize, and many factors compound the risk to students with nonmainstream learning preferences. True disabilities, limited diversity in available textbooks, the push towards standardization, and sheer time constraints handicap even the most talented and devoted teachers.

THE NEED FOR EMPOWERMENT

While all students can learn, there are, of course, students with bona fide disabilities. Physiological disabilities, including physical impairment and brain damage, present a significant challenge to both students and teachers. The visual learner who suffers from visual impairment and the student whose short-term memory has been damaged through an incorrect dosage of medicine require more assistance and more creativity on the part of the teacher than do students who simply have nonmainstream learning preferences. As to the fact that they, too, can be taught and that accommodation of learning profiles can improve their rate of success, I have ample evidence.

In the real world, teachers do not always have a choice of materials. Textbooks are usually oriented towards one learning style, typically the style of the author. "When are teachers going to have some concrete-random textbooks for teaching Russian?" a teacher asked me at a conference a few years ago. My answer was "Very likely only when you produce them yourself." Most textbook writers are college professors of the abstract-sequential variety. They are not likely to produce concrete-random textbooks instinctively. (Actually, a concrete-random textbook may be a contradiction in terms. The same thing can be said of other foreign languages and of other subject matter courses. Even if sometime, somehow, somewhere, someone produces a concrete-random textbook, then it will not be good for the abstract-sequential students in the class.

As mentioned earlier, the push toward standardization in all subject areas ignores the fact that students are different and pulls teachers away from teaching. Standardized tests often show little more about a student's knowledge, ability, or proficiency than how well he or she can take a standardized test. Some better tests may predict to some extent how well students will perform in traditional classrooms. They rarely, if ever, accurately predict how well a student will be able to perform on the job, contribute to a given domain, or even how he or she will perform in a nontraditional classroom. Global students routinely "undertest" on such exams, whereas their testwise particular peers often "overtest" (unless they are reflective learners, in which case, they, too, may "undertest"). Given the reality of standardized testing, teachers need to help at risk students testproof themselves through the acquisition of test-taking skills. This differs from teaching students the specific content of a test. Preparing students for a specific test by teaching the content of that test is a disservice to students insofar as test preparation takes time away from the learning of the subject matter, with the result that students may receive a high test score but not learn the content. Unfortunately, some outcomes-oriented programs tempt teachers to prepare students for test content rather than to teach them subject matter. *The astute teacher teaches the subject matter in accordance with students' learning styles and provides test-taking advice (and practice) to at risk students.*

Outcomes-based programs, another attempt at standardization (treating everyone the same but not equally), may ultimately improve education nationwide, but they need to be treated with caution at the moment. Questions to be asked are the following:

1. What is the purpose of the proposed outcome?
2. What kinds of learners will be advantaged or disadvantaged?
3. How do we accurately and fairly assess attainment of the desired outcome for all learner profiles?

Most of these questions have yet to be raised, let alone answered. *As an impulsive nation, we are pressing forward toward transmissionable values without reflection.*

The hoopla associated with new standards for the year 2000 (Bodell, 1994) exacerbates the tendency to teach only the information required by such standards. If tests are well-designed (they usually are not) and the objective is well-defined (it usually is not), then such standards can have a beneficial impact on instruction. Such is the case of the U.S. State Department's Foreign Service Institute (FSI) foreign language proficiency tests. The tests are flexible enough to accommodate many (although far from all) learner profiles, and the objective is clearly defined in terms of a follow-on job where the language will be used in specific ways. The FSI test is fairly unique in this respect. One would be hard pressed to find a parallel in academia, including the American Council on the Teaching of Foreign Languages (ACTFL) proficiency test, which evolved, and distinctly departs, from the FSI test.

Time as an obstacle can be a serious threat to a teacher's ability to individualize. Initially, assessing learning styles and adapting lessons require a substantial time investment. With increasing experience, the time investment significantly decreases, but there is no way to reach near-automation without the initial outlay. As an administrator concerned with the education of the whole class, I have tried to ensure that teachers have the time and support to develop these skills. For a number of reasons (both avoidable and unavoidable), not all administrators are so inclined.

For those educators who are able to break through these barriers, the step from accommodation to empowerment is a natural one, especially for those teachers who are already teaching in a facilitative way. Style conflicts do not have to result in lack of self-confidence, erosion of self-esteem, or other battle scars. They can, instead, result in the development of style flexibility in learners. Those who contend that learning styles are so resistant to change that the effort to teach style flexibility is not a useful endeavor are not fully justified in their beliefs. In fact, some elementary school teachers versed in style differences insist that they have observed style changes as some children mature, with some kinesthetic students, for example, becoming more comfortable with visual learning; these kinds of shifts have also been observed by some researchers (Parrill-Burnstein, 1981).[1] The question is: Did the preferred style change, or did students develop a strong secondary preference? I suspect that the basic style preference has not changed; it probably just went underground. As a closet kinesthetic for many years, I might have tested as a visual learner on a learning-styles test, depending on how I interpreted the intent of the test and the questions and depending on the content of the questions. If someone were to have observed me during high school and college days, they might have labeled me visual. However, now that I am old enough to be permitted eccentricity, I have reverted to my kinesthetic preferences—although I still might "test" visual on a learning-styles instrument. What my own experience, the experience of a number of elementary school teachers, and some psychological research make clear is that these kinds of secondary preferences can be developed as a result of classroom requirements (Halford et al., 1995; Koorland, 1986; Pressley et al., 1990; Serrapere, 1977). Strategy training can support this development where it occurs naturally and become a catalyst in those instances where it does not naturally occur.[2]

Strategy training is especially important for students who are truly inflexible in their learning styles. In addition to needing more accommodation in the activities assigned to them than do those who can at least bend a little, they also need more direct assistance in learning to be flexible. Usually, these students have a limited repertoire of learning strategies. Regardless of learner profile, such students need assistance in increasing that repertoire. *When students develop secondary learning style preferences as a result of strategy training, the effect on their learning is powerful, immediate, and motivational* (McCombs, 1988).

What researchers now know about learning strategies is that effective learning comes from selecting strategies that are appropriate to the task (Ehrman, 1996; Oxford & Leaver, 1996). This information contradicts earlier beliefs that a wide variety of strategies alone might be sufficient to develop successful learners. However, larger repertoires of strategies do have some advantages; they provide a wider choice of tools for the task and therefore greater comfort in working in an opposing learning style.

Through strategy training, students build comfort with working in an opposing style by discovering and learning to use the strategies that are associated with that style, as well as learning which strategies are appropriate to specific tasks (Oxford, 1989, 1990a; Pressley et al., 1990). This can occur both explicitly and implicitly. In a group of successful diplomats whom I interviewed in a study I conducted in 1984-

1985, there were a number of learners who had tested as having two diametrically opposed preferred learning styles: concrete-random and abstract-sequential. I might have dismissed this as a testing abnormality had a friend with whom I share a number of learning style attributes and I not tested the same way, and we are both style-aware and testwise. My interest piqued, I explored the reason behind the students' answers on the Gregorc self-report. As it turned out, all of these dual-style learners, like my friend and I, were actually concrete-random learners who had found their natural learning strategies unappreciated in the classroom and who in some way— either on their own, through the assistance of a parent or teacher, or through placement in unique educational settings conducive to some form of strategy training— developed the learning strategies associated with abstract-sequential approaches to learning, in time becoming so comfortable with those strategies that abstraction-sequentiality became a secondary learning style preference for them.

THE PATH TO EMPOWERMENT

Teachers in the past sometimes accomplished such strategy training unconsciously through a serendipitous combination of like and unlike styles. Students may have felt uncomfortable with some aspects of this mismatch, but the more style-flexible students apparently were able to increase their repertoire of strategies and, therefore, turn nonpreferred learning styles into secondary learning style preferences. In the real world, students do not necessarily need to feel comfortable all the time. In fact, Joyce and Weil (1972) note that "significant learning is frequently accompanied or impelled by discomfort" (p. 436).

A very effective teacher with whom I studied many years ago had few styles that intersected with mine. Recalling our behaviors, I would assess his styles approximately (I cannot vouch for the precision of a child's assessment, but I can vouch for moments of strongly felt cognitive dissonance) to be reflective (I am impulsive), converger (I am an accommodator), sequential (I am random), analytic (I am synthetic), introverted (I am extraverted), and intuitive-thinking (that fulcrum again!). There may also have been a modality match, kinesthesia, although I cannot be sure. In general, the differences were so disparate that theoretically there should have been no rapport and minimal learning. In reality, the opposite occurred: strong rapport and maximum learning. Why? The intersection of temperament, intuitive-thinking, may have been enough to create the rapport, and the possibly shared kinesthesia may have been enough to establish comfort in pacing, but what compensated for the extensive mismatches in cognitive styles? Certainly, I was aided by my own cognitive flexibility (present in some, but far from all, students), but that could not have explained everything. As I reflect on the instruction, I remember two key elements being present: 1) style acceptance and 2) style expansion. The teacher's intuitive apprehension of my cognitive "gaps" and gentle insistence through repeated opportunity that I fill them represented a form of strategy training (one that we would today label "implicit strategy training"). The instructor facilitated this by initially accepting my responses, then requiring more reflection and analysis under the rubric of thinking more critically, developing a personal opinion, or other kinds of deeper cognitive processing. In this way, he helped me to develop comfort with reflection, particularism, sharpening, and analysis. Because the teacher accepted my synthetic, global, leveling, and impulsive styles for some activities, I did not have to work entirely out of style; I could work partly out of style and partly in style, making the task of style expansion manageable. Whether that instructor— who was teaching before we knew anything about facilitative teaching or the development of critical thinking skills, let alone teaching the whole class through learning-style accommodation and learning strategy training—expanded my strategies consciously or, more likely, intuitively does not matter. What matters is that a form of strategy training did take place. The result was that I could feel intellectual growth, although at the time I had no label for it. That classroom, in spite of the impulsive versus reflective and synthetic versus analytic battles, inexorably drew me to its threshold day after day. I saw similar responses in other students whom I now recognize as possessing even other learning-style preferences.

The essence of this early form of facilitative strategy training lay in its two-pronged approach: response acceptance (essentially, style acceptance) followed by response clarification or complexification (essentially, style expansion). Teachers today can use this approach to accomplish strategy training more routinely, more effectively, and more consciously than was possible in the past. The development of style flexibility is an important part of TRT (Chapter 5), with style acceptance being associated with T (teaching and testing) and style expansion with R (review), and an important element in developing lifelong learning independence, self-confidence, and self-esteem in students. Style flexibility helps students do effective battle with hostile curricula, inscrutable teachers, and incomprehensible peers.

EMBRACING THE STYLE WARS

Some of my colleagues are likely to think I have marched right off the cliff of common sense and fallen into an abyss of pure nonsense with the following statement: style wars can be profitable. *Sometimes it is more strategic to stand and fight than to retreat from a style war.* Other times, surrendering to the enemy (the person with the opposing style) facilitates growth. Those who consider learning styles immutably entrenched may consider this impossible or undesirable, but it is neither. Accomplished intentionally, it results in learner empowerment.

Why should teachers strive to empower their students? One compelling reason is because learner empowerment enhances self-esteem and self-confidence. At one seminar, I was surprised during a discussion of impulsivity and reflectivity to hear a highly respected school principal say, "I'm not stupid!" No one I knew had ever thought she was. However, she had always been insecure on this point because she was reflective. At a subsequent session, I was conducting a short "data dump" (pure lecture at a rapid clip of speech available only to a native New Englander). Sensitive to this principal's reflectivity, I asked if she needed me to change my delivery style. Her response was no, now that she knew she was reflective she could handle such situations by taking notes and reflecting on them later, rather than trying to do both at once. She had empowered herself. Another individual who had also empowered himself was the kinesthetic high school dropout who decided to attend community college. The schedule he put together had courses from early morning to late evening, with 2 to 3 hours between each. His explanation? Knowing that he was kinesthetic, he arranged his day so that he could tolerate an hour of pure sitting from time to time—a scheduling option that was not available to him in high school. By empowering students to resolve learning-style conflicts on their own, we can give them the self-esteem and self-confidence that these two empowered individuals had gained. (And there is no need to wait until they are adults to do it!)

Effective outcomes of learning situations still rely heavily on the teacher: on the teacher's ability to assess the needs of students, design classroom activities to accommodate all students, find appropriate materials, and overcome the deleterious effects of standardization and limited time. In the ideal world, teachers can select instruction and activities to accommodate all students' learning styles. In the real world, teachers can make the accommodation task easier if they empower their students to become flexible learners and to recognize and resolve style conflicts on their own.

Underlying Concepts

Before discussing how to empower learners, it is important to understand some underlying concepts. These include the nature of learning strategies, the relationship of learning strategies to learning styles, and the relationship of learning strategies and styles to processes of memory.

What Are Learning Strategies?

Learning strategies are the specific techniques used to acquire new information. To use battlefield terminology, if learning styles are the avenues of approach to an objective, then the learning strategies are the tactics employed to ensure that the objective is attained; the range of what those tactics can be is dictated by the avenue of approach.

For reasons of elegance, I generally use the proposed four-category system for grouping learning strategies. These categories are metacognitive strategies, cognitive strategies (including memorization and coping strategies, which some specialists consider to be separate categories), social strategies, and affective strategies (Oxford, 1990b; Poulisse, 1989; Poulisse, Bongaerts, & Kellerman, 1984).

Metacognitive Strategies

Metacognitive strategies relate to how one thinks about one's own learning; in other words, they are strategies associated with thinking about thinking (McCombs, 1988). Metacognitive strategies include the following:

advanced organization	monitoring	homework planning
selective attention	evaluation	setting goals
self-awareness	anticipation	selecting tasks

Advanced organization means looking through the material ahead of time and determining how it is organized in order to prepare for an upcoming task. This is the student version of advanced organizers that students use on their own. The teacher form of advanced organizers is used in the classroom as pre-reading or pre-viewing activities (Ausubel, 1960). When teachers use advanced organizers in the classroom, they help students to understand material they are about to present. When students learn to use advanced organizers on their own as a metacognitive learning strategy, they prepare themselves to be more receptive to new information. When the Russian section at the Foreign Service Institute was using a principally auditory approach to grammar drilling, visual learners were encouraged to look at the drills (and explanations) in written form prior to coming to class. This is one kind of advanced organizer. Advanced organizers can be used for students of many learning styles to prepare them to cope with a nonpreferred style in class. With advanced organizers, students are actually learning through their preferred style (at home) and practicing through their nonpreferred style (in class). This approach works well only to the extent that students are capable and willing to do the learning on their own in advance of class.

Selective attention, sometimes called directed attention, means focusing on the important information or elements in a learning task and ignoring that which is not relevant. Selective attention is critical for a number of learning activities and does not seem to come naturally to particular learners, levelers, or to learning disabled students (Parrill-Burnstein, 1981; Ross, 1976).

Self-awareness means that students understand how they learn best, where they learn best, and when they learn best and use this understanding to create optimum learning conditions. Self-awareness comes more readily to NTs and NFs than to other temperaments (Oxford & Leaver, 1996).

Monitoring refers to listening for mistakes and correcting them, preferably before they slip out (Krashen, 1982). Monitoring as a learning strategy usually needs to be deliberately taught to global learners, who tend to focus on meaning to the exclusion of paying attention to verbal precision. Monitoring can be more than just paying attention to and controlling speech. It can include any behavior.

Evaluation involves checking on one's progress toward a goal. Critically reviewing one's success or reasons for failure comes naturally only to intuitive-thinking types (Keirsey & Bates, 1988). Other kinds of learners usually need to be taught how to do this and to make a habit of doing it.

Anticipation is a multipart strategy. It involves being prepared for the class, paying attention to what is going on in class, and developing a sense for what might happen next. Intuitives and inductives are better at this than other kinds of learners, for whom this strategy might be incorporated into in-class strategy training activities (Leaver & Oxford, 1993).

Homework planning is an area in which students can incorporate their understanding of their environmental preferences. Strategy training that includes the environmental preferences can be of great value to students in homework planning (Oxford, 1990b). It is more accessible to intuitive-thinkers than to other types.

Setting goals can refer to immediate goals for completion of one night's homework, longer term goals for completion of assigned projects, and career goals for subject matter learning that is of relevance to student ambitions. Goal setting comes naturally to judging types, not so naturally to perceiving types, who often rely on serendipity in their education and careers.

Selecting tasks is a metacognitive strategy that can be used only by those students who are in courses where teachers provide choices in task completion Style-aware students select those tasks which let them use their learning strengths.

Cognitive Strategies

Cognitive strategies are ones associated with the details of the thinking process. For a number of years now, researchers have focused on the cognitive strategies. Therefore, it is not surprising that we have isolated more strategies in this group than in other groups. There are so many cognitive strategies that one cannot begin to list them all here. The ones that are listed have been rather arbitrarily selected. None is really "better" than any other. All have an appropriate place and a requirement in some kind of learning activities.

elaboration	hypothesis formation	recombination	assembly
context expansion	hypothesis confirmation	recognition	disassembly
"extending the habit"	grapheme and phoneme conversion	looking for patterns	information location
clustering	rehearsing	comparison	sequencing
categorization	applying the known	paraphrasing	structuring

Context expansion refers to the ability to work with kernel information and ascertain a context for it. This strategy comes naturally to synthetic learners, but to those learners who need context for learning, context expansion can be difficult.

Elaboration (Reder, 1980) is often essential for comprehension and retention. It involves expanding in some way on the content of what one is reading or hearing. This strategy comes naturally to synthetic learners; in fact, they need to learn when to hold this strategy in check. It does not come as readily to analytic learners, but they can be taught it fairly easily.

"Extending the habit" (Goertzel, 1993) refers to the concept advanced by Pierce (1935) that people have a tendency to take habits, that is, to search for patterns, on the basis of which they construct models. We can apply this concept to the construction of any system. Levelers have some advantages when it comes to the strategy of extending the habit, although intuitive-thinkers of nearly any cognitive style also do this instinctively. Sensing types and sharpeners may need some strategy training in order to accomplish this on a routine basis.

For concept formation, **clustering** is often important. Global, synthetic, and leveling students have some advantages here. Where the opposite styles have some advantage is in **categorization**. Because clustering and categorization can be considered the leveling and sharpening side of one activity, training of both strategies is often in order (McCombs, 1988).

We tend to think of **hypothesis formation** and **hypothesis confirmation** as two-steps in one process. Usually, however, students possess one or the other strategy but not both. Hypothesis formation, which involves extradimensional shifting and intradimensional shifting, is associated with a synthetic learning style, whereas hypothesis confirmation, which involves dimension checking and stimulus differentiation, is associated with an analytic learning style. To activate the two-step process often means deliberate strategy training of the missing strategy (Hoskins, 1979).

Coping with letters and combinations of letters are required for a number of learning tasks. One related strategy is the **grapheme conversion,** in which the student sees the letters *h-o-u-s-e,* and the image of a house forms. Grapheme decoding is another strategy. In this case, the student sees the letters *h-o-u-s-e* and hears the word *house.* Yet another, related strategy is grapheme encoding. This strategy allows the student to hear the word *house* or see the image of a house, and then write the letters *h-o-u-s-e.* When there are difficulties in reading and writing, these are some of the strategies that may need to be trained.

Similarly, in **phoneme conversion,** sounds need to be converted into letters (encoding), and letters are converted to sounds (decoding). One strategy training device that helps with encoding is graph models for teaching spelling, in which the shape of the word is graphically represented together with the letters (D. Bolduc, personal communication, March 31, 1997).

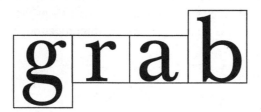

Rehearsing refers to practicing activities and tasks in advance. There is no particular learning style with which this strategy is associated. Nevertheless, many students need strategy training to use this strategy regularly (Oxford, 1990b).

Applying the known is another way of explaining the role of background knowledge in learning. Often, students, especially particular students, have the key to comprehension but cannot unlock the door because they do not know how to use the key. Strategy training that includes pretask discussions about background information is one way to develop this strategy (Oxford, 1990b).

Recombination means using pieces of old information in new, uniquely constructed ways. This relates to the third stage of memory: reconstruction. (This assumes that new information has passed through the comprehension stage into storage.) Students who have information in storage may still need assistance in combining the pieces into new entities. This is easier for synthetic learners than for analytic learners, whose tendency is toward recall. However, all students can be taught to recombine.

Recognition as a learning strategy has many tentacles. One must recognize letters in order to read. One must recognize words in order to understand a lecture. One must recognize cognates in a foreign language in order to use their existence to advantage. The kinds of recognition and the things that need to be recognized dictate what kinds of strategy training are needed and for whom (Leaver & Oxford, 1993).

Looking for patterns means examining a group of objects or ideas for their repetition of form or content. This activity comes easier to synthetic learners and levelers than to other learners, who might benefit from strategy training (McCombs, 1988).

Comparison means looking at two or more items and finding the likenesses or the differences. There are two components to this strategy: looking for similarities and looking for differences. Levelers use one of the components: looking for similarities. Sharpeners use the other: looking for differences. Both kinds of learners need to be taught each others' strategies. A suggestion that one teacher made to help levelers learn to handle differences is the use of Venn diagrams (partially overlapping circles, in which similarities are in the overlapping section and differences in the other sections). These help students visualize both similarities and differences. Levelers can be guided to find the differences in the outer, nonoverlapping areas of the two circles and sharpeners to find the similarities in the central, overlapping area of the two circles. (J. Leaver, personal communication, March 28, 1997)

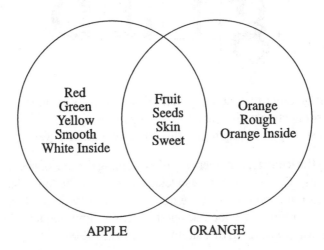

Paraphrasing means using other words to say the same thing. Paraphrasing is used in many subject areas upon occasion. However, its most significant use (and need) is in English, language arts, ESL, and foreign language classes. Being able to express one idea in many ways is the forte of the global-leveler. It is the bane of the analytic-particular learner. Often, analytic learners need help in developing this strategy.

Assembly means putting things together. This strategy is used routinely by synthetic learners but often needs to be taught to analytic learners.

Disassembly means pulling things apart. This strategy is used routinely by analytic learners but often needs to be taught to synthetic learners.

Information location implies being able to find the salience in a word, sentence, text, discourse, or image. This requires the ability to see the trees within the forest. This strategy comes easier to sharpeners than to levelers. Without this strategy, levelers find contemporary forms of comprehension testing difficult. They often must be taught the strategy of information location before they begin to perform well on multiple-choice comprehension tests. Given that LD students are more often levelers than sharpeners, they can also benefit from strategy training (Lester, 1974).

Sequencing means putting things into an order that is recognized by others as a bona fide order: chronological, alphabetical, and the like. Sequencing skill is obviously an inherent trait of the learning style of sequential learners. Although random learners may also be good sequencers, their forms of sequencing are not usually recognized by others as bona fide. Sequencing strategies can be difficult to teach to random learners, but for them to cope with many classroom tasks with ease, they will need to acquire them. Direct instruction does not seem to work as well with developing sequencing strategies as do extensive exposure, practice, and mechanical repetition.

Structuring also means putting things into an order, only it may not necessarily be an order that is recognized by others as a bona fide order. It can be hierarchical, circular, inverted, whatever the organizer wishes. Random learners are excellent at structuring information; sequential learners often become confused if information does not lend itself to chronological or logical structure.

As mentioned earlier, the strategies discussed above are only some of the cognitive strategies that can be taught. Readers are invited to explore other cognitive strategies that may be of equal and greater importance to their own students. Schmeck (1988a, 1988b) provides an overview of the field. Leaver and Oxford (1993) discuss strategies that are highly relevant to foreign language learning, as well as to other subject matter areas, including paraphrasing, adherence to the known, activation of passive knowledge, and cognate recognition. Ehrman (1989), Ehrman and Oxford (1990), Nyikos (1987), O'Malley and Chamot (1990), and Oxford (1989, 1990a, 1990b) discuss even more specifically strategies for successful foreign language learning and, in several instances, how to develop them. Ehrman (1996) presents a format for extensive and intensive analysis of strategy-related and other learning difficulties. Bastick (1982) proposes strategies related to analogy as an essential part of creativity and intuition. Kosslyn (1980) proposes a specific format of cognition: image versus propositional cognition, with young children more frequently using strategies related to image (generation of image, scanning an image, "zooming in" on one or more aspects of an image) and older learners using proposition, which requires symbolization. Nelson (1988) talks about strategies related to modes of organization, which he bases on principles of artificial intelligence. These strategies include categorization of paradigms and structures and scripting of syntagmas and world experience. He suggests that categories derive from scripts through strategies of substitution, ontogeny, and slot-filling. Anderson (1981, 1985) relates strategies to thought and memory; although his works are dated in the physiology of memory, the information Anderson provides on cognitive strategies serves as an excellent supplement to the information on cognitive strategies provided by others. A more updated version of the same topic as related to cognitive development but with the presentation of a different array of cognitive strategies can be found in Bideaud and Houdé (1991). Dunn and Dunn (1972) present more than two dozen cognitive strategies, some discussed above and some not, and provide examples for integrating these strategies into elementary classrooms.

Social Strategies

Social strategies are ones which relate to interaction with others. Social strategies include the following:

questioning	listening	cooperation
negotiation	involvement	empathy

 Questioning refers to using others to find out information. These others can be teachers, classmates, relatives, or experts (Oxford, 1990b). Extraverts and feelers are more likely to use the questioning strategy. Introverts and thinkers are more apt to search out the information in a reference volume.

Negotiation means working together with classmates or the teacher to determine meaning or to accomplish a task. Negotiation is a complex strategy; it involves component strategies of planning, goal setting, evaluation, and cooperation. In strategy training, the component strategies may need to be taught first.

 Listening means paying attention to what is said. It is an important strategy for sentient memory. Not all students are good listeners, yet this strategy is not complicated. It can be developed fairly quickly (Oxford, 1990b).

Involvement means spending time with the subject matter in a nonclassroom, nonhomework setting. Involvement could mean participation in extracurricular activities. Although listed as a social strategy, involvement could also be a loner activity. For example, extensive reading of unassigned texts could be considered using a strategy of involvement for English, ESL, or foreign language courses. Involvement can be encouraged and explained. It is a little more difficult to train than are some of the other social strategies. Sometimes, making a "contract" with a student to use a strategy of involvement during specific phases of a project can expose the student sufficiently to the involvement strategy that the strategy is added to the students' general strategy inventory, or repertoire (Dunn & Dunn, 1972).

Cooperation means working together with classmates on a common task. It is an essential strategy any time that cooperative learning is used as a method. However, it is not uniformly present in young children. Although it does naturally develop in many children, as they get older, it is a strategy that is more commonly associated with feelers and extraverts and less commonly with thinkers and introverts. If teachers wish to use cooperative learning as a method, they may need to conduct explicit strategy training for a large number of their students (Slavin, 1985).

Empathy means placing one's self in someone else's shoes and understanding how that person feels. Studying historical characters as people appeals to students who possess the strategy of empathy; it is less effective as a teaching technique for students without it. Empathy can be taught as a surface strategy—knowing what aspects of another's life to look at and how to evaluate those aspects without necessarily investing one's own feelings or values. As a deep strategy, because of the underlying values the strategy implies, it may be unteachable (and may not be needed for classroom use, anyway). This is a decision the teacher will need to make based on the mix of temperaments in the class. Intuitive feelers will have the strategy in spades, and others may simply be uncomfortable with the personalized form of it.

Affective Strategies

Affective strategies are those which relate to one's emotional state. Affective strategies include the following:

risk taking	self-talk
keeping a diary	discussion
deliberate relaxation	laughter
positive thinking	self-reinforcement
taking charge	cultural acceptance

Risk taking means not being concerned about making mistakes. Some kinds of learners are natural risk takers: accommodators, concrete-randoms, and, on an intellectual level, intuitive-thinking types. Others usually need some form of strategy training (Pellegrino, 1997).

Keeping a diary provides students with the opportunity to work through their reactions to their learning on paper. It also provides them with the requirement for self-reflection, a strategy that impulsive, global, synthetic students often do not possess. Some students resist keeping a diary and alternative strategies, such as group discussion, talk with a mentor, or quiet time for thinking, can provide options for those students who find diaries restrictive (Oxford, 1990b).

Deliberate relaxation means reducing stress in one's reaction to learning. Deliberate relaxation can take physical form, such as yoga, meditation, or sleep. It can also take the form of temporary avoidance (i.e., finding an alternative, unrelated activity), such as going to a movie, talking to a friend, and so on. Teaching students to do this is often a matter of giving them permission to do what they would like to do anyway.

Positive thinking means maintaining a positive attitude toward the class, the teacher, and the subject matter. This, of course, is easier where there is rapport because of like learner profiles and in situations where students are learning successfully. Here is where awareness strategy training is very helpful. It as important for students to realize that they do not have to like each other and their teacher (but they do have to display respect for all) in order to be a successful learner as it is for teachers to know this.

Taking charge means being responsible for one's own learning. This is a simple and obvious concept, but it is one that is often forgotten by students and teachers alike. After all, it is the students, not the teachers, who do the learning. Sometimes, it is difficult for teachers to allow students to take charge. For some students, it is easier to let the teacher take charge. Intuitive-thinkers, random processors, concrete-random learners, and accommodators usually possess a healthy portion of this strategy; in fact, sometimes this strategy overrides other strategies and causes some classroom difficulties, as in the case of one concrete-random LD student who refused to accept a new teacher's revised schedule, leading the rest of the class out of the classroom and to the library, gym, or other learning activity in accordance with the previous teacher's schedule. The new teacher ultimately had to use the social strategy of negotiation with the student in order to change the behavior. Teaching this strategy to students with other learning styles may require more than explanation with anticipated application. Contracts are one way to handle early practice of this strategy.

Self-talk is a strategy that nearly all students possess. Mruk (1995) considers self-talk to be a key ingredient in self-esteem, which is essential for successful learning. The problem is that not all students use positive self-talk. Many use negative self-talk. For these students strategy training is in order. The importance of this strategy cannot be overemphasized, yet far too many students do not possess it. Several years ago, the reason for one student's failure become clear to me at an Attrition Review Board (ARB) that had met to consider a faculty request to disenroll a student for lack of aptitude. When the student presented his side of the story, he related a dozen reasons why he could not learn, giving a litany of examples. His attitude had become a self-fulfilling prophecy: He told himself he could not learn, and as a result, he could not. The ARB turned down the request for disenrollment and suggested that the faculty concentrate on strategy training with this student, especially on helping him to replace the strategy of negative self-talk with positive self-talk. This was accomplished, and the student discovered that there were just as many reasons that he *could* learn successfully.

Discussion means talking to someone about one's learning experiences. For extraverted-feeling types, discussion comes more easily than for other types, for whom strategy training might help.

The strategy of **laughter** basically involves releasing tension by laughing and injecting humor in the learning process from time to time. This strategy is one that most students do possess but do not use in stressful situations—precisely the times when they *should* be using it. Explicit strategy training can help.

Self-reinforcement as a strategy can take a myriad of forms. A very effective form of this strategy is self-reward, something in which only students with good metacognitive strategies tend to indulge. For example, after a successful study period, students using self-reinforcement might reward themselves with a snack, a walk, or whatever else suits their environmental preference. As with the strategy of deliberate relaxation, teaching students to do this is often a matter of giving them permission to do what they would like to do anyway.

Cultural acceptance refers to understanding and respecting one's own background, as well as the backgrounds of one's peers and teachers. This means that strategy training needs to take into account cultural realities.

How Do Learning Strategies Relate to Learning Styles?

Every learning style has strategies which are naturally associated with it and other strategies which students with that learning style rarely use. Some combinations, as mentioned above, are obvious. Visual learners use visualization strategies; auditory and kinesthetic learners usually do not. Auditory learners more frequently use the strategies of rehearsal and repetition than do learners with other modality preferences. Extraverts tend to have the interaction strategies needed for cooperative learning classrooms; introverts frequently do not. Intuitive thinkers happily use assembly and disassembly; other personality types might not. Specifics of style and related strategy use are discussed more fully in the subject matter discussions that follow.

We do know that style flexibility comes from possessing more learning strategies, especially strategies associated with an opposing style. In this way, we were somewhat correct in our earlier assumption that numbers of strategies do count. This also provides some support for the importance of having a range of strategies at one's disposal, as suggested by Froumina and Khasan (1994), who, based on an instrument developed by Khasan, identify two kinds of learners: those who embrace cognitive dissonance and those who do not. They found that the more successful students in a Russian environment (and likely, also in an American environment) are those who are more willing to accept cognitive dissonance. They are referring to those students who are willing (or unwilling) to work through materials that are incongruous, incomplete, make little sense, or are ambiguous. This difference may be related to students' willingness to tolerate ambiguity (Chapelle, 1983), or it may be that those who accept cognitive dissonance probably can do so because they have more learning strategies at their disposal. The latter seems to be the case, because Froumina and Khasan also tested students on a learning strategies self-report instrument and found a significant difference between the number of strategies reported by students willing to accept cognitive dissonance (a high number of strategies) and those unwilling to accept cognitive dissonance (a low number of strategies). As mentioned earlier, however, possessing a large number of strategies alone is not enough. Applying them in effective ways at appropriate times can have a critical impact on learning success.

What Role Does Memory Play?

Memory is a complex matter, as we saw in Chapter 3. Based on what we now know about memory, even though our knowledge is as yet incomplete, we can make several statements about the role of learning strategies in memory or the role of memory in learning strategy use (Leaver & Thompson, 1997).

☞ *Rote memory is rarely an effective strategy for learning.*

Rote memorization, the typical learning strategy applied in all subjects for all activities in the past and in many programs even today, is rarely an effective strategy for learning, although it *can* work for a limited number students. It works for me, for example. Memorization of word definitions, formulae, grammar rules, and lists of any sort does not typically initiate the processes necessary for storage and recall/reconstruction. This is not to say that there is not a role for rote memory. However, rote memory cannot serve as the primary means to store and reconstruct information because its use is based on a faulty understanding of how memory works. Rote memorization assumes that one should be able to recall information holistically, and we now know that we usually reconstruct rather than recall. Rote memorization also assumes that memory is a location in the brain but we now know that memory is a process.

☞ *Selective attention is critical to memory.*

Selective attention as a learning strategy is critical to memory, regardless of learning style. To move information into short-term memory, it must enter sentient memory. For it to enter sentient memory, we must pay attention to it. Information that just passes through is far less likely to make any progress towards short-term and long-term memory than is information to which we pay attention. This means that students without this strategy, levelers (and frequently, LD learners), should benefit from the training of this strategy.

☞ *One needs to do something with received information.*

Selective attention alone is not enough. One often needs to do something with the information received as a result of focused attention, such as analyze it or synthesize it, in order to turn it into recognizable, useful information. Simply exposing students to new information with no manipulation of it is a hit-and-miss venture.

☞ *Recognition must occur.*

Sentient memory is associated with recognition. Cognitive strategies, such as application of background knowledge, comparison, and contrast, are also helpful in causing recognition to occur. Once recognition occurs, then short-term memory can work with the new information.

☞ *Establishing the significance of new information is helpful.*

Another strategy for retaining information in short-term memory is to hypothesize about the nature of new information and significance. Once the significance has been established, there is a pathway for associating the new information with older information already present in memory.

☞ *Memory releases extraneous information.*

One function of short-term memory is to release information after it has been used or when it is no longer needed; this is called forgetting. Sorting, categorization, and evaluating specific information are strategies that assist with good forms of forgetting and with remembering.

☞ *Memory retains information for future use through the application of cognitive strategies.*

Another function of short-term memory is to retain information for undefined future use. To do so requires the application of cognitive strategies, such as rehearsal, or repetition of the information. (It is important to realize that rehearsal occurs *after* recognition. This means that rehearsal is of information that has already been understood, not simply parroting of new information that may or may not yet be understood.) Rehearsal can occur from the outside, as in repeated exposures to the information, and it can occur from the inside, as one practices using it. With multiple rehearsals, the information gets entered into memory.

Sometimes, entering information into memory happens without effort. An example of this is an "aha" experience, an associative strategy. Making associations seems to take new information further toward long-term storage than does simple repetition. It is as if having schema on which to hang one's new knowledge helps fasten it into long-term memory easier than when it is floating through the brain unattached (Mayer, 1983, 1988). Teachers can facilitate the use of schemas by "scaffolding" (providing much help in the beginning and less help as students become more secure).

☞ *Long-term memory is the outcome of a process.*

Long-term memory is not a filing cabinet or a holding tank, as previously suggested. It is the outcome of a process that can take as long as 3 years. Disruptions of any sort (strokes, lack of reinforcement, etc.) during that time can result in an incomplete process, that is, no ultimate long-term storage of information. As a process, memory constantly feels the impact of neighboring activity or other processes.

☞ *Metacognitive strategies assist long-term memory.*

To assist long-term memory in retaining its original information and interpretations thereof, the metacognitive strategies of assessment, planning, monitoring, and self-awareness are helpful. Assessment is more common for NT learners. Other students can be taught assessment by tasks that require the answering of evaluative questions. Monitoring is more common for analytic, particular, and sharpening learners. Other students can be taught monitoring by having them listen to themselves. The cognitive strategies of reviewing, summarizing, and recording can also be helpful, as can social and affective strategies. Comparing notes with a peer or comparing current thinking with previous work can show inconsistency in memory.

☞ *Reconstruction encounters many obstacles.*

Reconstruction and even creation (new ideas seem to come from new arrangements of pieces of old information) are not necessarily an automatic outcome of the process of memorization. Beyond the tendency of the memory to forget and to alter, there are many problems that can occur with the return pathway, which does not appear to be the intake pathway in reverse. Rather, reconstruction appears to have its own pathway, which has yet to be examined closely enough to know where and how all this happens.

What is clear is that pieces of information get reassembled. Sometimes, there are blockages in the reassemblage, and they show up as speech defects. Disinhibition, a speech pathology, is an example of excellent reception and garbled production. Blockages also show up as productive speech that is less erudite than receptive speech. This also occurs frequently in foreign language and ESL classes, as it should—it is rather strange to be able to express more than one can understand, although that does happen in cases of memorized production in foreign language classes.

Strategies that can assist not only with accurate reconstruction but also in creation of language are recombination, paraphrase, synthesis, and activating receptive language. Recombination is more typical for synthetic learners. Other students can be taught recombination through games that ask them to recombine pieces of a story to develop a new story or to replace characters in one story with characters from another.

STEPS TO EMPOWERMENT (TEACHER)

The first series of steps to empowering students must usually be taken by the teacher. These steps are the following:

1. Collect information
2. Make a decision to adapt, capitalize, or compensate
3. Select scope of strategy training
4. Select scheduling of strategy training
5. Select mode of strategy training
6. Train

Information Collection

Step 1 involves collecting information. The information needed includes learning styles of students, the kinds of learning strategies currently being used by students, and an analysis of activities being used in class to determine what strategies are needed for successful learning of the materials.

Determining a Course of Action

Step 2 requires teachers to analyze the situation and determine a course of action. Based on the information collected, the teacher must make a decision to accommodate student learning styles by adapting the classroom materials; capitalize on students' learning styles where the materials, tasks, and learner profiles fortuitously coincide; or compensate for the materials by teaching students to do their own adaptation. The latter decision requires some form of strategy training.

Selecting the Scope of Strategy Training

Step 3, strategy training, can take many forms. It can be conducted as group instruction in the classroom, with individual students as counseling, or individually as homework. It can be scheduled as one-time training, as periodic training, or as long-term regular (durative) training (Oxford & Leaver, 1996).

The scope of strategy training will depend on the number of students needing strategy training and the extent to which classroom activities lend themselves to strategy training. If materials cannot be readily adapted and many students are at risk for failure to learn, then classroom training is warranted. If only one or two students need additional assistance, then counseling those students may be the most effective means of providing assistance to them. In all cases, homework assignments which include strategy-training activities can be very effective.

Scheduling Strategy Training

Step 4, scheduling of strategy training, determines the effectiveness of strategy training. The more durative the strategy training, the more likely it is that students will begin to use a wider range of learning strategies with more comfort. However, time constraints often do not permit long-term, regular strategy training, however desired it might be. In these cases, one-time training is better than nothing and serves to raise awareness. In such cases, teachers might provide manuals that students can use for learning more on their own. Training conducted regularly over an extended period is even better, and sometimes teachers can "sneak" such training into the curriculum via the homework exercises mentioned above.

Selecting the Mode of Strategy Training

Step 5, selecting the mode of strategy training, depends on availability of resources. Both time and expertise are needed for strategy training. The mode will also determine the results of the strategy training. The modes that exist include awareness, implicit, and explicit learning strategy. Research shows that of the three, the only really effective mode is explicit strategy training (Oxford & Leaver, 1996). However, sometimes there is no choice but to use either awareness or implicit strategy training. In such cases, a little *is* better than nothing at all.

Training

Once the mode of strategy training has been selected, the teacher has many ways in which to implement this training. The following sections contain some lesson plans that teachers may find helpful.

Awareness Training

Awareness training simply allows students to understand that there are learning strategies and that the application of appropriate strategies during the learning process will help them to learn more effectively. Awareness training is usually a matter of good intentions and great, unfounded hopes on the part of the teachers conducting the training that a "shot" up front will "vaccinate" their students for the semester or the year. A number of students may receive the benefit of improved self-esteem, and a few may be able to use the information to empower themselves. However, most will probably not be able to apply the information in the ways that teachers conducting the training had hoped (Druckman & Bjork, 1994). Ways in which awareness training can be conducted include reading, lecture, interactive lectures, discussions, experiential presentations, and journals. Although the depth of understanding that is needed for learner empowerment can rarely be captured in a short burst of these kinds of activities, imbuing students with the concept that they *are* "okay" can go far in helping them to *perform* "okay" and to look for ways to empower themselves on their own.

**AWARENESS TRAINING
PRIMARY SCHOOL LEVEL
LESSON PLAN**

1. Introduce the concepts of temperament.

2. Use an active self-report to determine temperament.

3. Provide students with a blue card, other students with a yellow card.

4. Introduce the concepts of modalitiesies.

5. Use an active self-report to determine modalities.

6. Provide auditory students with a blue card, others with a yellow card.

7. Compare cards.

8. Brainstorm ways to handle color conflicts.

An example of awareness training with elementary school children (yes, it can start that early) is to gather at least a dozen students (a larger number is fine) into a session in which a group leader presents the concepts of learning styles (albeit with titles that students can understand—I have learned never to underestimate the ability of even young children to handle seemingly sophisticated, terms, if these are personalized) through activities such as those described in the box to the left. Before class, the group leader obtains enough blue and yellow cards for each student to receive two of each and posts on four different walls the letters NT, NF, SJ, or SP (or some alternative description that is appropriate to the group being taught) and the words "eye" (visual learners), "ear" (auditory learners), "hand" (mechanical learners), and "body" (kinesthetic learners). For young children, pictures are a nice substitute for the letters and words.

The concept of temperament can be introduced briefly through talking about what is most important to students—being with other people (NF), doing what's right (SJ), having time to play (SP), or learning new things (NT). A short, situational questionnaire, based on the students' own life experiences, can be developed (three to four questions per temperament), and students can be asked to stand by the picture which best describes them. (I realize that my sensing colleagues who have labored to develop skill at statistical analysis will cringe at this oversimplified approach to assessment. In the ideal world, we would construct wonderful statistical matrices for each learner and his or her peers and learning environment. I would love to be transported on such clouds. In the real world, however, I often only have time to dash madly through mud puddles on my own two legs.) The children standing under the mainstream learning-style picture are handed a blue card; all others are handed a yellow card.

The group leader can then go on to repeat the process with the modalities or with any other learning styles that the group leader considers it important to include. With older students more styles can be included in one awareness session; with younger children, a couple of domains are enough. Once student styles have been determined and students are holding a set of cards, students can compare their colors with those of the teacher, their peers, and the "absolute" mainstream (all blue).

This activity shows students vividly how far their learning needs depart from what they can expect to experience. They can then brainstorm ways to handle color conflicts. For example, how might someone with two yellows work together with someone who has two blues or someone who has one blue and one yellow?

Awareness training for older students can take the form of pre-course activity sessions in which students are typed, learn the meaning of the various styles and style terms, and focus on which strategies they can use to capitalize on their styles in order to enhance learning and memory and which strategies they might need to develop. Sensing-judging and intuitive-feeling students might even be persuaded to set up notebooks and journals for keeping a record of their strategy development and strategy use during the course. Unfortunately, sensing-perceiving and intuitive-thinking students are less likely to do this—SPs because they view it as restrictive and NTs because they view it as directive. NTs, however, usually have good meta-cognitive strategies and, having been exposed to this new information, are likely to incorporate it into their ongoing internal evaluations of their performance in their own way. SPs usually need a more protracted and involved form of strategy training.

Implicit Training

Implicit strategy training results from teachers assigning activities that require students to use specific strategies that either are not in their personal inventory or are weak for them. The activities are assigned, and students are provided with the means of completing the activities without any accompanying discussion of what learning strategies are or how these are embedded into the assignments. The assignments can be either in-class work or homework.

An example of implicit training might be a foreign language classroom in which the teacher wants students (especially the particular learners) to start applying background knowledge. Teachers of such students have several options. They can provide students with authentic reading materials and require them to locate and circle information that they already know. As a pre-reading activity, they can provide students with a list of key words and ask the students to suggest the general content of the article to be read.

With implicit strategy training, there is no guarantee that the scaffolding associated with such assignments can ever be removed. Students may or may not begin to use these strategies on their own. In a study I conducted with short-term Russian students (6 months of intensive study) in 1987-1988, using three groups—a control group, an implicit strategy training group, and an explicit strategy training group—no significant difference was found in proficiency between the control group and students graduating in the previous 4 years, between the implicit strategy training group and previous students, or between the control group and the implicit strategy training group. However, explicit strategy training did seem to make a difference, with all of the students in the explicit strategy training group reaching a proficiency level of 2+ or 3 (on a 5-point scale), compared to an average level of 2 reached by previous students, the control group, and the implicit strategy training group. These results were in keeping with the results of other research in implicit strategy training (Oxford & Leaver, 1996).

Explicit Training

Explicit strategy training means that teachers explain what learning strategies are and which learning strategies are required by assignments designed to improve strategy use. In explicit strategy training, before completing assignments that require the application of new strategies, teachers present the strategies needed. After the assignments are completed, teachers discuss with the students what strategies they applied, how they went about applying them, and what difficulties they encountered. Based on student progress, teachers periodically return to this topic.

There are a number of ways to conduct explicit strategy training. Some programs provide students with a manual (e.g., the Defense Language Institute provides students with language-specific strategy training manuals). Some programs hold periodic strategy awareness and strategy training sessions and feedback sessions. Some teachers use student journals as a means of communication about strategy use and individualized strategy training. Some programs incorporate strategy training into direct instruction so that students receive strategy training on a regular, continuing basis interwoven with related classroom activities.

Teachers can also use students with opposing learning styles to conduct another form of explicit strategy training. Such assistance is easily effected through shared tasks. For example, a global learner paired with an analytic learner, given the task of evaluating the significance of a reading passage, can share strategies such as synthesis, application of schemas, contextizing, gisting, looking for known information, and comparison with the analytic partner. The analytic student can show the synthetic (or global) partner how to isolate details, look for differences, categorize, and decode.

STEPS TO EMPOWERMENT (STUDENTS)

Steps to empowering students are the following:

1. Awareness
2. Changing the situation
3. Changing one's self

These include making students aware of styles and strategies, then teaching them the skills to apply this knowledge to specific situations and developing the ability to make choices in how this knowledge is applied.

Becoming Aware

The first step that students must take to becoming empowered is to be aware of their own learning styles. They might do this through formal instrumentation (but they should always assess whether the results of the instrumentation are accurate), through discussion with a teacher conversant in styles and style determination, or through one of the informal assessment tools presented in this book.

Students must not only be aware of their own styles, they must also determine the styles of their teachers, the course materials, and their peers. In the same way that teachers can learn to observe and assess, students can also learn to observe and assess. In fact, because students are very much caught up in the style wars and often have strong emotions associated with them, they can sometimes assess the situation more quickly and more accurately than the teacher who is a little farther from the front. These assessments help students identify the locus and source of the conflict. The advantage of assessing the situation in this light is that students now have a value-free way to understand their difficulties. No longer do they have "bad teachers." No longer can they "not stand" the other students in the class. Rather, they are "yellows" working with "blues" or NTs working with SJs. I once overhead an eight-year-old, who had experienced more than his share of frustration with classmates, tell a friend, "I am not 'strange.' I am an INTJ. There are lots of INTJs in the world. There just aren't any other ones in our class."

Once students have identified a conflict, they can proceed to resolve it. At their disposal are two means of conflict resolution: change the situation or change themselves.

Changing the Situation

Changing the situation requires changing one of the following: the teacher, the materials, the peers, or the conditions. All are viable alternatives depending upon the situation itself. Each time each student must assess each situation anew in order to select the appropriate alternative.

Changing Teachers.

Teachers usually come part and parcel with a course, but sometimes it is possible to change the teacher. A clear example that we have encountered earlier comes to mind: Eliza (Chapter 2). Obviously, the teacher's lectures were the problem area for Eliza. Eliza did resolve her problem. She observed the teacher's teaching style and noticed that the teacher wrote information on the chalkboard wherever he happened to be standing at the moment, and being kinesthetic, there was no telling where he was going to stand next. For sequential Eliza, who expected to read left to right, top to bottom, the nonlinear organization of information on the chalkboard impeded her ability to take sequential notes and, therefore, to organize her lecture notes for effective review. Noticing also that the professor lectured from a detailed lesson plan and that he came to class a few minutes early, Eliza approached him, explained her difficulty, and asked to copy his notes before class started. The professor agreed, the conflict disappeared, and Eliza brought her grade up to an A by the end of the semester. (Of course, there is also the option at the college level of changing the teacher by dropping the course of a professor with an opposing learning style and adding the same course taught by a professor with a more similar learning style. I have known several students who have done this, some with conscious consideration of learner variables, others instinctively.)

Changing Materials

Instructional materials are perhaps the easiest way that students can compensate for style conflicts. If the textbook (and even the teacher) is presenting materials in ways that are out of style for the students, the student can obtain other materials (or a tutor) that are more in keeping with the student's preferred style—much in the way that Heather's mother (Chapter 2) found a global math tutor to assist Heather in learning about graphs.

Changing Peers

Changing peers is easier said than done and rarely an option outright, other than in the extreme case of changing schools, which can and does happen. Ironically, the parents of one SP student, assessed at the AGSI, had moved their daughter from a public school with an eclectic curriculum (and, therefore, exposure, albeit without outright accommodation, to several learning styles), where she was not faring well, to a very rigid parochial school with strong and exclusive SJ values, policies, and procedures. The parents did not understand why their attempt to buy a better education for their daughter resulted in even poorer grades and lower standardized test scores. I am certain that they did not welcome the recommendation of the assessor: return the daughter to the public school and work with her on learner empowerment issues.

There are less drastic alternatives than changing schools that can alleviate some of the distress that occurs when the class profile differs from that of the individual student. The student can seek out as study partners those students who match his or her learning styles. Or, the student can seek assistance from students with learner profiles that come closer to matching the class profile. ENTJ types (those whom Keirsey and Bates [1988] call "field marshals") have even been known to impress their learning-style preferences on their peers when the class profile has differed from their own.

Changing Conditions

Sometimes, specific conditions of how a class or test is conducted can make a significant difference. A university junior in a science and engineering program ran into trouble in an upper-level physics course. A reflective learner, she encountered

47 physics problems to be solved on the first exam of the semester. Unlike many students in similar situations, she did not assume that she was unprepared for the test because she could not complete 47 problems in 75 minutes. She knew that she was prepared and that she knew the information; she just would not be able to work fast enough to complete all the problems in the time frame allotted. In resolving this conflict, her first concern was to demonstrate beyond a doubt to the professor that her inability to complete the test was due to a style conflict and not to lack of knowledge. Therefore, she went through the entire test and wrote down the formula for each of the problems. Then she returned to solving the formulae. In all, she completed three problems. A day later, she made an appointment to talk to the professor in order to explain her strategy and why she had used it. Because she had all of the formulae correct, the professor immediately understood the essence of the style conflict and agreed to have a graduate assistant proctor future tests so that there would be no time limits, thus liberating all the reflective learners in the class to show what they knew.

Changing One's Self

The alternative to changing the situation is to change one's self. Remember the reflective high school student who dramatically increased her SAT score by practicing filling in dots faster? This is what changing one's self is about: developing the strategies that are associated with one's nonpreferred learning styles so that one can have access to the strategies needed when specific style demands are made by learning situations. To change one's self requires both the development of additional strategies and practice in style shifting.

Development of Additional Strategies

Following teacher-presented strategy training, students can continue to add to their style repertoires on their own. They can do this through completing homework in tandem with other students known to have a different learning style. They can do this by using student manuals—there are few available, so teachers may need to develop some of their own. Once they have developed the strategies of disassembly and brainstorming, students can analyze various tasks presented to them and determine which additional strategies they will need to develop.

Practice in Style Shifting

Simply identifying needed strategies and learning how to apply them is rarely sufficient to create comfort in using opposing learning styles. Most students need much practice in using the nonpreferred style. The opportunity to do this during class review sessions can make a big difference in students' ultimate comfort in style shifting.

EMPOWERING STUDENTS TO SUCCEED WITH TEACHERS

The strategies that students need to apply differ depending on which style conflict they encounter. Some potential conflicts and how to teach students to defuse them are given below. Obviously, it is not possible to cover all possible conflicts in this section. The examples given, however, can serve as models for similar conflicts with different styles and strategies.

◆ *sensing students studying with intuitive teachers*

Intuitive teachers do not pay attention to the details that fascinate sensing students, and they expect the students in their classes to be creative. Sensing students can be taught strategies for empathy, projection, and analogy.

◆ *deductive learners studying with inductive teachers*

In working with an inductive teacher, students may need to apply a number of strategies that do not come naturally to deductive learners. These include clustering, information location, looking for similarities, and looking for patterns.

◆ *synthetic and analytic teachers and students working together*

In order to work with synthetic teachers, analytic students need to be taught the strategy of assembly. Conversely, in order to work with analytic teachers, synthetic students need to be taught the strategy of disassembly. In my experience, these cognitive styles are so ingrained that it is difficult to teach these strategies in isolation. The most effective way I have found to teach assembly to analytic learners is to group them with synthetic students and provide them with a synthetic task. Likewise, the most effective way I have found to teach disassembly to synthetic learners is to group them with analytic learners and provide them with an analytic task. *Sometimes, students teaching students is far more effective than teachers teaching students.*

◆ *working with teachers from other cultures*

Although we have only barely touched on this topic in previous chapters, there is ample evidence that cultures have a dominant learner profile, the same way that individuals have a learner profile and classes have a learner profile (Bickley, 1989; Dunn & Griggs, 1995; Paredes & Hepburn, 1976; Ramirez & Castanedo, 1974; Wallace, 1970). At the risk of taking a politically incorrect stance, I suggest that in the same way that teachers in teaching and testing often need to accommodate the nonmainstream learning styles, they also need to accommodate the culture-specific and subculture-specific learning styles that minority and foreign/emigrant students bring to their classrooms. However, the importance of going beyond accommodation to empowerment with these groups cannot be overemphasized. Coping with mainstream expectations is a dilemma that these students will face each time they are taught by a teacher who is not style-aware. Members of minority groups who in the past have reached levels of accomplishment *in any society* equivalent to their dominant-culture peers have usually either possessed a learner profile more in keeping with mainstream expectations or have been flexible enough to shift styles.

Typically, the strategies needed are those associated with left-hemisphere preference, visual and auditory modalities, analysis, sharpening, impulsivity, and particularism, as well as with the SJ temperament. This is especially true of Afro-American populations, which have been found to be more right-hemisphere preferent, global, and kinesthetic than mainstream populations (Boykin, 1983) with cultural values more reminiscent of people with SFP personality types. This is also true of Native American populations, which have been found to be generally more global (Huber & Prewardy, 1990); Asian populations, which have been found to be more ISTJ and abstract (Flynn, 1991; Melton, 1990; Tsang, 1983), and Latino populations, which have been found to be more EF for both genders (Lennon, 1988).

Although I suggest accommodation and empowerment for all of these groups, including awareness training, I simultaneously offer here a very serious word of caution not to let race or ethnic group alone create assumptions about learner profiles. The assumption that any one individual will match the average or typical profile suggested for the culture or subculture to which that individual belongs is false and can waste the teacher's time in cutting a path through the wrong forest (to use Covey's image). Although there are tendencies among cultures, as noted above and earlier in this book, to foster the development of one set of learning-style attributes over another, no one individual within that group can be considered to reflect these attributes *per se*. Within cultures and between cultures, learners are individuals. Each learner has his or her own learning profile. That profile may or may not reflect typical attributes of his or her cultural heritage. Therefore, assessment must be done on each student as a separate and unique entity if one wants to have accurate information upon which to base strategy training. *Knowledge of a learner's subculture profile can inform the assessment; it cannot determine the assessment*.

What is considered "mainstream" and what kinds of strategies should be the focus of strategy training depend very much on where students are located. Russian emigrant populations enrolling in Israeli schools were found to possess a larger number of memorization strategies compared to their Israeli counterparts and a lower number of compensation strategies (Levine, Reves, & Leaver, 1996); within Israeli classrooms, then, compensation strategies should become the focus of strategy training for Russian students who fit the emigre profile. In some southwestern schools in the United States, where the school population is 90% or more Hispanic, students who would otherwise be considered the mainstream may find that they lack the kinds of learning strategies needed to succeed in classes where the class profile does not reflect mainstream learning styles. Strategy training for them may focus on those strategies which are associated with non-Western learning styles, such as global, leveling, and synthetic traits. For students in such classes, paraphrase, comparison, and assembly are the strategies to be trained. *No matter where one is located or how the class is constituted, the "bottom line" remains the same: How does "the one" fit with "the many?"* (Fitting "the one" and "the many" together in any given classroom is discussed in Chapter 7.)

A second word of caution is also in order here. In training strategies to help students cope with mainstream teaching styles, orientation of material, or with a particular class profile, we should always keep in mind that the strategies we are training are not necessarily any better than the strategies that students are using. Otherwise, we run the risk of implementing actions similar to the following suggestion that was made to use a form of strategy training to eradicate introverts from American society, a trait considered a deficit in a socialized, industrialized society (and, ironically, in today's high-technology, information-age environment considered an asset): "Can a civilization through vicarious activities set up a series of socially acceptable and safe means of 'draining off' of those traits that are of danger to others?" (Plant, 1966, p. 155).

The learning strategies that we choose to teach should have three characteristics. First, they should be associated with the student's nonpreferred learning style. Second, they should comprise the dominant learning styles (whatever they are in the current environment). Third, they should expand upon, rather than replace, students' own strategies.

Empowering Students to Succeed With Subject Matter

The reason that students with specific learning styles experience more success with some subjects than with others can be attributed in part to the fact that some subjects by nature require a specific set of learning strategies associated with one style or another. The situations described below consider the nature of the subjects, apart from the nature of the teachers teaching those subjects. Not every learning style combination is discussed. I have focused on those which appear to cause the most difficulty in a classroom setting and the strategies that students of those styles will need to develop to overcome those typical difficulties.

In the English or Language Arts Classroom

Reading. A number of strategies are needed for reading. They include grapheme decoding, grapheme encoding, letter recognition, and semantic integration of antecedents, among several other strategies. Nonvisual learners may need assistance with all of these, and random learners may need training in integrating referents and antecedents sequentially.

If comprehension checks are to be conducted in traditional ways, synthesizers and global learners can be taught analysis (disassembly) and selective attention. They can also be taught memory strategies associated with holding information in short-term memory long enough to answer discrete item test questions. (I hope that eventually these kinds of comprehension checks will not be used with synthetic and global readers; however, experience shows that right now, they dominate in many classrooms.)

Composition. Levelers may need to develop sharpening strategies, including identification of differences in color, size, shape, location, and so on among similar and dissimilar items. One way to accomplish this is to assign a composition for which students receive a model to follow. The model may be a description of a summer scene, for example, and the task may be for students to describe the same location in winter. Levelers may need to have a picture to look at and specific questions to answer that point out potential differences. With time, experience, and the emergence of sharpening strategies, such cognitive scaffolding can be removed. Other strategies that levelers will need to develop along the way include classification (categorization) and organization. Similar kinds of scaffolding can be provided until levelers have acquired these strategies.

Spelling. Auditory and kinesthetic learners may need to learn visualization strategies. We have discussed the reason for this before (Chapters 4, 6). One way in which this can be accomplished is to give one student a picture and have him or her describe it for another student, who, then, draws the scene.

Grammar. Synthetic, global, and inductive learners may need to learn the strategy of hypothesis testing to ensure accuracy. They might also benefit from learning memorization strategies, if they are enrolled in a course where grammar is taught as a system and application of rules.

In Foreign Language and ESL Classes

Culture. Sometimes, NT and SJ students, more than anything else, need to use affective strategies (which they may even resist developing because they do not value them). Examples of these include keeping diaries and positive self-talk. Building affective strategies can go a long way toward helping NT and SJ students establish rapport with foreign cultures—something that their NF classmates do instinctively.

Grammar. Global students continue to make grammatical mistakes, even at very high levels of proficiency. They even make grammatical mistakes in their own language because they are focused on meaning, not on how that meaning is expressed. Often, their grammatical mistakes are not particularly noticed because proper intonation makes it easy to talk to them. Proper intonation comes easier to global learners, who tend to be right-hemisphere preferent, than to particular learners, who tend to be left-hemisphere preferent. Global learners would do well to develop the strategies of monitoring, disassembly, classification, and questioning.

Pronunciation. Because visual learners usually learn from reading, they experience more difficulty in pronunciation than other kinds of learners because they constantly guess (usually incorrectly) at pronunciation. (This is also an attribute of their first-language acquisition, although over time, they ultimately hear most of the words they use and change their pronunciation accordingly.) The strategies that they need to develop are selective attention to grapheme-phoneme correspondences, questioning (and any other social strategies), and recording (either on tape or written transcription). They can be taught grapheme-phoneme correspondence by giving them an accompanying script when they listen to broadcasts and films. Questioning and recording can be included as routine classroom or homework activities.

Listening Comprehension. Visual students experience the greatest difficulties in listening comprehension. Because they often speak like they read, when they hear a word pronounced correctly, rather than mispronounced in their own way, they may not recognize it. Elisions represent special problems for visual learners, who are used to seeing words written as separated items. More than anything else, they need to develop selective listening strategies, down to the phoneme level. Cloze forms of scripts (i.e., scripts with some words removed and replaced with blanks), especially where blanks are provided for elision and regressive assimilation, can help visual learners to acquire better listening skills, especially those associated with selective attention. When given the full script along with the cloze text, they can quickly determine where their own listening difficulties occur and make the appropriate adjustments.

Reading. Particular readers also need strategy training but in different ways. They are easily located in any foreign language classroom in which students are reading silently. These are the students who are reading the text with a pencil in one hand. This pencil is actively writing English equivalents above each of the foreign language words—including the ones that the students know well. Once particular students acquire foreign language reading strategies, they have less need for translation support. These include an understanding of locus of meaning in a sentence (e.g., in Russian sentences there is a relative importance of morphology over syntax); the location of meaningful information in a discourse (e.g., in English texts the most important information comes at the beginning of the text and topic sentences at the beginning of paragraphs, whereas in Arabic texts the important information is recycled throughout the text); and recognition of journalistic cliches.

Synthetic-global learners often fare better in reading than their analytic peers in the beginning stages of language study because they are willing to give up a need to understand every word. They are more likely to use strategies such as guessing from context, application of background knowledge, and assembly. Where they run into harm's way is in overgeneralization from what they know and think to what is actually written. Hypothesis formation is a strategy they usually possess in spades. Hypothesis confirmation is a strategy they typically lack. There are several ways to teach the strategy of hypothesis confirmation. They can be asked to check their work; specifically, they can be told to ask themselves, Does what I say match reality as I know it? (For example, one student summarized a television broadcast from Moscow: "Gorbachev and the Canadian Prime Minister met at the Montreal Airport in Moscow." Contrary to common student opinion, foreign languages do make sense!) Students can ask a peer or native speaker to check their work. They can check a reference book. Often, a well-constructed task will indicate to them the accuracy of their hypothesis, because an incorrect hypothesis will not permit them to complete the task.

Speaking. Many analytic learners are unwilling to speak until they feel in control of the language. This can delay production quite some time (but it helps to keep in mind the various studies on delayed oral production that indicate greater ultimate success in grammatical and lexical precision). To speak with comfort, analytic students need develop the cognitive strategies of paraphrase and recombination.

In the Mathematics Classroom

Concepts. To understand math concepts fully, students need the strategies of hypothesis formation and hypothesis testing. Although inductive and synthetic learners usually have the strategies they need for concepts taught in inductive courses, where the concepts are conducted deductively, these students need to be taught sequencing and disassembly strategies.

Calculations. Traditional calculations appeal principally to particular, mechanical, some analytic, and some abstract learners. These students possess the strategies needed to decontextualize information and work symbolically. Other learners can first be provided the scaffolding needed to develop these strategies by making calculations based on information from a periodical or personalized information. As strategies develop, more and more of the scaffolding can be removed.

Word Problems. Sometimes, something as seemingly simple as changing the situation from the one in the book to one related to the student's personal environment, family, or experience can provide the support needed.

Graphs and Charts. We have discussed this particular feature of mathematics classes at length. Readers are reminded of Heather's needs. If global-synthetic learners are to deal with graphs and charts taught in particular, analytic ways, rather than being accommodated in their learning-style preference as Heather was, they usually must first be taught the strategy of disassembly.

In the Science Classroom and Laboratory

Concepts. In general, the same skills are needed to cope with science concepts as are needed to cope with mathematics concepts.

Experimentation. Science experiments appeal mainly to concrete learners, at least in the way in which they are typically implemented at the high school level. At higher levels, there may be some appeal to abstract learners, especially if the learners are given the opportunity to design their own experiments. (Concrete-random learners, if they deign to be in the classroom, like this aspect, too.) Strategies that need to be taught at times include sequencing strategies for random learners, hypothesis formation for analytic learners, and hypothesis confrimation for synthetics.

In Social Studies and Social Sciences Classes

Concepts. The subject matter areas of psychology, sociology, and history are full of concepts. Although these concepts are more philosophically-oriented, the same strategies are needed as are needed for math and science.

Historicity. Dates and chronologies are easier for sequential students. Often, for random students, organization by time is an arbitrary system for understanding events. Random students need to develop strategies of chronologization (sequencing in time order). Random-kinesthetic learners sometimes have to be physically shown how to create timelines by having them line up in order of a date or event that each personalizes.

Trends. Trends are easier for levelers to understand than for sharpeners. Sharpeners often need to be shown how to look for likenesses and patterns rather than for differences.

EMPOWERING STUDENTS TO SUCCEED ON TESTS

Throughout their academic careers, students encounter several kinds of assessments. These include, at a minimum, achievement tests, performance tests, proficiency tests (for some subjects), prochievement tests, and portfolios.

Succeeding on Achievement Tests

Achievement tests come in a variety of forms. They are usually based on the acquisition of abstract knowledge and the ability to display that knowledge out of its normal context. Depending on the format, students of various learning styles may receive inappropriately low scores. Multiple-choice questions, which particular students love, are the bane of global students. Fill-ins are not much better. *Global students want to create, using the knowledge they have acquired, not guess at what their teacher has created or fill in someone else's creation.* To do well on achievement tests, global learners need to develop the strategies of deduction, classification, analysis, comparison, and contrast.

In order to succeed on typical, timed achievement tests, reflective learners need to develop time management strategies (such as cutting back on neatness); sometimes, even this is not enough, and they simply need to find an alternative means of showing that they know the material. A prime example of such an alternative means was the case of the reflective physics student described earlier.

Succeeding on Performance Tests

Performance tests ask students to demonstrate that they can do something. Abstract performance tests ask students to develop paper models, to answer essay questions, and so on. Concrete performance tests ask students to carry out an experiment, task, or procedure. Performance tests allow students with some of the less commonly addressed learning styles (kinesthesia, globality, field dependence) to show what they can do more fairly than achievement tests allow. On the other hand, students who by nature are very abstract and visual are handicapped on those performance tests that depend on gross and fine motor control. Strategies that these students need to learn to use are repetition and rehearsal, because doing so will help them develop the necessary motor control.

Succeeding on Proficiency Tests

Proficiency tests are a variant of performance tests. They work well for extroverts and impulsives. Introverts fair poorly because they rarely have much to say. Reflectives often wait too long to start talking, and it takes them too long to write. All the strategies mentioned for learning to speak well are applicable for students who do not do well on proficiency tests. In addition, since this is a test, not a context-embedded discussion or reading, students without the skills for handling discourse out of context need to develop the strategies of analysis and disassembly.

Succeeding on Prochievement Tests

These are the latest in the family of foreign language tests. They are not yet very widespread, but their ultimate success holds much promise for testing in other subject matter areas. They combine the best features of proficiency and achievement tests. They are performance tests and can be either abstract or concrete in nature. The questions that are presented on the test expect students to use the language in resolving a problem or accomplishing a task; the structure (grammar and vocabulary) that is needed to carry out this assignment reflects the structure that has been presented in the classroom prior to the test, but the authentic texts used for the questions are ones that students have not seen before. Thus, students use the vocabulary, grammar, and content information that they already know, but they use it to accomplish new things. These tests can be designed in ways to accommodate a range of learning styles, especially if tasks are designed to reflect a variety of styles and if students are allowed to choose between tasks. Strategies that students will need to develop will depend on the content of the tests. In some cases, if the test is well designed, there will be a minimal onus on the student.

Succeeding With Portfolios

An alternative to testing that has become popular in the last decade is the use of portfolios. In such cases, a variety of "instruments" are used to determine student grades. These include oral and written reports, oral and written tests, homework assignments, and projects. Some teachers allow students to select which items will comprise their portfolios. One advantage of portfolios is that they paint a more detailed picture of student performance. Some of the strategies in which students in portfolio courses may need training include any cognitive strategies related to the content of the portfolio, as well as a number of metacognitive strategies, such as setting goals and self-evaluation.

EMPOWERING STUDENTS TO SUCCEED WITH HOMEWORK

Students can be empowered to succeed on homework that requires them to work in nonpreferred learning styles in the same way that they can be empowered to use strategies associated with nonpreferred styles in the classroom and on tests. In fact, homework can be used as a form of explicit strategy training, in which students learn about the strategy, then have the opportunity to practice it when they complete their homework.

IN SUMMARY

Although accommodation of student learning style is highly encouraged, if not essential, during teaching and testing, teachers have a wonderful opportunity during periods of review to help students develop flexibility in learning styles. They do this through a variety of kinds of learning strategy training: awareness training, implicit strategy training, and explicit strategy training. Explicit strategy training is the most involved and the most effective, especially when it is long-term and regular. The value of expanding students' learning styles through strategy training is reinforced by the consideration that students who have a large inventory of learning strategies that they use appropriately are going to be better students, regardless of their so-called "academic potential." *Teachers who train their students not only in the content of their courses but in the strategies needed to live and succeed in the real world truly give their students the tools that they need to continue on alone as lifelong learners.*

Practice Exercises

1. Develop a lesson plan for learning-styles awareness training for your class.

2. Develop explicit strategy training activities for use in homework assignments in the subject matter area you teach.

3. Identify two or three strategies from each of the strategy groups. Make a plan for including each of them in upcoming lessons as explicit in-class strategy training.

4. A junior high class of mostly deductive learners working in a science course based on the inquiry method of instruction is having difficulty. What strategy training might you try?

5. A subgroup of random-kinesthetic learners in a high school English class needs to improve writing skills; however, these students cannot even put together a reasonable outline. What strategy training might you try?

6. An elementary school social studies class is studying the American West. The concrete-randoms are finding the textbook dry and are not learning the contents well. What strategy training might you try?

Notes

1. The issue of nature versus nurture in the area of learning styles is far from resolved. As of the writing of this book, the majority of learning-styles specialists agree with Jung that styles are inborn and mature along with the individual.

2. Strategy training, while providing a powerful assist to students, is not an alternative to accommodation. Each has a role, and each has its season. Furthermore, although strategy training can be accomplished in off-campus environments, the most effective strategy training is conducted by teachers in the classroom as an element of teaching the whole class.

7

Reducing the Risk:
Teaching the Whole Class—Sanely

Preparing 30 or 40 separate lesson plans to meet all student needs is neither necessary nor sensible in the real world. This is not the kind of individualization that whole-class teaching promotes. Teaching the whole class is about establishing conditions under which all students can learn successfully. Teaching the whole class is a matter of accommodating and empowering all students as part of a specific class, while identifying and directly assisting those individual students who truly need additional accommodation or empowerment (i.e., those students who are experiencing the most severe style conflicts with teachers, peers, or materials).

In managing risk, *the teacher can take one or both of two approaches: (a) to reduce the risk of failure in learning "for the many" or (b) to reduce the risk of failure in learning "for the one."* Either approach is legitimate; used together, all students can benefit. Each approach creates conditions under which *most* students are working in their preferred learning style most of the time. *Taken together, these approaches create conditions under which all students are working in their preferred learning style most of the time; this is the goal of whole-class teaching.* In my experience, teaching for the many means that the teacher is reaching about 50% of the students very well, 30% well, and 20% poorly. This is a significant improvement over situations where teachers teach only in the way that they learn. It is also a significant improvement over situations where an 8-part or 4-part system is used so that all students are taught in style 12% to 25% of the time. Teaching for the one, in addition to teaching for the many, allows teachers to add the students in the 20% group to the remaining 80% of the class, in essence, creating a situation in which all of the students are learning most (perhaps even nearly all) of the time.

Reducing the risk for the many requires the teacher to look at the composite of learning styles in the classroom (i.e., at the class profile) in order to make decisions in lesson planning, materials selection, and teaching methodology.

Reducing the risk for the one requires the teacher to look in depth at those students who are at particular risk in a given classroom environment or in working with specific materials and to assist them individually. The kinds of assistance offered may vary, depending on the student's learning-style flexibility, the degree to which he or she differs from the class profile (i.e., from the other students), and the planned materials/activities. Assistance can range from counseling to learner empowerment to lesson adaptation. Although teachers usually cannot devote inordinate amounts of time to every unusual learning style that appears in their groups of students, they can take care of "the one" in a number of ways that are not overly time consuming. These include the following:

1. Homework assignments
2. Strategy training
3. Counseling
4. Empowerment to change the nature of input
5. Permission to voice needs
6. Small group placement
7. Choice in multifaceted tasks
8. Affective support

Homework assignments can be individualized to allow the odd student out to complete the assignment successfully by using his or her preferred learning style. These "odd students" can be given strategy training (either individual strategy training or strategy training presented "for the many") so that they develop learning strategies that allow them to work in nonpreferred styles. They can receive counseling on their learning styles and be shown ways in which they can cope with input that comes via other styles. They can also be shown ways in which they themselves can change the nature of the input they receive, as in the case of a visual learner who is taught to visualize auditory input, process it visually, and turn it into auditory output, as Jacqueline (Chapter 3) did. They can be encouraged to voice their needs in class, as in the case of a visual learner who asks the teacher to write the information on the board or an auditory learner who asks the teacher to read something aloud. The teacher can also take extra care in placing at-risk students for small-group work. If at-risk students are placed with students who share at least one of their learning preferences, they may be able to find intersection with their peers in one learning-style domain that encourages them to seek and accept assistance from peers in other learning-style domains. The teacher can also prepare multifaceted tasks for the classroom and for homework that allow students a choice in assignment according to the learning styles present in the classroom. Finally, the teacher may need to work on the affective domain of students who find themselves a sample size of one. These students may need to be "class-proofed" vis-à-vis other students.

In some cases, teachers may be able to send "the one" to a learning skills center (this option is more likely to be available to a college professor than to a K-12 teacher), where learner styles are understood and students can be empowered. Traditionally, however, these centers (as well as a number of counseling centers and private concerns that offer study skills courses) have taught analytic skills for synthetic learners, left-hemisphere processing strategies for right-hemisphere-preferent students, linear organization for random students, and abstract thinking skills for concrete students. In short, they teach the student who does not fit mainstream profiles to work in a manner consistent with mainstream requirements. Many, if not most, instructors in these programs do not understand or teach learner empowerment. Essentially, they teach behaviors associated with mainstream learning styles as "right" approaches, the implication being that anything else is "wrong." This attitude can confuse students with nonmainstream learning styles and seriously undermine their self-esteem. Without accompanying strategy training, including style awareness, students are simply implementing superficial, rote behaviors. Teachers can have a far more significant impact and produce far greater results simply by teaching to the class composite, accommodating the at-risk students directly, and including learner empowerment instruction in their courses.

For those students who are sent away further than the doors of a learning skills center, all the way to the isolation of special education classrooms, the likelihood of being helped becomes even more remote. (Although graduate schools of education are teaching full inclusion, many schools still assign students to restrictive environments.) Strangely, the least amount of accommodation to learning styles appears to be offered in special education classrooms. Considering that most children in these classrooms have already displayed a rigidity in their learning style, it is ironic that relatively few instructional materials available for the special education classroom compensate for nonmainstream learning styles. Although learning-styles instruction is now a component of most certification and faculty development programs in special education, too few practicing special education teachers are aware of learning-style differences and their impact on students' ability (or inability) to acquire new information, and even fewer deliberately incorporate them into their instructional practices. Literature (especially textbooks) for special education teachers refer to learner differences too infrequently, even more rarely give teachers concrete suggestions for incorporating style differences into their lesson plans, and almost never provide help in identifying student styles without cumbersome instrumentation. At one university library which boasts more than 600 tomes for the special education teacher, only one of those volumes discusses learning styles. Course materials prepared for teachers of the learning disabled tend to be highly analytic, particular, and sequential. Style-aware special education teachers are forced into creating their own materials on a regular basis. Even avenues for sharing these are limited. The search among administrators of special education programs, as in regular education, is typically for a method (not yet discovered) that will be a panacea. If one considers the wondrous array of learner profiles in any classroom, including special education classrooms, it is not reasonable to wait for such a panacea.

FORMULA FOR WHOLE-CLASS TEACHING

To teach the whole class, teachers might apply the following formula:

1. Determine the students' learning styles.
2. Enter each student profile onto a chart.
3. Determine what styles represent the class average.
4. Determine who does not fit the majority profile.
5. Determine the teacher's teaching style and note conflicts with students' learning styles.
6. Determine the orientation of the materials and note conflicts with students' learning styles.
7. Assess the severity of conflicts in styles (3 or more mismatches).
8. Determine ways to include the at-risk students.

1. Determine each student's learning styles.

The first step in using the formula is to determine each student's learning profile. This can be done by instrumentation (the list of tests in Resource A might help), or it can be done by observation (the checklists in Resource B might help).

2. Enter each student profile onto a chart.

Once each student's learner profile has been identified, the profile may be entered on plotting charts like the ones provided in this book, or teachers may use any other format that they find comfortable. I say "may be entered" rather than "should be entered," because once teachers are skilled in the concepts and practice of teaching the whole class, the kinds of support being suggested here (instrumentation, observation check lists, and plotting charts) usually can be eliminated. In fact, skilled teachers of whole classes rarely work through this formula; they recognize students' needs from the first hour of interaction and simply proceed to meet those needs. That ability, however, often takes several classes and some experimentation to develop. In the interim, the support system suggested does seem to help.

3. Determine what styles represent the class average.

Once all students' learner profiles have been plotted on the chart, teachers need to determine which styles comprise the class profile. This is a simple majority rule process. Whichever style dominates in quantity (i.e., in numbers of students who possess it) represents part of the class profile.

The class profile will not match the learner profile of all students. In fact, it may not match the learner profile of even one student. The class profile simply reflects a listing of the dominant trait in each of the domains selected by the teacher for use. The important issue is to determine who deviates from it most and in what ways. Most students will have enough learner traits in common with the class profile that teaching to the profile works for them.

In addition to class profiles, there are subgroups. Subgroups usually represent profiles shared in common by more then 25% of the class but less than half the class. These subgroups provide support to each other, and on some occasions interact positively with the teacher's learner profile or with the learner profile of the materials. They are part of the whole class, and their presence must be considered, especially their influence on instruction.

4. Determine who does not fit the majority profile.

The next step requires that teachers analyze how each student deviates from the class profile and determine the level of risk for that individual student. What we are looking for in this analysis is the identification of those students who do not fit with this year's or this semester's peers. If the conflict is small (e.g., most of the peers are impulsive-visual learners, and the student is an impulsive-kinesthetic learner), there is probably little to be concerned about. The student will interact with peers on a cognitive level but not on a modality level. However, if a given student differs from peers in modality, personality type, and cognitive style, the negative influence on that student's ability to learn in this class is likely to be high. (This, of course, is a judgment call; making such judgments becomes easier with growing experience in teaching the whole class.) Such deviation should be marked as one area of risk for that student (student-class conflict).

5. Determine the teacher's teaching style and note conflicts with students' styles.

Next, the teacher needs to assess his or her own learner profile and follow the same analysis as for the class profile. Which students do not match the teacher's learner profile in one or more learning-style domains? How significant a difference is the mismatch? Does the student have secondary preferences or style flexibility upon which he or she can rely? If a given student significantly deviates from the teacher's learner profile, once again this student should be marked as being in one area of risk (student-teacher conflict).

6. Determine the orientation of the materials and note conflicts with students' styles.

The next step in the application of the formula is to determine the orientation of the materials to be used in the classroom. These materials include textbooks, workbooks, any handouts to be given, reports, materials that students may be sharing with each other, audiovisual aids of any sort—anything that the students will be using in support of learning. Here, too, the teacher needs to analyze the difference between each student's learner profile and the learner profile of the materials. Where do the deviations occur? How significant are they? If they are significant enough to cause learning difficulty, then the student possessing them should be marked as being in one area of risk (student-material conflict).

7. Assess the severity of conflicts in styles.

Once these three analyses have been made, the identification of at-risk students becomes very easy. Those students who have significant conflicts in none or only one of the areas discussed above (class profile, teacher profile, profile of materials) either fare well or can cope. Students who have conflicts in two areas or a very significant conflict in one area (such as one reflective student in a class of 90% impulsive students) will experience a moderate risk of failure. Those students who have conflicts in all three areas are at grave risk for failure.

8. Determine ways to include the at-risk students.

Once the at-risk students have been identified, then ways to assist those students can be determined. There are many options. The choice will depend on teacher inclination, size of class, situational factors (e.g., access of the student to external help, such as a learning skills center versed in style wars), time, availability of other kinds of materials, and so on. Some ways in which adaptation can be made include the following:

1. In-class task adaptation
2. Creative grouping in small-group work
3. Student choice in tasks
4. Individualized homework
5. Student counseling

FOR THE MANY

Teaching for the many means that teachers teach to the class profile. It means that more than one set of materials is available, teachers adjust lesson plans to the class profile, and they assess their students' strengths and weaknesses not in accordance with how they test (with high test scores identifying "good" students) but in accordance with how they learn (learner profile).

The class below represents a sample of what a teacher might find in a classroom. A hypothetical class constructed by random selection, it represents the situation that teachers face at the beginning of the school year or semester—an unknown, random collection of learner profiles. The class size has been reduced to 10 for ease of discussion. However, the same principles apply to much larger groups.

On the charts below (either type), a set of learner profiles is graphically portrayed. Teachers can elect to include those styles they consider most important.

1. The class:

Grace: A S G Syn Imp E NF V	Gloria: A S P An Imp I SJ V
Godfrey: C S G Syn Imp E NF Aud	Guadelupe: A S P An Imp I SJ V
George: C R G Syn Imp E SP Kin	Gary: A S P An Imp I SJ V
Gerald: C S G Imp E NF Kin	Goshen: A R P An Ref NT Mech
Glenn: A S P An Imp E NT V	Grant: C S P An Imp SJ Mech

Style	Students
Abstract	Grace, Glenn, Gloria, Guadelupe, Gary, Goshen
Concrete	Godfrey, George, Gerald, Grant
Sequential	Grace, Godfrey, Gerald, Glenn, Gloria, Guadelupe, Gary, Grant
Random	George, Goshen
Global	Grace, Godfrey, George, Gerald
Particular	Glenn, Gloria, Guadelupe, Gary, Gosen, Grant
Analytic	Glenn, Gloria, Guadelupe, Gary, Goshen, Gary
Synthetic	Grace, Godfrey, George
Impulsive	Grace, Godfrey, George, Gerald, Glenn, Gloria, Guadelupe, Gary, Grant
Reflective	Goshen
NF	Grace, Godfrey, Gerald
NT	Glenn, Goshen
SJ	Gloria, Guadelupe, Gary, Grant
SP	George
Visual	Grace, Glenn, Gloria, Guadelupe, Gary
Auditory	Godfrey
Mechanical	Goshen, Grant
Kinesthetic	George, Gerald

2. The teacher, Mr. Abbot: abstract, sequential, particular, analytic, reflective, visual, introverted, intuitive-thinking

3. The course materials: abstract-sequential

This group as a whole is particular, analytic, impulsive, visual, abstract, sequential, and extraverted, with no dominant temperament. We can tell this by counting the traits on either of the above charts.

The teacher's style, the class profile, and the materials all share much in common. Given this coincidence of styles, all students whose style match or come close to matching the class profile should be readily served.

Of the obvious subgroups, the global-synthetic students, while not fitting into the class profile, are not endangered because they make up 40% of the class and are all impulsive extraverts. As such, they will make their needs known. At worst, they should be vocal enough that Mr. Abbott may find himself intuitively including more synthesis than normal, focusing on concepts rather than details.

The concrete-sequential subgroup matches both teacher and materials on sequentiality. Where they will need assistance, either in lesson adaptation or in learner empowerment, is on concretization of the abstract elements of the course.

Although there is not a dominant temperament in this class, there are more SJs than other types. These students will probably prevail upon the teacher to provide the structure and deadlines that they need. The teacher is likely to be more unorthodox than SJs are accustomed to, but they will likely manage that by asking for deadlines, assignment specifics, and what is going to be on the test. The NT profile, the second largest group of students, will want to work on systems, patterns, and rules—all of which will be easily provided by the teacher, whose own personality type matches that of these students—and the materials which are abstract-sequential in nature. The NFs, a definite minority, will miss their necessary interaction unless the teacher overtly promotes the development of interpersonal relations; injects cultural activities in foreign language, ESL, or social studies classes; and incorporates small-group work or individualized teacher-student activities in other classes. The SP, of course, is a loner and is at great risk.

When teachers work with the many, they adapt the lesson plans to meet the needs of the many. In the case of this sample class, the lesson plans are likely to be highly abstract. They will directly meet the needs of 50% of the class, who match the class profile: Grace, Glenn, Gloria, Guadelupe, and Gary.

Another three students come close to the class average and represent only a moderate risk. They are students Godfrey, Gerald, and Grant. Like the rest of the class, they are impulsive. They are also all extraverts. This combination means that they are likely to express their needs in ways that get those needs addressed.

In this class, only two students are at severe risk. A rule of thumb that I have discovered in working with whole classes is that, *if a teacher teaches to a class profile (teaching for the many), only 10-20% of students will need additional assistance (teaching for the one)*. The students at risk in this class are George and Goshen. In a typical class, where a teacher is unaware of differences in learning styles, it is likely that George would be removed from the class for disciplinary reasons and Goshen would be removed for reasons of academic failure. However, both can succeed if the teacher addresses their areas of difference.

In this particular class, the teacher is likely to find himself at risk, or at least, frequently fatigued. The preponderance of extraverted impulsive learners is apt to wear out his introverted, reflective patience!

FOR THE ONE

When teachers work with the one, they must first determine the level of risk of failure that each student faces. They do this by comparing each student's style with the class profile, the teaching style (or the teacher's learning style), and the style of the curricular materials. (With practice, the time required for this analysis becomes almost nil; a glance at a class chart or an hour of teaching the students makes the patterns and individual deviations obvious to the teacher experienced at teaching the whole class. Initially, this kind of analysis takes some effort.)

In the above class, Grace shares her visual, impulsive, extraverted, abstract, and sequential learning styles with the class profile, her abstract-sequential style with the materials, and only abstract-sequentiality and visual learning with the teacher. Grace is an NF; to some extent, this student's desire to please and to create rapport with the teacher will help compensate for those learning traits that differ from the class profile and the teacher's learner profile as long as the teacher recognizes her need for praise and interaction. However, Mr. Abbott is an NT. It is not likely that he will instinctively provide Grace with the amount of interaction she needs. If he is style-aware, he will provide this interaction consciously; otherwise, Grace will lack an important ingredient for her learning success.

Godfrey, on the surface, looks like a student in trouble. He shares many of Grace's deviations: global, synthetic, NF. In addition, he is concrete and auditory. What will help Godfrey is the power of the sequential learning style, which will make the abstract-sequential material, the teaching style, and peer learning preferences more accessible than if he were a random learner. Furthermore, he belongs to a strong subgroup likely to make its presence and needs known: the extraverted globals. Without this subgroup, Godfrey would likely struggle and would definitely be at risk for failure.

George has several risk factors. His cognitive processing styles are diametrically opposed to those of his teacher, the materials, and his peers. This puts him at risk for academic failure. However, something even more significant distinguishes him. George is the only SP in the class and one of only two kinesthetic students. His difficulty will lie in concentrating for long periods of time on rules and explanations and working out the systems that will absorb the majority of the class. The combination of SP and kinesthetic means that he will probably have a low tolerance for boredom and for pen-and-paper tasks. Within minutes, his mind will probably be focused on something outside the window, his fingers tapping, and his legs bouncing. An uninitiated analytic, reflective, NT teacher might quickly become irritated at this student's inability to settle down. With academic difficulties reinforcing George's lack of desire to be in any classroom, let alone this one, his behavior may become intolerable, and Mr. Abbott might well be tempted to drop him from the class for improper behavior. However, if Mr. Abbott is style-aware, he can accommodate George's styles by changing the activities frequently; even if the majority of activities are planned for visual, analytic learners, kinesthetic SP students can surprisingly often tolerate them and learn from them if the variety is sufficient to retain their attention. Another way that the teacher can accommodate George's learning needs is to change the composition of small groups periodically. Giving George permission to stand or stretch when needed may also help, as may the interspersion of more physical activities. If gross motor use in the classroom or lesson plan is out of the question, writing activities can sometimes serve as a weak substitute. Whether this technique will work with George needs to be tested in the classroom. Use of video and computer instruction can sometimes provide sufficient kinesthesia for kinesthetic SP students—just notice how long they can sit still at home watching adventure movies on television! George will definitely need some assistance in the form of adapted homework that allows him to apply concepts learned in class to concrete situations. Learner empowerment training will help him develop strategies related to sharpening, selective attention, focusing on details, and disassembly, among others.

The intersection of sequentiality in Gerald's learner profile with the class profile and the teacher's learner profile will provide some battle relief for Gerald and may make his kinesthetic nature less noticeable and less troublesome. *Of all the cognitive styles, one of the most critical to learning success, in my experience, is the student-teacher intersection of learner profile in the sequential-random domain.* In this domain, Gerald is in good shape. Moreover, his NF personality may prompt him to accept some style discomfort for purposes of establishing rapport and maintaining harmony. If Mr. Abbott is style-aware, Gerald will be more comfortable. As an NT, if Mr. Abbott is not style-aware, he may provide insufficiently frequent feedback to Gerald on his efforts and behavior, and Gerald may feel unappreciated and insecure.

Glenn matches the class profile in every domain. This is unusual and certainly fortunate for Glenn. Teaching to the class profile is teaching Glenn, and teaching Glenn is teaching to the class profile.

With the exception of introversion, Gloria matches the class profile in all domains. As an introvert, she may appear especially quiet in this particular class. As an SJ, she belongs to the most populous subgroup among the temperaments. As an SJ, she will accept course requirements and will strive to implement them because that is what she "should" do.

As far as learning styles are concerned, Guadelupe and Gloria are twins. They, too, will appear to be members of the silent minority, and they will work hard to do as they are told.

Gary makes a triplet with Gloria and Guadelupe. It is unusual to have so many students with identical learner profiles. This concurrence makes this class easy to teach because this subgroup comes close to the class profile and is composed of students with the same learning styles. In this case, treating students the same and treating them equally are synonymous.

Goshen has several risk factors: He is reflective, mechanical, and random. In fact, he is the only reflective student in the class. In another class, being the only reflective student would be highly detrimental to his potential success. However, in this class, he is lucky. His teacher is also reflective; he may instinctively relate to Goshen, include some time in the schedule for processing information, and know what kinds of results to expect on tests. With an impulsive teacher and the same class profile, Goshen would probably fail academically. The student's mechanical needs, like those of Grant below, may be taken care of as homework and as an opportunity to copy information from the board. Again, in this same class with an auditory or kinesthetic teacher, Goshen's limited access to mechanical activities might compound his other differences and lead to academic failure. Where Mr. Abbott will need to pay some individual attention to Goshen's learning needs is in the abstract-random combination. It is likely that too much learning will be based on reading and too little on observation. Mr. Abbott can deal with this by showing films periodically and by routinely assigning tasks to be completed in small groups, at least for Goshen, the NFs in the class (Grace, Godfrey, and Gerald), and the extraverts; other students can be given similar tasks to be completed independently.

Grant is mechanical. In this, he differs from the rest of the class, but all his other learning styles match the class profile. Since Mr. Abbott is visual, he will probably spend time writing on the board, giving Grant the opportunity to copy from the board, allowing him to access his mechanical memory. It is also likely that Mr. Abbott, being a visual, abstract-sequential teacher, will assign much written homework, also allowing Grant to use his mechanical learning style.

MORE EXAMPLES

Now, let's take some classes in subject matter areas and the specific lessons associated with them. The same general principles apply as in the generic subject class described above, but the concrete situations can show in greater detail how whole classes work together—or encounter trouble together.

The following three classes, with their teachers and instructional materials, have not been structured in any preconceived way. Rather, they have been composed in the same way that most classrooms are—through random selection. What I have done in the following sections is to put on paper the thinking process that whole-class teachers or administrators would go through should they encounter these combinations in their classrooms. There are no right and wrong answers in teaching the whole class. There are many different ways to accommodate, group, and empower students and to interpret the relative importance of various combinations of learning-styles variables. If these were real classes, readers could try out various options and let the resulting effectiveness or failure guide their next steps. The fluid nature of teaching the whole class will undoubtedly frustrate SJ readers, or at least those who do not tolerate ambiguity well. Unfortunately, often students and their behaviors require interpretation and initial interpretation is not always accurate. Finally, class size has been held to 10 students in order to include several examples.

Sample Class One: Foreign Language

The topic for this lesson is forms of transportation. The grammar inherent in using the topic is verbs of motion. Verbs of motion (in those languages where these differ grammatically and semantically from English) have traditionally been taught in textbooks as abstract-sequential rules and systems or as concrete-sequential hands-on application and practice. Depending on the class profile, the teacher may need to select one approach over another or develop a new approach.

1. The class:

Frank: A S An P ENTP Ref V I	Fred: C S G Syn ENTP Imp Aud III
Fran: C S G Syn INFJ Imp Kin III	Freda: C S An P ESFJ Imp V III
Fawn: A S An P ESFJ Imp V IV	Felicity: C R G Syn ENTJ Emp Kin IV
Francis: C R G Syn ISTP Ref Kin IV	Freeman: A R An P INFJ Imp V I
Fannie: C S An P INFP Ref V III	Flora: C S An P ESTJ Imp Aud III

2. The teacher, Ms. Bailey: concrete, sequential, analytic, particular, ENFJ, impulsive, visual, converger

3. The materials: authentic: magazines, newspapers, television, and personal letters

The class profile is concrete, sequential, analytic, particular, impulsive, extraverted, visual, converger. This is a combination hands-on reading class. Preferences will likely be for a majority of applied activities, once concepts are acquired through reading or other visual means. Intake (sentient memory) in this class may best be enhanced through students' eyes and storage (short-term memory and long-term memory) through their hands. In this way, the class is slightly bifurcated in its preferences and reflects the same needs as would an individual student with a discontinuous learning style.

The subgroups are reflective, kinesthetic, and synthetic learners. One third of the students are reflective. They may disappear somewhat into the background, but they do have an extravert in their midst, whose other learning styles better match the class profile. There are three kinesthetic students (one third of the class; given the number of extraverts and kinesthetic learners in the class, this is likely to be a "noisy" class). The synthetic learners comprise 40% of the class. This is a sizable subgroup and one that Ms. Bailey would do well to include in any lesson plan. No temperament predominates. With the exception of the lonely SP, there is an even spread of temperaments.

The teacher's learner profile matches the class profile in several domains: concrete, sequential, converger, impulsive, extraverted, visual, and analytic. This is an excellent match, better than usually can be hoped for. Ms. Bailey will probably have an easier time teaching this class than Mr. Abbott will have with the sample class!

It is clear that given a choice of materials, Ms. Bailey can succeed with traditional concrete-sequential approaches, such as applied tasks and exercises associated with using verbs of motions—role plays, skits, treasure hunts, map work, and real-life applications. The authentic materials provide the teacher with an excellent means of doing this. Train schedules and similar items provide an ideal means of having concrete-sequential converger students practice using information that requires verbs of motion for expression. However, Ms. Bailey will most likely need to construct the tasks carefully. In my experience, the particular-analytic profile usually defines groups that feel insecure with authentic materials (they want to translate every word) and encounter difficulties in listening comprehension (requiring some cogent prelistening activities prior to introducing the television material).

In this class, Frank will survive. Although he might prefer more theoretical and textbook-based approaches, he is analytic and visual like the teacher and the class profile. Many of the concrete-sequential tasks and exercises assigned by the teacher are apt to be analytic and visual in nature. He also shares a preference for sequentiality with teacher, peers, and materials. His NT temperament should allow him to develop an overall system for understanding and processing verbs of motion, although it may also cause him to become bored with and derisive of the applied activities. If this is the case, the teacher will soon know, because Frank is an extravert. His reflectivity may make him seem slow to the teacher. If he feels slow to himself, then there can be accompanying behavior issues, because NTs need to feel competent and are their own greatest critics. In Frank's case, a little patience, a little time, and homework that allows Frank to work on theory before he has to come to a class where nearly everything is applied can go a long way toward incorporating him successfully into this class.

Fran mostly matches the class profile. She deviates in three ways: global, synthetic, kinesthetic. Given the course materials, she should not suffer from the global-synthetic deviation. In fact, she will probably handle the authentic materials much better than the rest of the class. As a kinesthetic learner, learning a topic like verbs of motions is natural, and a good instructor will find ways to capitalize on that, such as allowing her to act out or role play the motions. An NF, Fran will try to please the instructor, even if it means working via a nonpreferred style.

Fawn's only significant deviation from the class profile is her concrete-random style. This might normally get in the way because it is such a marked style. However, Fawn is also an SJ (the CR-SJ combination is somewhat unusual). The SJ personality type will likely check the more egregious of CR behaviors.

Francis is quite clearly at risk. He deviates from the teacher's learner profile and from the class profile, as well as from the profile of the material. As a perceiver, he may find the teacher reaching closure too soon for comfort. The concrete-random, global, and synthetic attributes will help make accessible the authentic materials, but because accurate use of verbs of motion relies on making minor distinctions, Francis may need some strategy training as part of a class activity or on homework to start seeing those distinctions. He may also need to practice seeing these distinctions during review periods; he is not likely to be able to use sharpening as a learning tool, at least, not in the beginning. Because the teacher is likely to develop tasks that are appropriate for convergers, the use of the materials may be made harder for Francis than he would normally experience with authentic materials. Furthermore, although there are many ways that verbs of motion can be taught kinesthetically, it is not likely that Ms. Bailey, a visual learner, will choose to use these. If she does, then the modality preference of Francis will not be a detriment to his learning; if she does not, then the modality needs of Francis will not be met. Because there are three kinesthetic learners in the class (enough to comprise a subgroup), Ms. Bailey might try having them scout out a walking trip for the class and write down the instructions. To do so, of course, requires appropriate use of verbs of motion. (Ms. Bailey will want to check on the accuracy of usage before handing over the instructions for the rest of the class to follow!)

Fannie is likely to fade from view in this class. As an introverted-reflective learner, her reflectivity will appear as slowness. As a perceiver, she may appear disorganized. She will certainly not be ready for the quick closure that will typify the class as a whole. Her learning *per se* may proceed without too much impairment, because she does share the converger and visual styles. However, this class is not likely to give her a chance to blossom. Accommodation that needs to be made is mostly in the area of speed. She needs time to observe, think, and come to closure. All those traits interact with each, and so her need for longer response time is even stronger than it would be with only one of those styles. She is not likely to be able to "hold her own," or even to want to, with other members of the class. If Ms. Bailey wants Fannie to succeed, she may need to provide her some extra help and moral support. If Fannie knows that the teacher believes in her, then it is more likely that she will not interpret her own need for response time as incompetence.

Fred also has some moderate risks in this class. His learning style profile deviates from both the class profile and the teacher in some aspects. He may need more auditory input that he will be receiving as part of this class. He could be provided auditory materials for homework and in preparation for class, such as listening to someone describe his or her journey on tape and drawing it on a map. His greatest problem will be his tendency to merge the distinctions between the verbs of motions. Strategy training for sharpening and analytic strategies might be advisable.

Freda is a fortunate student. Her learning-styles profile very closely fits the class profile. If Ms. Bailey teaches to the class profile, she will automatically include Freda.

Felicity has an excellent learning-styles profile for language learning and a risky profile for this particular class. All of her styles (modality, personality, and cognitive) do not match the class profile, the teacher's learning-styles profile, or the materials. Circumstance has created a square hole for this round, and likely talented, peg. No amount of strategy training is going to help this situation—there would be too many strategies to train. Accommodation, and in large doses, is required. If the teacher does not accommodate, then Felicity may turn into a behavior problem. Being extraverted, impulsive, and kinesthetic, she is a naturally "noisy" learner and will be noticeable, even in this classroom. As an NT, she is likely to be critical of teaching method. She will probably understand the authentic materials quickly but find any applied activities boring. As the only "leader type" (ENTJ) in the class, her disaffection is apt to infect other students, particularly those students who are already experiencing some forms of discomfort. The important point for Ms. Bailey to understand is that she must cope with Felicity somehow. The best way is through accommodation of her learning styles. As an ENTJ, Felicity can be trusted to lead the kinesthetic "away team" in their trip-scouting activities; the other members, an NF and an SP, will accept her leadership. On a more cerebral level, Ms. Bailey might have Felicity use verbs of motion to create. Felicity could create compositions (if she has a visual secondary learning style preference). Otherwise, she could use authentic materials on her own to create exercises for others (such as map trips, where she writes a script and the other students listen to the script and draw a map). The three accommodators in this class might make a subgroup to create exercises that might later be used with their peers or subsequent classes.

Freeman comes very close to fitting the class profile and being able to work well with the teacher and the materials, except that he is an introvert (so he will disappear into the background in this class) and a diverger. The latter learning style can be accommodated by using the television materials frequently. If he needs to watch more than other students do (very likely), videotapes could be loaned to him for homework assignments (assuming that he has access to a VCR).

Flora fits the class, teacher, and materials profiles even more closely than Freeman. She shares with him his need to watch. In fact, the diverger and the auditory learners in this class can be combined into a subgroup and given watching activities, while other students are busy with reading activities.

Sample Class Two:

The topic for this lesson is fractions. Students have not yet formally been introduced to the concept of fractions, or anything less than a whole.

1. The class:

Rain: A S II ESTJ Imp V An Ded	Stormy: A S II ESFJ Imp V An Ded
Sky: A S II ISTJ Ref V An Ded	Forest: C S III ISTJ Ref V An Ded
Moss: C S III ENFJ Imp Mech Syn Ind	Aspen: C S III ESTJ Imp Kin Syn Ind
Autumn: C S III INFJ Ref Aud An Ind	Summer: C S ISTJ Ref V An Ded
Spring: A R ESTJ Ref V An Ded	April: C R INTJ Ref V Syn Ind

2. The teacher, Mr. Gray: concrete, sequential, converger, ESFJ, impulsive, visual, analytic, particular, deductive

3. The textbook: deductive explanations, calculations, and word problems

The class profile is abstract, sequential, assimilator, introverted, NF, reflective, visual, analytic, and deductive learning. This is a class that learns well through traditional forms of instruction. The introverted, reflective aspects of the class profile will give this group the appearance of being very quiet and a little slow. The NF dominance can create an atmosphere of harmony. For students with mainstream learning styles, this is a pleasant group in which to be placed.

The subgroups in this class are concrete learners, inductive learners, and reflective learners. The concrete learners match the teacher's profile and, therefore, their needs are likely to be met on that level. The inductive learners could be handled rather easily by grouping them and letting them work on hypothesis formation, using examples of fractions in action, while the other students receive explanation. Reflective learners, as a subgroup, are not easy to group in supportive ways. They might best be handled as individuals, with one reflective learner seeded into each cooperative learning group. That way, each can reflect while others in the small group are working and be ready to respond after some time. The problem with a group of reflective learners is that all the students have to take time to reflect, so activities do not get accomplished nor do the students have other students to observe in this kind of like-group organization. (Reflection, especially introverted reflection, is not usually a group activity.)

The teacher's learning profile deviates from the class in three important traits, but in this particular class-teacher combination, the deviance should have limited consequence for the students. Although Mr. Gray is concrete, he is concrete-sequential, which places him on the same axis as the abstract-sequential class profile. The deviance will more likely have an impact on Mr. Gray and his reaction to this class. The reflectivity of the class, compared to his impulsivity, may make it seem like he is really struggling to get the students to accomplish anything, and the NF personality profile may make these students seem to take more time for and place more emphasis on relationships than Mr. Gray, an SJ, considers proper, although he is not likely to feel any conflict with their need for personalization because he, too, is an F. There are three SJ students in this class; all three are Ts. It is difficult to predict whether there will be greater rapport with the feeling students who match Mr. Gray's feeling type or with the SJ students who match his temperament but are thinking types. On some level there should be natural rapport with both subgroups. In fact, this class in general should have excellent rapport with this teacher.

The learning profile of the materials are abstract, sequential, assimilative, introverted, reflective, and visual, just like the class profile. As such, they are ideal for this class, even if they do not reflect contemporary teaching methods. This means less accommodation will be needed to teach to the class profile. It also means that those students who differ from the class profile may experience greater difficulties than otherwise, because they will also differ from the style of the materials.

Rain matches the class profile and the materials in all but two respects, in which she matches the teacher: SJ personality type and impulsive cognitive style. She will likely be perceived as a good student. Because she is one of the few impulsive students, she is likely to attract Mr. Gray's attention and develop rapport easily.

Sky matches the class profile even more closely than Rain, and in the one variance, SJ, she matches the teacher. If the teacher teaches to the class profile, Sky will be in excellent shape.

Moss has two learning styles that may be a little problematic: mechanical and inductive. However, given the nature of the subject matter and of the materials, Moss should have plenty of mechanical applications in the short-term memory and long-term memory storage stages. The comprehension/intake stage is a little more problematic, since Moss may need to have concepts introduced mechanically (somewhat difficult) or inductively (easier). For Moss's sake and the sake of the other inductive learners, Mr. Gray should set up the inductive subgroup discussed above.

Autumn, like Moss, has a modality that differs from the class profile (auditory), as well as a cognitive style that differs (induction). The classroom explanations that go along with traditional presentations of arithmetic concepts are likely to satisfy Autumn's auditory needs, at least at the sentient (comprehension) and short-term memory (storage) stages. Again, if Mr. Gray sets up an inductive subgroup, Autumn's second area of difference will be less of a problem.

Spring may be in for a more difficult experience than some students. Her randomness may well be unappreciated by a sequential teacher, and the sequential mode of learning which is likely to emanate from both teacher and materials and resonate with the class may bore her at best. Confusion and frustration are equally probable reactions. Furthermore, she is the lone diverger in the class. Unless Mr. Gray is very careful, she is not likely to get the amount of observation and demonstration that she needs for learning. Because sequential learning strategies will help her in working with the materials and in developing comfort in working in an assimilator mode (she is already abstract), which is the profile of the class, she might well benefit from strategy training in this area.

Stormy differs from the class profile only in her impulsivity and her SJ personality type, both of which match her teacher's profile. Stormy should find this class a calm haven.

With the exception of his reflectivity, which matches the majority of his classmates, Forest comes very close to matching his teacher's profile perfectly. For him, as with many students in this class, the topic and the year will probably be one that he remembers with fondness.

Aspen has quite an unusual combination of learning styles. Normally, one does not see the combination of assimilator and synthetic learner or the combination of assimilator and kinesthetic learner. Of course, these combinations can and do happen. Aspen may need to learn how to rely on his assimilator learning style (if he does not already know this) in order to fit more comfortably with the class profile. Because he is the only kinesthetic learner and also impulsive, he may appear to be hyperactive. (Remember Rory, Chapter 2?) In another class, he would be less noticeable. It will be important for Mr. Gray to keep in mind that Aspen needs movement and find ways to include movement for him during class time. (Mr. Gray might as well accommodate this learning style of Aspen's, because Aspen is not going to be sitting still, anyway.) Some of the mechanical computations will help, but gross motor muscles are going to be yearning to move. Board work can help. Learning stations can help. Manipulatives, although they involve fine motor muscles more frequently than gross motor muscles, can help and lend themselves well to such topics as fractions.

Summer is a happy combination of class profile and teacher learning style profile. Like a number of the other students in this class, she should find this year to be a pleasant experience.

April, on the other hand, is very likely to be an "unhappy camper." The only NT in the entire class, and an introverted one, she is likely to wonder if there is something wrong with her because the interests and relationships of her peers are going to be based on very different kinds of interactions (interpersonal, authoritative) than she would like them to be (intellectual). She is not likely to find a mentor in her teacher, especially because her first reaction will be to question authority, which he takes as a matter of course. Beyond that, her accommodator style will drive her to experimentation, and Mr. Gray is likely to rein her in. Even if she does participate in an inductive subgroup (definitely a positive way to assist her), her other styles are so far from the class and teacher learning-style profiles that the overall effect of this accommodation may be small. Her visual modality, while matching her peers and the teacher, is also nearly meaningless, given the strength, direction, and quantity of mismatches in personality and cognitive style areas. As a minimum, if Mr. Gray wants to teach April as part of the whole class, she should receive awareness training so that she understands that there is nothing wrong with her, that the learning environment at the moment is just not felicitously structured for her needs. As an NT and a natural scholar and as an accommodator and independent learner, she may have suggestions for how to handle her own learning; these should be listened to, even if, as with the ideas of many accommodators, they appear radical to the converger teacher. Some combination of small group and independent-study learning situations might work better for her than full-time inclusion in all-class activities.

Sample Class Three: Social Studies

The topic for this lesson is Latin American countries and their exports. The purpose of the lesson is for students to understand the diversity in Latin America.

1. The class:

Hayward: A S II INFJ Ref V An P	Holly: A S II ENFJ Ref V An P
Heath (twin of Heather): A S II INFP Ref V An P	Heather (twin of Heath): A S II INTJ Ref V An P
Heidi: C R IV ENTJ Imp V G Syn	Mary: A S II ENTJ Ref V An P
Larry: A R I ENFJ Ref V G Syn	Barry: C S III ISFP Ref Mech G Syn
Harry: C S III ISTP Imp Kin G Syn	Hilary: A S II ISFJ Ref V An P

2. The teacher, Mr. Daly: concrete, random, synthetic, global, accommodator, ENTJ, impulsive, kinesthetic

3. The materials: textbook and authentic (reference materials, experts, and field trips)

The class profile is abstract, sequential, assimilator, introverted, NF, reflective, visual, and analytic learning. This is another class that, with the exception of introversion and reflection, fits Western mainstream learning styles.

The subgroups are extraverted, impulsive, and synthetic learners. These subgroups are large and contain "noisy" students. Their presence will be felt. The materials, too, fit better with the subgroups than with the class profile.

The extraverts do not match the class profile, but there are 40% of them. Furthermore, they match their teacher's profile not only in extraversion but in other domains as well. This should make their learning experience tolerable; with a another teacher (one who is not style-aware), they would probably not fare as well.

There are only two impulsive learners. This hardly constitutes a subgroup. However, in this particular group, they have the potential to stand out, so it is worth discussing them here. Under normal conditions in a class with this profile, these impulsive students would appear "jumpy" or "hyperactive." However, this is less likely to be the case because the teacher is also impulsive. The reflective style of the class majority may make the class pace seem slow to the teacher, and these two impulsive students may provide relief. Without these two students, the teacher would likely feel discouraged at the end of each class from not accomplishing as much as he had planned.

A large subgroup of students, 40%, is global and synthetic. These learning styles also fall in line with the teacher's learner profile. With another teacher, these students might have some serious risk factors. However, this teacher and the materials that this teacher is likely to present counteract the negative aspects of being part of a minority profile.

As noted already, the teacher's learner profile is somewhat unusual for a classroom teacher. The difficulty with this teacher-class combination is that the teacher's learner profile does not match the class profile in any domain. If Mr. Daly is not style-aware, students and teacher are likely to be very unhappy in this class. Even a style-aware Mr. Daly will be hard-pressed to teach to a class profile that differs so strongly from his own profile. Ironically (and positively), Mr. Daly may find himself allied with some students who would otherwise be at risk for failure in this class but whose learning styles come closer to matching his own. Although the extraverted subgroup might trouble a teacher with a different learner profile, Mr. Daly will probably enjoy this group. They are likely to challenge him, and he is likely to be up to that challenge—and even relish it. In fact, Mr. Daly may very well enjoy the subgroup more than he enjoys the majority of the class. Because the learner profile of the subgroups is highly compatible with Mr. Daly's own learner profile, there may be a strong tendency to teach these subgroups rather than the class profile, putting the majority of the class at risk.

The materials represent the kinds of materials that many teachers with this teacher's learner profile would be likely to use. However, with the exception of the textbook, they will be difficult for this class profile to use. If Mr. Daly wants the whole class to succeed, he will have to style-shift in order to accommodate the class profile.

Hayward matches the class profile. If Mr. Daly accommodates the class profile in his teaching methods and materials adaptation, Hayward will learn well. If Mr. Daly does not accommodate the class profile, Hayward will experience serious difficulties, as will the majority of the class. Mr. Daly might think about using the textbook first, or assigning textbook readings as homework assignments prior to introducing topics in the class, so that those who need the sequential input can have it in some form before they have to deal with the randomness of the authentic materials. He might also do prereading and prelistening activities in class before beginning to work with the authentic materials. Before going on field trips or bringing in experts, he might have the assimilator students put together charts of countries and products with questions to ask of the experts.

Heath is close enough in learning styles to be as much of a twin to Hayward as he is to Heather. He also matches the class profile, and his success in the class will depend directly on how Mr. Daly decides to cope with the learning style conflicts between the majority of the class members and his preferred ways of teaching.

Heidi does not at all match the class profile, but she does match her teacher's profile. She is one with whom the teacher is apt to feel strong rapport. Given that she is an ENTJ (leader type), she may run into direct conflict with the other ENTJ in the class, Mary, whose learning style profile matches the class profile. The Heidi-Mary split very much symbolizes the teacher-class split. These kinds of splits can set up near-physical conflict and create very troubled group dynamics in the classroom. If this class is to succeed, Mr. Daly must recognize this split very soon after the class begins and actively manage the split through equal instruction for members of the class represented by Heidi and for members represented by Mary. It is unlikely that anyone can make the split disappear or that teaching this class will ever be a comfortable experience, but students can complete the course feeling successful and unaware that the split existed. Cooperative learning may be the method of choice for Mr. Daly in accomplishing this, because it will allow him to put together like groups; if Mary and Heidi are in different learning groups, they are more likely to compete for (and gain) leadership within the small group and cooperate in the class. Heidi is more likely to be willing to march off and interview an expert. Mary is more likely to want to research opinions and prepare surveys for the interviewing of experts. Heidi and Mary can combine these interests in completing a project together amicably.

Larry is the only diverger in the class. He may share his randomness with the instructor, but that is not likely to help much because of the mismatch between abstraction and concreteness. He should be able to handle the naturally synthetic-global nature of the teacher's instruction and the authentic materials, unless Mr. Daly decides to teach exclusively to the class profile, which would omit Larry from this domain, too. Larry will definitely find more rapport with his peers, many of whom are also NFs, than he will with Mr. Daly, who is an NT. Depending on how Mr. Daly decides to balance the competing needs of the class, Larry will need both accommodation for divergence (perhaps working in a subgroup with concrete-randoms, where he can first observe, will help) and strategy training for either concretization or for sequencing (or for both). As a diverger, Larry should enjoy watching programs on television (or videotapes) about Latin American countries and sharing that information with the rest of the class. Mr. Daly should be able to individualize Larry's homework assignments to accommodate his divergence.

If Larry seems to be a problem vis-à-vis the class profile, Harry has even more problems. He is a converger (one of only two), kinesthetic (perhaps Mr. Daly, being kinesthetic himself, will intuitively accommodate this modality preference), and an SP. He doesn't want to be in any classroom, let alone this one. Keeping him on task would not be difficult for Mr. Daly, if he had a full group like this. Because Larry is in the minority, Mr. Daly's best option is to use cooperative learning, structuring groups in accordance with learning-style profiles and putting Harry in the global-synthetic group, giving this group modality choices in activities as well as mixed modality activities. Mr. Daly might consider putting Harry together with Barry, the other converger, for specific projects. However, for routine activities, both can fit well into a larger, global-synthetic learner subgroup.

Holly matches the class profile. Like that of others in the class, her success very much depends on how Mr. Daly decides to handle the conflict between his learning-style profile and the class profile.

Like Hayward, Heath, and Holly, Heather matches the class profile. Like them, she will either succeed well or fail miserably, depending on accommodation.

Mary, too, matches the class profile in cognitive style and modality preference. The only difference is personality type. As mentioned earlier, her likelihood of encountering conflicts with Heidi are high, depending on whether activities are the same for the whole class or whether there is some individualization by group. If Mr. Daly does not teach to the class profile, Mary can become a formidable problem, especially given her NT nature to not respect authority, unless she has a reason to do so.

Barry, as mentioned above, is the other converger in the group. He and Harry share many traits, with the exception that they have different kinds of motor memory. Nevertheless, they should work well together on specific projects. They do match their teacher in several ways, including concreteness, globality, and synthesis. They can certainly be expected to work successfully in a global subgroup of the class. The materials, too, should be fairly accessible to them, unless Mr. Daly so adapts the materials to the class profile that they lose their original properties. Convergers dealing with topics such as countries and products often enjoy map-making projects. Perhaps Harry and Barry could be assigned such tasks in support of a larger project that is more accommodator or assimilator by nature.

Hillary, like so many other members of the class, matches the class profile but differs from her teacher. As the class as a whole fares, so will Hillary fare.

IN SUMMARY

In the real world, teaching the whole class means first knowing who is in the class. As noted earlier, teachers of the whole class focus on individual traits and needs, accepting students where they are and accepting students for who they are. Knowing this much allows teachers to see the variations and patterns among members of a class, between the dominant styles in the class and the teacher's own styles, between the styles of any one student and those of the teacher, and between each of the students' learning styles and the orientation of the proposed materials.

Once a teacher has this knowledge, whether it is gained through observation or through instrumentation, a world of options and opportunity opens up. As we have seen in the four classes above, each time the variables take a different shape; a different teacher with any one of those classes or one or two different students in the class would result in a very different learning environment and very different accommodation and empowerment needs. However, there is always a way to accomplish both accommodation and empowerment.

Whether with any given class or any given student the choice is made for accommodation or empowerment or some of both depends on the learning environment and the resources available. In some cases, learner empowerment will make no difference in the short-term, although it might have some benefit for the next class and the next teacher. In other cases, accommodation is not possible, but learner empowerment is. Examples of criteria used to make the choices for accommodation or empowerment appear in the classes discussed above. These can be used as models for other classes. Nevertheless, every situation is unique. Every student is unique. Each time the decision to empower or accommodate must be made anew. Teachers who know when to accommodate and when to empower and who do both leave their students with an invaluable inheritance. ***Through accommodation, teachers give students a gift for the duration of their course; through empowerment, teachers give students a gift for a lifetime.***

Right now, for some readers, teaching the whole class in the fullest form, accommodating and empowering, as shown in the classes above, may seem impossible, especially with a class of 30 or more students. Yet it is precisely with such classes that whole-class teaching is most needed and most beneficial. It is not essential to begin with all the domains (modalities, personality types, and a range of cognitive styles) at once or to start out by working with "the many." There is some wisdom in starting out with one or two style domains or with working with "the one." In time (and sooner than many teachers predict), most teachers are comfortable working with a wide array of styles and all students. As with anything else, the first step and the first time is the most difficult.

PRACTICE EXERCISES

1. Use the Formula for Whole-Class Teaching to evaluate the following classes. In each case, (a) determine the class profile, the profile of the subgroups, the teacher's learner profile, and the profile of the materials; (b) determine which students do not match each of these learner profiles; (c) determine which students are at gravest risk; and (d) suggest how the at-risk students can be helped.

a. Class #1

Class:

Hayward: A S II INFJ Ref V An P	Holly: A S II ENFJ Ref V An P
Heath (twin of Heather): A S II INFP Ref V An P	Heather (twin of Heath): A S II INTJ Ref V An P
Heidi: C R IV ENTJ Imp V G Syn	Mary: A S II ENTJ Ref V An P
Larry: A R I ENFJ Ref V G Syn	Barry: C S III ISFP Ref Mech G Syn
Harry: C S III ISTP Imp Kin G Syn	Hilary: A S II ISFJ Ref V An P

Teacher: analytic, particular, random, introverted reflective
Materials: abstract-sequential

b. Class #2

Class:

Alicia: An P S I Ref	Rocky: An P S E Imp
Louetta: An G R I Imp	Ricky: An P S I Ref
Drake: Syn P R E Imp	Micky: An P S E Imp
Darin: Syn G R E Imp	Dick: An P S E Ref
Marci: Syn G R I Ref	Lisa: Syn C R Imp

Teacher: concrete, random, impulsive, inductive, right-hemisphere preferent
Materials: concrete-sequential

2. Look at Lisa's interaction in each of the classes. Lisa has not changed, but the peers, teachers, and materials have. How does Lisa's learning style profile fit into each of the environments.

3. Reexamine each of the above classes, but replace the given teacher's learner profile with your own learner profile. How does this change who is most at risk and what can you do to create a safe learning environment for these students?

4. Try this same procedure with a class that you are currently teaching. If the class is large, look at a random sampling (the first three rows, etc.) or use a limited number of learning style variables (perhaps two of the cognitive styles), unless you feel comfortable working with the larger number.

8

Epilogue

Perhaps the easiest way to summarize what teaching the whole class is all about is to compare a traditional teaching approach to an approach which keeps in mind whole-class principles. The following story illustrates these approaches in action.

A TALE OF TWO LORDS

In a faraway land in a faraway time there lived two lords, each with his own fiefdom, His Excellency Dejan and His Excellency Mejan. Now Dejan and Mejan each hoped to wed the king's daughter and ensure security and riches for their own fiefdom. The price of the bride was to make a present to the king of the best honor guard in the whole kingdom, as determined by the most successful completion of an unknown task to be assigned to all contending honor guards.

In preparation, Lord Dejan and Lord Mejan each gathered together 99 of the best soldiers in their fiefdom for training as honor guards. They determined that members of the honor guard needed three skills: marching, firing, and collecting intelligence. So, each selected 33 soldiers with strong legs, 33 with strong eyes, and 33 with strong ears.

Lord Dejan put his chief administrator in charge of the training for the soldiers in his fiefdom. The chief administrator agreed immediately; he had a number of ability and achievement tests that his staff had been developing that he would be able to use in the service of his lordship.

The chief administrator first tested all the men nominated for the honor guard on ability and found two thirds of them lacking in marching skills, two thirds lacking in firing skills, and two thirds lacking in listening skills. He immediately found three remedial instructors, one for each subject area. Soldiers with strong legs spent most of the next six months in remedial firing and remedial listening classes. They sat for most of the day, and their legs grew weak. Soldiers with strong eyes spent all day in remedial marching and listening classes. They marched to the point of fatigue, and their eyes clouded over. Soldiers with strong ears were sent to remedial marching and remedial firing classes. The noise of the weapons dulled their hearing. After six months, great progress had been made. All of the soldiers tested "average" in all skill areas on achievement tests.

The chief administrator knew that "average" would not be good enough for Lord Dejan, so he implemented a motivation program, associated with periodic progress testing. For testing, he used multiple-choice test items based on a componential analysis of each of the three skills, as well as hypothetical tasks. When soldiers assigned to a particular instructor exceeded their previous percentile scores by more than 10%, the instructor received a bonus. Soon, the instructors were familiar enough with the test items that they could begin direct instruction of the soldiers in the specifics of those items and how best to handle the test questions. The instructors initiated an incentive program for the soldiers: the higher the test score, the more privileges a soldier would receive. The scores of the soldiers began to rise dramatically, and the chief administrator was immensely pleased. When the scores reached nearly 100% for all soldiers, the instructors received a big bonus, and they were immensely pleased. The instructors handsomely rewarded the soldiers with lavish benefits for their high scores, and the soldiers were immensely pleased.

Nearly a year had passed, and the time for the competition for the king's daughter neared. Lord Dejan, assured by his chief administrator that objective test results proved that these were the very best soldiers in the entire kingdom, proudly presented his honor guard to the king for the competition. As the king prepared to reveal the unknown task to the honor guard, the soldiers looked at each other nervously, wondering if the task would match any that had been on their tests and what would happen if they failed to be the best honor guard in all the kingdom.

Now, during this same time, Lord Mejan also established a training program for his soldiers. First, he approached a retired general, who had been known for his exemplary service and multiple soldiering skills; they had been tested and honed in some very fine battles. He asked this old general to oversee the training program for the new soldiers. The general, at first, declined, "Sire, I am too old. I no longer walk well, let alone march. I no longer see well. I no longer hear well. How can I train your soldiers to be good marchers, good marksmen, and good intelligence collectors?"

Lord Mejan would not listen to the general's demurring. He replied, "You do not have to march or to walk or to see or to hear. I have 33 soldiers with the strongest legs in the kingdom; they will carry you. I have 33 soldiers with the best eyes in the kingdom; they will see for you. And I have 33 soldiers with the best ears in the kingdom; they will listen for you. You have been the best of all my soldiers. You have accomplished remarkable feats. You can share your ways of soldiering with these new soldiers. They, not you, must now do the marching, the firing, and the intelligence collection; they need you to support them in doing this the best way that they can.

And so, the old general agreed to teach the new soldiers. He knew that they would all need to be able to do all three skills well, so he organized them into groups of three. In each group there was a soldier with strong legs, a soldier with strong eyes, and a soldier with strong ears. When the soldier with strong eyes could not march well, the soldier with strong legs guided him into a marching rhythm. When the soldier with strong ears could not fire well, the soldier with strong eyes helped him aim his weapon for better marksmanship. When the soldier with strong legs could not collect data well, the soldier with strong ears showed him how to use his legs to get just close enough and positioned well to hear better.

To help the new soldiers, the old general selected the best marcher, the best marksman, and the best intelligence collector in the fiefdom and gave them roles as counselors. When individual soldiers determined that they needed extra help or simply wanted assistance, they could come to these counselors to practice under their mentorship, to receive individualized instruction, or to have questions answered. The counselors' roles were to serve as mentors and role models, as well as to foster the growth of skills and confidence in each soldier by observing how each soldier went about soldiering, making him aware of what he still needed to know (and why he needed to know it), showing him the best strategies for improving his soldiering skills, and encouraging him to take risks and to experiment with his own training program.

When all the soldiers had improved their weaker skills, the general tasked them to complete meaningful missions. Often, these missions involved going to far parts of the fiefdom where information on subjects' living conditions could be brought back to Lord Mejan. The soldiers had to march there, use marksmanship skills to forage for food, and listen well to bring back accurate intelligence to his lordship. Sometimes, when they had done this, Lord Mejan would send a detail of soldiers back to those same subjects to bring to them the supplies and assistance they needed. The soldiers felt good about this—they were helping their countrymen, and their countrymen loved them. Their confidence grew, and they became better marchers, marksmen, and intelligence collectors.

The old general sometimes went with them, and they did carry him. Sometimes, he stayed behind and allowed them to fend for themselves, debriefing them and making suggestions when they reported back to him. Sometimes, he gave them detailed instructions in advance. Other times, he simply provided general information and let them determine what they needed to do. What he gave them and asked of them depended upon what he knew they could do and where they still needed support. With time, he removed more and more of the support. With time, they stopped relying upon him and began relying upon themselves and their developing skills.

The old general did not check the soldiers' knowledge through standardized exams; instead, his observations served as informal "tests." He would have examined the soldiers objectively, had Lord Mejan required it, but then he would have used the test results only to supplement his observations. He watched the soldiers complete their missions. He listened to their descriptions. He evaluated their successes. He analyzed their failures. Where he found the soldiers lacking, he provided individual or group instruction or practice, as need dictated.

In a year, when the time for the competitions for the king's daughter neared, he approached Lord Mejan. "Are my soldiers the best in the kingdom?" asked Lord Mejan.

The old general answered his lordship, "Sire, *best* is a relative word. Those with strong legs are still the better marchers, those with strong eyes the better marksmen, and those with strong ears the better intelligence collectors, but all the soldiers possess strategies for accomplishing all these tasks both independently and as one unit. Sire, these soldiers are capable today, and they will not disappoint you. But more important, they have the knowledge and skills to become better tomorrow and even better the day after that. Your soldiers have competed not against peers but against their own potential. They have cooperated in helping each other become better. They have the thinking skills to handle both the known and the unknown and enough self-confidence to take any risk. They are ready for this competition."

Lord Mejan marched with his soldiers to the castle and presented his honor guard to the king. Standing at their head, carried there by the soldiers with the strong legs, was the old general. As the king prepared to reveal the unknown task to the honor guard, the soldiers looked at each other in anticipation, wondering what exciting challenge might lie in store for them today.

Now, I won't tell which honor guard won the competition. That is pretty clear, and if it is not, the words of Brophy and Evertson (1976) should help:

> Effective teaching is not simply a matter of implementing a small number of "basic" teaching skills. Instead, effective teaching requires the ability to implement a very large number of diagnostic, instructional, managerial, and therapeutic skills, tailoring behavior in specific contexts and situations to the specific needs of the moment. (p. 139)

TRAINING THE BEST HONOR GUARD

Teaching diagnostically, managerially, and therapeutically, whole-class teachers ignore the fads—the direct-instruction approaches of yesterday (that have not yet disappeared), the multiple-intelligences approaches of today, and the highly-touted outcomes-based approaches for tomorrow. Whole-class teachers do not seek such panaceas. They know that the magic pills offered by scripted, specific methods don't take away all the problems—in fact, most don't come close to taking away many of the problems at all.

Teaching the whole class can come much closer than magic pills to eliminating most learning problems and ensuring learning success, but a word of caution is· always in order: Commonsense should dictate how that is done. I have focused in this book on learner profiles related to various kinds of learning styles: modality preferences, personality type and temperament, and cognitive styles, with some mention of environmental preferences. At the same time I admit that physical health, home environment, peer influence, social values, and a number of nonacademic factors can also play immensely important roles in student success. Teachers should always be aware of factors external to the classroom in determining how best to teach students. Evaluating the source of difficulty, no matter where it is found, is part of that first step in teaching any member of the whole class.

With these external variables in mind, I have sympathy for high school teachers who are struggling to teach the whole class. They often inherit unsuccessful students who have found alternative avenues for success in street gangs, alcohol, and narcotics trade or who have developed plain old bad attitudes. Getting these students back on track when teachers see them for only an hour a day is a great challenge. (This statement does not dismiss the challenges that elementary school teachers and college professors have, nor does it ignore the successes that style-aware elementary school teachers achieve in changing student failure to student success in the early years. It simply admits the unique challenges that face high school teachers beyond those of elementary school teachers, who generally have students for longer periods of time, before the hormonal deluge, and before students have decided that most adults have less of value to convey to them than do their chronological peers.)

Winning the style wars or developing the best honor guard can be accomplished humanely and successfully by understanding how students learn, accepting who and where they are, leading or sending them to where they need to go, and giving them the tools and skills they need for continuing on alone. As noted in the acknowledgments to this book, this is how skilled teachers have developed skilled students for many years. This is how whole-class teachers develop whole classes of students into learners who excel (not into average students). They win the style wars through learner accommodation, and they build the best honor guards through learner empowerment. They accommodate when they teach and when they test, and they empower when they review. Whole-class teachers facilitate the learning of their students. They do not learn for them, but they support them every step of the way.

In Summary

I am very aware of the damage that has been done by the tendency today to force specific learning-styles systems on teachers in the same way that specific teaching methods historically have been forced on teachers. My first task in working with any group of teachers or administrators has often been to defuse the pain and frustration that has come from taking a magic pill and finding it a placebo. Of course, anything that is imposed on a classroom and a teacher from outside that class has little chance to help teachers teach the whole class. The "outside" has very limited understanding of this year's or this semester's "inside." This book is not about predicting the "inside." It is not about an a priori instructional design or syllabus or set of lesson plans. I don't believe that any a priori instructional design can be effective. Although it is messier, less formal, and more difficult for educational administrators to evaluate, post hoc instructional design, based on the actual students present in one-of-a-kind classrooms, is the best hope that teachers have of teaching all of their students most of the time. To do that requires instructional programs that promote teaching the whole class: accommodating learner profiles and empowering students for lifelong learning.

In fact, this book is not about implementation of any extant teaching method or technique. Most methods and most techniques work for some students some of the time and for other students none of the time. Teaching the whole class requires selecting from among the many choices of methods and techniques to match specific student needs. *This book is about giving the learning process back to those to whom it has always belonged: the learners. It is about understanding how each student learns and using that understanding to help each student learn successfully.*

Glossary

This glossary has three parts. Part 1 provides the full terms for the acronyms used in this book. Part 2 provides a definition of various terms used in this book. Part 3 shows the icons used as "trail markers."

Part 1

AR: abstract random

AS: abstract sequential

CR: concrete random

CS: concrete sequential

DISTAR: Direct Instruction System for Teaching Arithmetic and Reading

E: extravert

F: feeling type

FD: field dependent

FI: field independent

GATE: gifted and talented education

I: introvert

J: judging type

LD: learning disabled

N: intuitive

P: perceiving type

S: sensing type

T: thinking type

Part 2

abstract: conceptual, symbolic

accommodator: one who learns through trial and error and through experimentation

activated memory: memory that feeds information from permanent memory and long-term memory into short-term memory for the purposes of construction and reconstruction

affect: emotional variables

affective strategies: strategies related to how one feels and one's emotional responses

analog: metaphoric

analysis: finding details and pieces within one whole item

analytic: one who breaks wholes into parts

artisan: sensing-perceiving type

assimilator: one who learns through textbook and lecture

auditory: one who learns through audition (listening or talking)

aural: one who learns through hearing

authentic materials: in foreign language classrooms, refers to materials written by native speakers for native speakers; in other classrooms, refers to materials/activities that are not prepared specifically for the classroom: reference books, films, field trips, input from experts

bifurcated: split into two pieces

cerebral dominance (also called hemisphericity): in describing learning styles, refers to preferences for specific kinds of input and interests; right-hemisphere dominant individuals prefer gestalt, synthesis, music, and art; left-hemisphere dominant individuals prefer details, analysis, speech, and science

classification: here, finding the "umbrella" category to which an item belongs

cloze: scripts with some words removed and replaced with blanks

comparison: here, looking for similarities

concrete: hands-on, pragmatic

continuous learning styles: learning styles that do not change according to stage of memory

contract learning: 1) an independent study program, in which students contract to complete a certain amount and kind of study; 2) agreements made by teachers with students in the classroom to complete a certain amount and kind of study

contrast: looking for differences

converger: here, someone who learns by hands-on application

cooperative learning: learning together with others via active interaction in small groups

deduction: applying the rule

deductive: a learner who prefers to be presented a rule, then apply it

digital: literal (as opposed to metaphoric)

direct instruction: teaching students everything: the big picture and the application; often associated with the DISTAR method; uses a deductive approach to teaching

discontinuous learning styles: learning styles that change depending on stage of memory

diverger: here, one who learns by watching and vicarious experience

durative: applied to learning strategy training, refers to training that is regular and long-term

ectenic: the characteristic of perceiving phenomena as composites

error: in foreign language, an incorrect utterance that occurs because the speaker or the writer does not know a correct way of expressing the thought

extravert: one who gains energy through interaction with other people (spelling of the term in accordance with the Myers-Briggs Type Indicator usage)

facilitative teaching: learner-centered teaching in which the teacher assigns tasks and assists students as needed and only as needed in completing them, observing how students are learning and helping them fill cognitive gaps

field dependent: unable to separate foreground from background; context-dependent

field independent: easily separates foreground from background; context-free

four-handed dialogue: two teachers conduct an unrehearsed conversation on the topic under study, while students listen and ascertain specific information

global: someone who sees the forest, the big picture

guardian: a sensing-judger; someone who maintains and passes on social values

hemisphericity: (see cerebral dominance)

idealist: an intuitive-feeler; someone who places greatest value on relationships and the common good

imagist: a visual learner who "sees" pictures

impulsive: learns through trial and error marked by immediate response to stimuli

induction: building a rule through examples

inductive: one who builds a rule through examples

introvert: one who loses energy through interaction with other people

intuitive: one who lives for tomorrow; reacts in accordance with internal values

islands: memorized segments of discourse

kinesthesia: learning by gross motor application

kinesthetic: one who learns by using gross motor muscles

learner-centered instruction: instruction that focuses on class and individual student needs; often permits student input into course design

Kolb types: type I is a learner who needs to observe the group and experience in order to learn; type II is an abstract sequential learner, learns readily from lectures and textbooks; type III needs hands-on experiences; type IV is a highly independent learner; see also diverger (I), assimilator (II), converger (III), and accommodator (IV)

learner-focused approaches: any of the approaches that focus on the learner as the central player in instruction: facilitative instruction, learner-centered instruction, diagnostic teaching, differentiated instruction

learning style: an approach to organizing comprehension, acquisition, storage, and reconstruction of information

leveler: one who finds similarities between two items

long-term memory: memory that lasts from several minutes to several years

mainstream learning style: learning style that matches the expectations of the society in which it is found

MBTI: Meyers Briggs Type Indicator; classifies personality types in four domains (see individual listings):

> extraverted-introverted
> sensing-perceiving
> thinking-feeling
> perceiving-judging

manipulatives: physical objects used for instruction

mechanical: learns by writing

mistake: an incorrect utterance that occurs when the speaker or the writer knows the correct way of expression the thought but misspeaks or miswrites

monitor: refers to the internal "device" or process by which students pay attention to the grammatical accuracy and lexical precision of their verbal communication (especially in using foreign language)

NF (intuitive-feeler): learns through interaction with people, interested in culture

NT (intuitive-thinker): learns through interaction with ideas, interested in systems and models

oral: learns by talking

particular: pays attention to details

permanent memory: memory that lasts for the duration of one's lifetime

power test: any test that does not have a time limit and that is graded based on what students have completed (not on what they have not completed)

random: organizes in a non-linear way

rational: intuitive-thinking type

reflective: requires time to internalize and process

scaffolding: providing learning strategies or background knowledge to students to assist them in learning tasks

sensing: exists in the here and now; notices details; needs time for response; tends to work towards accuracy

sentient memory: awareness of surroundings; initial intake of information

sequential: organizes in a linear way

sharpener: finds differences between two items

short-term memory: storage area for incoming information, lasting from a few seconds to a few minutes

SJ (sensing-judging): expects organization; needs structure and deadlines

SP (sensing-perceiver): expects flexibility; needs change

speed test: any test that has a time limit in completion and that is graded based upon completion of the entire test; a timed test, in which unanswered questions are considered to be incorrect responses

style wars: (coined by Oxford, Ehrman, & Lavine, 1991) a conflict between a student's learning style and 1) his/her teacher's teaching style, 2) the orientation of textbooks and classroom materials, or 3) the learning style of his/her classmates

synoptic: the characteristic of perceiving phenomena as wholes

synthesis: finding relationships among disparate items

synthetic: builds whole from parts

trifurcated: split into three pieces

TRT: a system in which students are taught in accordance with their learning style preference, materials are reviewed in accordance with students' non-preferred learning styles, and students are tested in accordance with their preferred learning styles

verbalist: a visual learner who sees words

visual: learns by seeing

whole-class teaching: instruction that accommodates students' learning styles and empowers them to develop style flexibility

word attack: breaking words into their components (roots, stems, etc.) in order to understand their meaning

Part 3

Icons

Cognitive Styles

Personality Types

Sensory Modalities

Resource A
Learning-Styles Tests

The list below describes some of the more widely used learning-styles instruments. The list is far from exhaustive but should provide readers with some choice in testing for environmental preferences, sensory modalities, cognitive styles, and personality type.

AMERICAN GLOBAL STUDIES LEARNING STYLES ASSESSMENT TEST (ALSAT)

The ALSAT is a self-scoring, computerized test that measures the following cognitive styles: random, sequential, concrete, abstract, impulsive, reflective, global, analytic. It also measures sensory preferences: visual-imagist, visual-verbalist, motor-kinesthetic, motor-mechanical, auditory-oral, auditory-aural. It is the only test that breaks the sensory preferences into component parts (imagist, verbalist, etc.). The test is being validated; for now, it should be considered unvalidated. It can be obtained from the American Global Studies Institute Press, 14 Spreckels Lane, Salinas, CA 93908. In cases where teachers are willing to assist with validation, copies of the test may be made available free of charge.

THE BARSCH LEARNING STYLES PREFERENCE FORM

Developed by Jeffrey Barsch, this test measures modality preferences: visual, kinesthetic, and auditory. It does not further break down the modalities into the various types: verbalist, imagist, and so on. As a first step to determine general preferences in modality, it can be used by teachers who are not yet ready to identify students through personal observation. The test is in the public domain, is used widely in California community colleges, and can be obtained from its author at Ventura Community College, Ventura, CA.

COGNITIVE PROFILE

This profile examines seven cognitive domains: reflective-impulsive, analytical-global, focus-nonfocus, complex-simple, narrow-broad, sharpener-leveler, tolerant of ambiguity-intolerant of ambiguity. The reader should be aware that Letteri makes value judgments about these styles, with the first of the two components of each dimension being considered a good style and the second not a good style. By good style, he simply means useful for most traditional school learning. He is one of the only researchers in learning-style theory who attaches value judgments to learner variables. This test, as far as I know, is in unpublished form. I refer readers to Dr. Letteri, School of Education, University of Vermont, Burlington, VT.

DUNN AND DUNN

This test measures the environmental preferences. Since the publication of the original test, Dunn and Dunn have added one cognitive dimension: right-brain/left-brain differences. A version of the test was published in Dunn and Dunn (1978).

HERMANN PARTICIPANT SURVEY

This is a longer brain hemisphericity test (machine scorable) than the Torrance test described below (Your Style of Learning of Thinking). It is fairly expensive, and there is a requirement to become trained in the Hermann system of evaluating brain hemisphericity. More information can be obtained from The Whole Brain Corporation, Lake Lure, North Carolina.

HIDDEN FIGURES TEST

This variant of the embedded figures test is well-known in the academic community, and some version of it has been used for more than three decades. The test measures spatial forms of field dependence and field independence. It is available from Educational Testing Services, Princeton, New Jersey. There is a small charge for using it.

ILLINOIS TEST OF PSYCHOLINGUISTIC ABILITY (ITPA)

The ITPA is more than a learning-styles test, but it does contain learning-styles elements. It tests auditory reception, visual reception, visual sequential memory, auditory association, auditory sequential memory, visual association, visual closure, verbal expression (encoding), grammatical closure, manual expression, auditory closure, and sound blending. The ITPA may be obtained from the University of Illinois Press in Urbana.

INFORMATION ACQUISITION PREFERENCE INVENTORY (GREGORC)

Developed by Anthony Gregorc, this test is a short instrument that determines the following styles: abstract-sequential, abstract-random, concrete-sequential, concrete-random. The test was published in Kolb, Irwin, and McIntyre (1971).

KEIRSEY TYPE SORTER

This instrument tests both personality types and temperaments. The test is available on paper in Keirsey and Bates's (1988) book, *Please Understand Me*. It is also available on self-scoring disk. Both book and disk may be purchased from Prometheus-Nemesis Book Company, P. O. Box 2748, Del Mar, CA 92014.

LEARNING AND STUDIES STRATEGIES INVENTORY (LASSI)

The Learning and Studies Strategies Inventory (LASSI) comes in two versions: paper and electronic, or computer-based. The computer-based version is called the E-LASSI. The LASSI assesses the use of learning and studies strategies. It is diagnostic and prescriptive and focuses on both overt and covert strategies from each of the learning strategies categories discussed in Chapter 6 (metacognitive, cognitive, social, and affective). It also includes traditional study skills questions. The domains include attitude, motivation, time management, anxiety, concentration, information processing, selecting main ideas, study aids, self-testing, and test strategies. Published in 1988, the E-LASSI is available from H&H Publishing Company, 1231 Kapp Drive, Clearwater, FL 34625.

LEARNING STYLE PROFILE

The Learning Style Profile was developed as a joint effort of the National Association of Secondary School Principals (NASSP), a task force of experts, three universities, and a large number of participating schools. Of the styles inventories available for K-12, it is one of the best researched and most comprehensive. It assesses a composite of styles, strategies, and skills, including 23 learner characteristics, the more important of which include: analytic skill, spatial skill, discrimination skill, categorizing skill, sequential processing skill, memory skill, verbal-spatial preference, perceptual response (visual, auditory, and emotive), persistence orientation, mobility preference, posture preference, sound preference, lighting preference, temperature preference, study time preference, verbal risk orientation, manipulative preference, and grouping preference. Although it is more appropriate for K-12 students, it could be used at the junior college or even university level for some purposes. The test may be obtained from NASSP, 1904 Association Drive, Reston, VA 22091.

LEARNING STYLES INVENTORY (LSI)

The LSI, developed by David Kolb, is based on four stages of the learning cycle: concrete experience, reflective observation, abstract conceptualization, and active experimentation. The LSI produces information about four types of learners: divergers, assimilators, convergers, and accommodators. The test is available from McBer and Company, 137 Newbury Street, Boston, MA 02116, telephone (617) 437-7080.

MYERS-BRIGGS TYPE INDICATOR (MBTI)

The MBTI is one of the best-known of the personality types tests. It tests the personality type variables discussed throughout this book. Validation statistics are overwhelming in their copiousness. The MBTI must be administered by a certified MBTI specialist, but the actual test cost is low. The test is machine-scorable, and results come with an interpretation. More information on the MBTI can be obtained from Consulting Psychologists Press in Palo Alto, California.

PERSONALITY RESEARCH FORM

Developed in 1974 by Jackson, the most interesting aspect for those involved in learning styles should be the Impulsivity Scale, designed to measure differences between impulsive and reflective learners. It was published by Research Psychologists' Press in Goshen, New York and may be available from local libraries.

PROBLEM INTEGRATION STRATEGY TEST

Developed by Allen Weinstein, this is the only test I know that assesses sequential and random learning styles separately from other domains. It is an unpublished test, and the only place it is available is in the appendix to the book, *Understanding Second Language Learning Difficulties*, by Madeline Ehrman. The book is available through Sage Publications, Inc., 2455 Teller Road, Thousand Oaks, California 91320-2218.

READING STYLE INVENTORY

Developed by Carbo, this instrument assesses many of the same dimensions as the Dunn and Dunn instrument, but it focuses exclusively on reading. It is a questionnaire. Dimensions involve mostly the environmental preferences and sensory modalities. The Reading Style Inventory is published by the National Reading Styles Institute, P. O. Box 737, Syosset, NY 11791.

YOUR STYLE OF LEARNING AND THINKING (SOLAT)

The SOLAT was designed by Paul Torrance. The Torrance test looks at three kinds of brain hemisphericity: right-brain dominance, left-brain dominance, and integrated dominance. A copy of this test appeared in Torrance, Reynolds, Riegel, and Ball (1977).

Resource B
Check Lists

The following charts may assist in determining the learning preferences of individual students. To use them, select the desired domain(s), then check off the blocks that illustrate the behavior(s) of the student(s) in question. Because students rarely possess purely one style, the dominant style will be evident from the spread of check marks, as will any deviations from the dominant style. A class profile can be prepared by filling in the number of students falling into each block on the charts.

These charts are not intended as alternatives to validated learning styles instruments. They are simply guides to ways in which students can be observed and a means to develop awareness and intuitions about learner profiles. They are "scaffolding" to help with observation tasks initially. With experience, this scaffolding should become dispensable and the observer fully independent.

As an intuitive learner, I naturally trust the results of observation and intuition over empirical results, but I realize that the sensing readers of this book will invariably be drawn to test results. Based on fifteen years of using both observation and testing, during which good observers have routinely provided more accurate assessments than has instrumentation, I suggest to my sensing colleagues, as well as my intuitive colleagues who have been swayed by today's push to quantify absolutely everything, that they consider at least trying it both ways and that in all cases where they choose instrumentation that they interview students to confirm the accuracy of the instrument's results before establishing a lesson plan that teaches the whole class. (It is somewhat difficult to teach the whole class effectively, if some members of the class are incorrectly profiled.)

Readers will note that the personality types and temperaments are not included here. This is because the extant tests are valid, reliable, readily available, and inexpensive. Further, Keirsey and Bates (1988) include descriptions that can be used as charts similar to the ones I have presented on the next pages for sensory preferences and cognitive styles.

SENSORY PREFERENCES

	Visual	Auditory	Motor
what they say or write	following verbal explanation: "What are we supposed to do?" "Would you spell that?" (verbalist) "Would you write it down?" (verbalist) use visually descriptive words: colors, details use words related to vision: see, view, appear ask for repeat of oral information	following visual explanation or demonstration: "What are we supposed to do?" "Would you repeat that?" "How do you pronounce that?" use words related to sounds: hear, quiet whisper to get help from others "May I tape the lecture?"	following verbal explanation: "What are we supposed to do?" "Would you spell that?" (mechanical) use action words and verbs (kinesthetic) use limited number of adjectives (kinesthetic) ask for repeat of oral information "May I try?"
what is difficult for them	lack of visual support for lectures removing scripts that have become crutches	visual and mechanical work remaining quiet independent reading	visual and verbal explanations sitting still reading silently in their seats
what they do	read while teacher is talking (verbalist) look at pictures while teacher is talking (imagist) write down everything (verbalist) doodle like demonstrations copy words from text ask for repeats of materials presented orally read voraciously	talk aloud (oral) whisper to peers (oral) use computer sound options (auditory) subvocalize read aloud rarely need repeats of material presented orally	squirm (kinesthetic) body action (kinesthetic) drop writing implements (kinesthetic) write down everything (mechanical) walk away occasionally (kinesthetic) choose computer learning when available copy words from text (mechanical)
where they excel	spelling (verbal) reading tasks	oral reports listening tasks	spelling (mechanical) performance tasks

COGNITIVE STYLES: IMPULSIVE/REFLECTIVE

	Impulsive	Reflective
what they say or write	"hurry up" quick speech	"let me think" tempered speech
what is difficult for them	careless mistakes sloppy, scribbled work	giving superficial answers meeting short time lines
what they do	quick response interrupt finish tests quickly display impatience with programmed learning	tempered response pause before responding check their work partial completion of timed tests patient with programmed learning
where they excel	finishing tests and projects quickly fluidity of thought	accuracy complexity of thought

COGNITIVE STYLES: GLOBAL/PARTICULAR

	Global	Particular
what they say or write	"in sum" "What's the main idea?"	precision in speech and writing
what is difficult for them	work lacks detail propositions are unsupported make wild guesses malapropisms abound display simple grammatical inaccuracy in native speech and in writing make careless errors in spelling	miss the main idea provide too many details provide unconnected details can't always find the "big picture" among the details
what they do	base conjecture on background knowledge repeat larger pieces of information but with inaccuracy in specific information read and use context	base conjecture on details presented repeat small pieces of information (e.g., language laboratory work) look up words in the dictionary write native-language translation above foreign words
where they excel	working without instructions developing new ways to organize fluency (ESL/foreign language) concepts (math) trends (social sciences) essay tests	precision grammar (ESL/foreign language) calculations (math) dates and events (social sciences) multiple choice tests

COGNITIVE STYLES: LEVELER/SHARPENER

	Leveler	Sharpener
what they say or write	talk in terms of categories: "I see fruit."	talk in specifics: "I see apples."
	talk about patterns, trends, common elements	talk about specifics and differences
	approximate speech	precise speech
	shorter compositions	longer compositions
	generalize	specialize
what is difficult for them	analogies	finding relationships
	finding differences	finding patterns
what they do	find similarities	find differences
where they excel	tasks that require them to find relationships, comparisons, trends	tasks that require them to contrast
	making connections among disparate topics	math calculations and word problems

COGNITIVE STYLES: SYNTHETIC/ANALYTIC

	Synthetic	Analytic
what they say or write	"If you combine..."	"If you break this into pieces..."
	"If you put X+Y together..."	"If you analyze..."
what is difficult for them	miss authorial intent in reading	difficulty reshaping ideas
	add information that was not given and think it was given	difficulty in developing something unique from traditional information
	miss information necessary for renarration	
what they do	use computer programs in new way	use computer programs as prescribed
	create new things	take things apart
	construct	reconstruct
where they excel	invention	description and explanation
	creative assignments	critical analysis

COGNITVE STYLES: INDUCTIVE/DEDUCTIVE

	Inductive	Deductive
what they say or write	ask for examples talk about patterns	ask for rules ask for explanations
what is difficult for them	tend to overgeneralize sometimes make incorrect hypotheses	misunderstanding of the rules incorrect applications of rules
what they do	guess from context use insight	look new words up in dictionary use logic
where they excel	discovering rules developing new approaches	applying rules applying traditional approaches

COGNITIVE STYLES: KOLB TYPES

	Type I	Type II	Type III	Type IV
what they say or write	"Why is it important?" "Show me." "Why does it work this way?"	"What do I need to know for the test?" "What is this all about?"	"How do I go about doing this?" "What is the next step?" "Would you draw that?" "Is there an illustration?"	"What if I do it another way?" "Why could it not work another way?" "I want to do it myself." "my opinion" "How else might this be used?"
what is difficult for them	sequencing errors difficulties in one-on-one situations	don't take risks, even when important dislike hands-on applications	difficulties with abstractions difficulties with developing and understanding metaphoric thought	not a good listener, unless planning to use the ideas many errors while learning; error as a learning device
what they do	watch others watch media avoid reading seek group interaction	obtain explanation, then practice read for information, explanation, theory seek tutoring arrangements for greater depth	seek meaningful application try things out read for instruction, facts, examples seek tutoring arrangements for hands-on assistance	experiment create new things read for new ideas, hypothesis confirmation select own readings seek independence play hooky, cut class
where they excel	art reviews group work	critical essays tests rote work	instruction manuals projects	original works experiments unique soultions and creations

COGNITIVE STYLES: CONCRETE/ABSTRACT

	Concrete	Abstract
what they say or write	use real-life examples use actual materials ask for applications	talk and write about concepts use symbols ask for explanations
what is difficult for them	misunderstand symbols theoretical misunderstandings	application of symbols to real activities is difficult
what they do	put things into context try things out to learn explicate applications and examples	extrapolate from context read books and textbooks to learn explicate ideas
where they excel	working without instructions developing new ways to organize	careful organization that others understand precision

COGNITIVE STYLES: RANDOM/SEQUENTIAL

	Random	Sequential
what they say or write	don't ask order or organization questions "What does the end product look like?" "Is there a picture or description?"	use order words (first, second) use organizational words (before, next) "What comes first?" "Where are the instructions?"
what is difficult for them	traditional sequence chronology, steps outlining organizing in expected ways	confusion in absence of external sequence difficulties with nonhierarchical organization
what they do	provide unique organization work from key concepts, words test questions answered out of sequence	apply traditional organization outline answer test questions in sequence
where they excel	working without instructions developing new ways to organize	careful organization that others understand precision

Always question the motivation behind the behavior. Things are often not what they seem to be!

Resource C
Answers to Practice Exercises

CHAPTER 3

1. The profiles for Shawn and Shane are as follows:

Shawn	Shane
impulsive	reflective
global	particular
synthetic	analytic
visual imagist	visual verbalist
accommodator	assimilator
leveler	sharpener

2-3. These responses will vary. As a guide, use the chart above for Shawn and Shane and think about the types of activities discussed in "When Twins Aren't Twins." This should help identify some of the styles. The observation checklists in Resource B might also help.

4. Although information is somewhat limited, there are some "guesses" that can be made fairly confidently about each student's style. These guesses are a starting point. The next step would be to confirm the accuracy of the guess before planning any instruction based on learning styles. Confirmation can be made through further observation, interviews with the students, and specific tasks that require students to work in one style or another (there the accomplishment of the work will make it clear with which style the student is most comfortable).

    a. The first attribute to check out is whether student A is an inductive learner. The differences between quiz and test grades might result from the student having the time to work on the material at home with an inductive approach. (We do not know how the material is being presented in the classroom. The assumption is that the material is being presented in a traditional, deductive fashion.)

    b. Perhaps student B is a sharpener and a particular learner. He works in concrete ways, proposing emendations of actual laws. Perhaps he is also a concrete-sequential and/or a converger. His strategy—memorization—is not in keeping with his learner profile, especially the converger domain.

c. Student C is likely a particular learner. She is lost in the trees and cannot find the forest.

d. Student D is likely a sharpener or a particular student.

e. Student E is likely either a mechanical or a visual learner. Further information is needed to make that determination. He may be copying the information because the feel of the words as he writes them helps him to remember them. On the other hand, he may be copying them so that he can review them by reading them later.

f. Student F may be an assimilator or abstract-sequential learner and likely a visual learner as well. As such, it is difficult for him to hold long pieces of aural information in his head at one time. If he is also visual, this compounds the difficulty.

g. Student G is probably analytic, perhaps particular.

h. Student H might be an introvert.

Chapter 4

1-2. These responses will vary. Look for the typical conflicts: a family of Js that tries to organize the one P, an NT with SJ parents (they expect the NT to obey their authority, and the NT does not consider the parents to have much authority), etc.

3. There is enough information to make some initial hypotheses about these students. Further investigation will be required to confirm the hypotheses.

a. This student apparently operates from two modalities: visual and auditory. Which is primary and which is secondary is not clear. It is likely that the conflict between teacher and student is in the cognitive dimension and likely in the concrete-abstract domain.

b. The conflict here is likely in the synthetic-analytic domain. The student wants to create his own world; the teacher wants him to translate someone else's world.

c. This student is clearly impulsive. Because we do not know the teacher's style in this domain, we do not know whether there is a conflict here. Apparently, the teacher uses small-group work. The student would appear to be concrete-sequential. The need for one-on-one work and for practical application would indicate that. The teacher, being abstract, is likely not to give enough practice in application for this student.

d. This student may be an SFJ. The need for guidelines seem to suggest the SJ temperament, and the need for emotional appeal suggests the F. It is a little odd that an SJ teacher is not providing enough structure for this SJ learner; this is something that would need to be explored further. The T-F conflict is fairly obvious.

e. This student may be an accommodator. The existence of only one right answer would frustrate an accommodator, who can find multiple answers to any question. Applied activities interest the student, and the student is clearly self-directed. The conflict is likely in the AS-CR domain. The concrete-random/accommodator will want much more autonomy than an SJ abstract-sequential/assimilator is likely to allow.

    f. This is likely a concrete learner. He or she is not interested in practicing the grammar—answering "where" questions when the content of the answer is obvious. The student wants abstract practice sessions to be more connected with real life. That is, the student is asking for more concretization in classroom activities. The teacher, as we know, is abstract. The conflict is likely in the abstract-concrete domain.

4. This answer will vary. You might test your conjecture through a discussion with the student selected.

CHAPTER 5

1-3. These answers will depend on your own Kolb type.

4. This answer will vary depending upon your personality type and the learning styles of the students in a particular class.

5. This answer will depend on the student you select.

CHAPTER 6

1-2. These lesson plans will vary by class. The key to a good learning-styles awareness plan is to define the strategies required by the materials and tasks to be used in the classroom and determine which of those strategies are lacking among the students. Then the generic training plan presented in Chapter 6 can be applied.

3. This answer will vary, depending on the strategies you selected.

4. These students will need to use an inductive learning style, Therefore, they will need help with hypothesis formation and confirmation, as a minimum.

5. They will need sequencing and visualization strategies.

6. They will need strategies related to reading and sequencing, as well as ways in which to concretize the abstractions that they find in the textbook.

CHAPTER 7

1. For each class, suggestions are provided below. As in any complex situation—and all classroom situations are complex—there can be many "right" answers. To determine the applicability of the answer, the teacher would have to be teaching this particular class and try out the answer. If the response is not as anticipated, then the answer can be adjusted.

    a. In this class, the teacher and the materials have the same styles. They match half the class. The class profile is somewhat analytic and particular. Otherwise, there is a pretty even mixture of styles. With such an even split of styles among the students in the class, this teacher might best work in a way that was *not* recommended in the chapter: by giving everyone a little of everything. It is not a perfect solution but given the composition of this class, it may be the best solution available.

b. The class profile is abstract, sequential, reflective, left-hemisphere preferent, and deductive. This group does not match either teacher or materials. If the teacher wishes not to lose the majority of students in this class, he or she will need to teach out of style much of the time. However, there is a large subgroup that matches the style of the teacher and materials. The teacher will do well to ensure that this group does not get treated as the class profile. Setting up small group instruction will help, given the size of the subgroup. Some strategy training is also advisable for both groups of students.

2. Lisa may have a slightly easier time in class #1 than in class #2. In class #1, the teacher will probably end up accommodating all kinds of learners because of the balance in the class. In class #2, the teacher will be teaching to the majority of students, who do not share Lisa's styles. Therefore, the work in this class may be more of a stretch for Lisa, unless she spends time with the subgroup, assuming that the styles of the subgroup will be accommodated.

3. The answer will vary, depending upon your own profile. Follow the procedures for analysis that were presented in Chapter 7.

4. Here is the pudding in which you will find your proof. Follow the steps outlined in Chapter 7, and you should be able to begin to implement the concepts underlying whole-class teaching.

References

Aliev, N. N., & Leaver, B. L. (1993). A new age in two lands: The individual and individualism in foreign language instruction. In N. N. Aliev & B. L. Leaver (Eds.), *Learner-centered instruction* (pp. 1-14). Salinas, CA: AGSI Press.

Anderson, J. R. (1981). *Cognitive skills and their acquisition.* Hillsdale, NJ: Lawrence Erlbaum.

Anderson, J. R. (1985). *Language, memory, and thought.* Hillsdale, NJ: Lawrence Erlbaum.

Asher, J. (1988). *Learning another language through actions: The complete teacher's guidebook.* Los Gatos, CA: Sky Oaks Productions.

Ausubel, D. P. (1960). The use of advance organizers in the learning and retention of meaningful verbal material. *Journal of Educational Psychology, 51,* 267-272.

Bandler, R. (1985). *Using your brain—For a change: Neurolinguistic programming.* Moab, UT: Real People Press.

Bastick, T. (1982). *Intuition: How we think and act.* New York: John Wiley.

Beadle, M. (1970). *A child's mind.* Garden City, NY: Doubleday.

Bickley, V. (Ed.). (1989). *Language teaching and learning styles within and across cultures.* Hong Kong: Institute of Language in Education.

Bideaud, J., and Houdé, O. (1991). *Cognition et développement: Boîte à outils théoriques* [Cognition and development: Theoretical tool-box]. Berne: Peter Lang.

Binet, A. (1980). *The development of intelligence in children.* Nashville, TN: William's Printing Company.

Blackburn, J. E. (1976). *One at a time all at once: The creative teacher's guide to individualized instruction without anarchy.* Pacific Palisades, CA: Goodyear.

Block, J. H. (1971). Introduction to mastery learning: Theory and practice. In J. H. Block (Ed.), *Mastery learning: Theory and practice* (pp. 2-12). New York: Holt, Rinehart & Winston.

Bloom, B. S. (1968). Learning for mastery. *UCLA-CSEIP Evaluation Comment* [Monograph].

Bloom, B. S. (1971). Affective consequences of school achievement. In J. H. Block (Ed.), *Mastery learning: Theory and practice* (pp. 13-28). New York: Holt, Rinehart & Winston.

Bodell, H. (1994). *Goals 2000: A national framework for America's schools.* Arlington, VA: Educational Funding Research Council.

Bogen, J. E. (1975). The other side of the brain, VII: Some educational aspects of hemispheric specialization. *UCLA Educator, 17,* 24-32.

Borgen, W. A., & Rudner, H. L. (1981). *Psychoeducation for children: Theory, programs, and research.* Springfield, IL: Charles C Thomas.

Boykin, A. W. (1983). The academic performance of Afro-American children. In J. T. Spence (Ed.), *Achievement and achievement motives: Psychological and sociological approaches* (pp. 321-371). San Francisco: Freeman.

Briggs-Myers, I. (1980). *Introduction to type.* Palo Alto, CA: Consulting Psychologists Press.

Brophy, J. E., & Evertson, C. M. (1976). *Learning from teaching: A developmental perspective.* Boston: Allyn & Bacon.

Bruffee, K. A. (1993). *Collaborative learning: Higher education, interdependence, and the authority of knowledge.* Baltimore, MD: Johns Hopkins University Press.

Bruner, J. S. (1963). *The process of education.* New York: Random House.

Cafferty, E. (1980). *An analysis of student performance based upon the degree of match between the educational cognitive style of the teachers and the educational cognitive style of the students.* Unpublished doctoral dissertation, University of Nebraska, Lincoln.

Calvin, W. H., & Ojemann, G. A. (1994). *Conversations with Neil's brain.* Reading, MA: Addison-Wesley.

Carbo, M. (1997). Reading styles times twenty. *Educational Leadership, 54,* 38-42.

Carroll, J. B. (1993). *Human cognitive abilities: A survey of factor-analytic studies.* Cambridge, UK: Cambridge University Press.

Chapelle, C. A. (1983). *The relationship between ambiguity tolerance and success in acquiring English as a second language in adult learners.* Unpublished doctoral dissertation, University of Illinois, Champaign-Urbana.

Claxton, C. S. & Murrell, P. (1987). *Learning styles: Implications for improving educational practices.* College Station, TX: Association for the Study of Higher Education.

Connor, R. (1976). *Relationships between conceptual styles of middle school pupils and their success with individually managing learning activities.* Unpublished doctoral dissertation, University of Pittsburgh.

Cooper, L. A. (1994). Probing the nature of the mental representation of visual objects: Evidence from cognitive dissociations. In S. Ballesteros (Ed.), *Cognitive approaches to human perception* (pp. 199-221). Hillsdale, N.J: Lawrence Erlbaum.

Cornett, C. E. (1983). *What you should know about teaching and learning styles.* Bloomington, IN: Phi Delta Kappa Educational Foundation.

Covey, S. R. (1990). *The seven habits of highly effective people: Restoring the character ethic.* New York: Simon & Schuster.

Dallman, M. (1971). *Teaching the language arts in the elementary school.* Dubuque, IA: William C. Brown.

Damasio, A. (1989). Time-locked multiregional retroactivation: A systems-level proposal for the neural substrates of recall and recognition. *Cognition, 33,* 25-62.

Damasio, A., Damasio, H. Tranel, D., & Brandt, J. (1990). Neural regionalization of knowledge access: Preliminary evidence. *Cold Spring Harbor Symposia on Quantitative Biology , 55,* 1039-1047.

Damasio, A., & Tranel, D. (1993). Nouns and verbs are retrieved with differently distributed neural systems. *Proceedings of the National Academy of Sciences (U.S.A.), 90,* 4757-4760.

Dilts, R. B. (1979). *Neuro-linguistic programming I.* Cupertino, CA: Meta Publications.

Druckman, D., & Bjork, R. A. (1994). *Learning, remembering, believing: Enhancing human performance.* Washington, DC: National Academy Press.

Dunn, R. (1988). *Quiet revolution in American secondary schools.* Reston, VA: National Association of Secondary School Principals.

Dunn, R. (1992). *Teaching elementary students through their individual learning styles: Practical approaches for grades 3-6.* Boston: Allyn & Bacon.

Dunn, R. (1993). *Teaching secondary students through their individual learning styles: Practical approaches for grades 7-10.* Boston: Allyn & Bacon.

Dunn, R. (1996). *How to implement and supervise a learning styles program.* Alexandria, VA: Association for Curriculum and Development.

Dunn, R., Beaudry, J. S., & Klavas, A. (1989). Survey of research on learning styles. *Educational Leadership ,46,* 50-58.

Dunn, R., & Dunn, K. (1972). *Practical approaches to individualizing instruction: Contracts and other effective teaching strategies.* West Nyack: NY: Parker.

Dunn, R S., & Dunn, K. (1978). *Teaching students through their individual learning styles.* Englewood Cliffs, N.J: Prentice Hall.

Dunn, R. S., Dunn, K., & Pizzo, J. (1990). A sound approach to improving reading: Responding to students' learning styles. *Journal of Reading, Writing, and Learning Disabilities International, 6,*(3), 249-260.

Dunn, R. S., & Griggs, S. A. (1995). *Multiculturalism and learning style: Teaching and counseling adolescents.* Westport, CT: Praeger.

Ehrman, M. E. (1989). *Ants and grasshoppers, badgers and butterflies: Qualitative and quantitative investigation of adult language learning styles and strategies.* Ann Arbor, MI: University Microfilms International.

Ehrman, M. E. (1996). *Understanding second language learning difficulties.* Thousand Oaks, CA: Sage.

Ehrman, M. E., & Leaver, B. L. (1997, March). *Sorting out global and analytic functions in second language learning.* Paper presented at the annual meeting of the American Association of Applied Linguists, Orlando, FL.

Ehrman, M. E., & Oxford, R. (1990). Effects of sex differences, career category, and psychological type on adult language learning strategies. *Modern Language Journal 73,* 1-3.

Englemann, S., & Bruner, E. (1968). *DISTAR reading level I*. Chicago: Science Research Associates.

Entwhistle, N. J. (1981). *Styles of learning and teaching: An integrated outline of educational psychology for students, teachers, and lecturers*. New York: John Wiley.

Eysenck, M. W. (1974). Extraversion, arousal, and retrieval from semantic memory. *Journal of Personality 42*,319-331.

Feuerstein, R. (1972). Alleviation of retarded performance. In H. P. David (Ed.), *Child Mental Health in International Perspective* (pp. 185-201). New York: Harper & Row.

Flynn, J. R. (1991). *Asian Americans: Achievement beyond IQ*. Hillsdale, NJ: Lawrence Erlbaum.

Froumina, Y., & Khasan, B. (1994). *Attitudinal, learning style, and gender influences on language learning strategy selection in Siberian students of English: Implications of tolerance-conflict, global-analytic, and male-female differences*. Unpublished manuscript.

Gabala, P. M., & Lange, D. L. (1997). Multiple intelligences: Multiple ways to help students learn foreign languages. *Northeast Conference Newsletter, 41*, 29-34.

Gardner, H. (1983). *Frames of mind: The theory of multiple intelligences*. New York: Basic Books.

Gardner, H. (1991). *The unschooled mind: How children think and how schools should teach them*. New York: Basic Books.

Gardner, H. (1993). *Multiple intelligences: The theory in practice: A reader*. New York: Basic Books.

Gary, A. L., & Glover, J. (1976). *Eye color, sex, and children's behavior*. Chicago: Nelson-Hall.

Goertzel, B. (1993). *The structure of intelligence: A new mathematical model of mind*. New York: Springer-Verlag.

Golub, J. (1988). *Focus on collaborative learning*. Urbana, IL: National Council of Teachers of English.

Goroshko, N., & Slutsky, L. (1993). Four-handed teaching. *Dialogue on Language Instruction 9*,49-53.

Gould, S. J. (1981). *The mismeasure of man*. New York: Morton.

Gregorc, A. (1982). Learning style/brain research: Harbinger of an emerging psychology. In J. Keefe (Ed.), *Student learning styles and brain behavior*. Reston, VA: National Association of Secondary School Principals.

Griggs, S. A. (1985). *Counseling students through their individual learning styles*. Ann Arbor, MI: ERIC Counseling and Personnel Services Clearinghouse.

Guilford, J. P. (1956). The structure of intellect. *Psychological Bulletin, 53*,167-193.

Guilford, J. P. (1959). Traits of creativity. In H. H. Anderson (Ed.), *Creativity and its cultivation* (pp. 142-161). New York: Harper & Row.

Guilford, J. P., & Hoepfner, R. (1971). *The analysis of intelligence*. New York: McGraw-Hill.

Halford, G. S., Smith, S. B., Dickson, J. C., Mayberry, M. T., Kelly, M.. E., Bain, J. D., & Stewart, J.E.M. (1995). Modeling the development of reasoning strategies: The roles of analogy, knowledge, and capacity. In T. Simon & G. S. Halford (Eds.), *Developing cognitive competence* (pp. 77-156). Hillsdale, NJ: Lawrence Erlbaum.

Hamilton, V. L., Blumenfeld, P. C., Akoh, H., & Miura, K. (1989). Japanese and American children's reasons for the things they do in school. *American Educational Research Journal, 26*, 545-71.

Hamm, M., & Adams, D. (1992). *The collaborative dimensions of learning.* Norwood, NJ: Ablex.

Hashway, R. (1992). *Cognitive styles: A Primer to the literature.* San Francisco: EM Text.

Hatch, T. (1997). Getting specific about multiple intelligences. *Educational Leadership, 54*, 26-29.

Hermann, N. (1983). Whole brain teaching and learning. *College Industry Education Conference Proceedings,* 188-190.

Hermann, N. (1984). *Hermann participant survey.* Lake Lure, NC: The Whole Brain Corporation.

Hermann, N. (1984). *Hermann participant survey.* Lake Lure, NC: The Whole Brain Corporation.

Hicks, C. (1980). The ITPA visual sequential memory task: An alternative interpretation and the implications for good and poor readers. *British Journal of Educational Psychology, 50*, 16-25.

Hill, P. J. (1986). *Teaching, learning, and communication.* Dover, NH: Croom Helm.

Hodgin, J., & Wooliscroft, C. (1997). Eric learns to read: Learning styles at work. *Educational Leadership, 54,* 43-45.

Holt, J. (1989). *Learning all the time.* Reading, MA: Addison-Wesley.

Holzman, P., & Gardner, R. (1959). Leveling and repression. *Journal of Abnormal Social Psychology, 59*, 151-155.

Hoskins, B. B. (1979). *A study of hypothesis testing behavior in language disordered children.* Unpublished doctoral dissertation, Northwestern University, Evanston, IL.

Huber, T., & Prewardy, C. (1990). *Maximizing learning for all students: Review of literature on learning modalities, cognitive styles, and approaches to meeting the needs of diverse learners.* Norman, OK: Wichita State University Press.

Itsines, N. (1996). *The life and work of Hippocrates.* Unpublished manuscript.

Jackson, D. N.. (1974). *Personality Research Form, manual.* Goshen, NY: Research Psychologists Press.

Jacobson, S. (1983). *Meta-cation: Prescriptions for some ailing educational processes.* Cupertino, CA: Meta Publications.

Jarsonbeck, S. (1984). *The effects of a right-brain mathematics curriculum on low achieving fourth grade students.* Unpublished doctoral dissertation, University of South Florida, Tampa.

Jenkins, J. (1989-1990). *Learning style profile handbook.* Reston, VA: National Association of Secondary School Principals.

Johnson, D. W., Johnson, R. T., & Smith, K. A. (1991). *Cooperative learning: increasing college faculty instructional productivity.* Washington, DC: George Washington University Press.

Joyce, B. R., & Weil, M. (1972). *Models of teaching.* Englewood Cliffs, NJ: Prentice-Hall.

Jung, C. G. (1971). *Psychological types.* Princeton, NJ: Princeton University Press.

Kagan S., Zahn, L. G., Widaman, K. F., Schwarzwald, J., & Tyrrell, G. (1985). Classroom structural bias: Impact of cooperative and competitive classroom structures on cooperative and competitive individuals and groups. In R. Slavin, S. Sharan, S. Kagan, R. H. Lazarowitz, C. Webb, & R. Schmuck (Eds.), *Learning to cooperate, cooperating to learn* (pp. 277-312). New York: Plenum.

Kaplan, S. N. Kaplan, J.A.B., Madsen, S. K., & Taylor, B. K. (1973). *Change for children: Ideas and activities for individualizing learning.* Pacific Palisades, CA: Goodyear.

Keefe, J. W. (1979). *Student learning styles.* Reston, VA: National Association of Secondary School Principals.

Keefe, J. W., & Monk, J. S., with Letteri, C. A., Languis, M., & Dunn, R. (1989). *Learning style profile.* Reston, VA: National Association of Secondary School Principals.

Keirsey, D., & Bates, M. (1988). *Please understand me.* Del Mar, CA: Prometheus.

Keirsey, D., & Bates, M. (1990). *Versteh mich, bitte.* [Please understand me]. Del Mar, CA: Prometheus.

Kempwirth, T., & MacKenzie, K. (1989). Modality preference in word learning: The predictive ability of the SWMI and ITPA. *Educational Research Quarterly, 13,* 18-25.

Keogh, B. K., & Donlan, McG. (1972). Field dependence, impulsivity, and learning disabilities. *Journal of Learning Disabilities, 5,* 331-336.

Kiernan, C., Ed. (1979). *Student learning styles: Diagnosis and prescribing programs.* Reston, VA: National Association of Secondary School Principals.

Kolb, D. (1984). *Experiential learning: Experience as the source of learning and development.* Englewood Cliffs, NJ: Prentice Hall.

Kolb, D. (1985). *Learning-style inventory.* Boston: McBer & Company.

Kolb, D., Irwin, S. & McIntyre, J. D. (1971). *Organizational Psychology: An Experimental Approach.* Englewood Cliffs, NJ: Prentice Hall.

Koorland, M. A. (1986). Applied behavior analysis and the correction of learning disabilities. In J. K. Torgeson & B.Y.L. Wong (Eds.), *Psychological and educational perspectives on learning disabilities* (pp. 297-328). New York: Academic Press.

Kosslyn, S. M. (1980). *Image and mind.* Cambridge, MA: Harvard University Press.

Krashen, S. (1982). *Principles and practices in second language acquisition.* New York: Pergamon.

Kreitler, S., & Kreitler, H. (1990). *The cognitive foundations of personality traits.* New York: Plenum.

Kroeger., O., & Thuesen, J. (1988). *Type talk.* New York: Delacorte.

Languis, M. L., & Miller, D. C. (1988). *Topographic brain mapping and learning disorders.* Unpublished manuscript, Ohio State University.

Lawrence, G. (1993). *People types and tiger stripes.* Gainesville, FL: Center for Applications of Psychological Type.

Leaver, B. L. (1986). Hemisphericity of the brain and foreign language teaching. *Folia Slavica, 8,* 76-90.

Leaver, B. L. (1988). *Brain hemisphericity, language aptitude testing, and the prediction of success in foreign language learning.* Paper presented at the Foreign Service Institute's Invitational Symposium on Language Aptitude Testing, Arlington, VA.

Leaver, B. L. (1990). *Znachenie dominiruyushchego polushariya v obuchenii russkogo yazyka uchashchimsya* [The significance of hemisphere dominance in the teaching of Russian as a foreign language]. Paper presented at Seventh World Congress of Teachers of Russian Language and Literature, Moscow.

Leaver, B. L. (1996) Teachers and textbooks: Today's teaching techniques. In M. Lekic, K. Gor, & T. Kirsh, *Teachers' manual: Live from Moscow!,* Chicago: Kendall Hunt.

Leaver, B. L. (1997). *Sravnitelnyj analiz sistem lingvodidakticheskogo testirovniya i testovykh materialov ispolzuemykh v ramkakh programm po izucheniyu inostrannykh yazykov v SShA* [A comparative analysis of pedagogical language testing and testing materials used in U.S. foreign language programs]. [Brochure]. Moscow: Russian Language Testing Center, Ministry of General and Professional Education of the Russian Federation.

Leaver, B. L., & Granoien, N. (1997). Educational philosophies: Why we teach the way we do. *ACTR Letter, 23,* 1-2, 24-25.

Leaver, B. L., Jones, W., & Johnson, F. (1996). *Learning style continuity in normal and learning disabled high school students.* Unpublished proposal to the U. S. Department of Education.

Leaver, B. L., & Oxford, R. (1993). *Learning strategies: A manual for students.* Salinas, CA: AGSI Press.

Leaver, E. E., & Leaver, B. L. (1996). Memory: Fact and hypothesis. *ACTR Letter,23*(1), 1-2, 8, 12, 23.

Leaver, E. E., & Thompson, K. (1997). Memory enhancement. In PRC, Inc., *Language awareness course* [CD-ROM]. Prepared under contract to the Central Intelligence Foreign Language Committee under the direction of the Defense Language Institute, Monterey, CA.

Lennon, O. (1988). Cultural variations, cognitive styles and education in Latin America. *Prospects, 18(3),* 13-20.

Lesser, G. S. (1976). Cultural difference in learning and thinking styles. In S. Messick and Associates (Eds.), *Individuality in learning* (pp. 137-160). Washington, DC: Jossey-Bass.

Lester, D. (1974). *A physiological basis for personality traits.* Springfield, IL: Charles C Thomas.

Levin, J. R., & Pressley, M. (1985). Mnemonic vocabulary instruction: What is fact, what is fiction. In R. F. Dillon (Ed.), *Individual differences in cognition,* (Vol. 1, pp. 145-169). Orlando, FL: Academic Press.

Levine, A., Reves, T., & Leaver, B. L. (1996). Relationship between language learning strategies and Israeli versus Russian cultural educational factors. In R. Oxford (ed.), *Language learning strategies around the world: Cross-cultural perspectives* (pp. 35-46). Manoa: University of Hawaii Press.

Levy, H. B. (1973). *Square pegs, round holes; The learning disabled child in the classroom and at home.* Boston: Little, Brown.

Lewis, A. C. (1991). *Learning styles: Putting research and common sense into practice.* Arlington, VA: American Association of School Administrators.

Long, K. (1977). *Johnny's such a bright boy, What a shame he's retarded.* Boston: Houghton Mifflin.

Lowery, R. (1982). *Letteri's information processing as related to cognitive structure.* Paper presented at Washington Junior High/Middle School Principal's Association Conference, Tacoma, WA.

Luus, C.A.E., & Wells, G. L. (1991). Eyewitness identification and the selection of distracters for line-ups. *Law and Human Behavior, 15,* 43-57.

Mangan, G. (1982). *The biology of human conduct: East-West models of temperament and personality.* New York: Pergamon Press.

Mayer, R. E. (1983). *Thinking, problem solving, cognition.* San Francisco: Freeman.

Mayer, R. E. (1988). Learning strategies: An overview. In C. Weinstein, E. Goetz, & P. Alexander (Eds.), *Learning and study strategies: Issues in assessment, instruction, and evaluation* (pp. 11-22). New York: Academic Press.

McCarthy, B. (1987). *The 4 MAT system: Teaching to learning styles with left/right mode techniques.* Barrington, IL: Excel.

McCarthy, B. (1996). *About learning.* Barrington, IL: Excel.

McCarthy, B. (1997). A tale of four learners: 4MAT's learning styles. *Educational Leadership, 54,* 46-51.

McCombs, B. (1988). Motivational skills training: Combining metacognitive, cognitive and affective learning strategies. In C. Weinstein, E. Goetz, and P. Alexander (Eds.), *Learning and study strategies: Issues in assessment, instruction, and evaluation* (pp. 141-170). New York: Academic Press.

McGuinness, D. (1985). *When children don't learn: Understanding the biology and psychology of learning disabilities.* New York: Basic Books.

Melton, C. (1990). Bridging the cultural gap: A study of Chinese students' learning style preferences. *RELC Journal: A Journal of Language Teaching and Research in Southeast Asia 21,* 29-54.

Messick, S. (1984). The nature of cognitive styles: Problems and promise in educational practice. *Educational Psychologist, 59,* 59-74.

Messick, S., & Associates. (1976). *Individuality in learning.* Washington, DC: Jossey-Bass.

Miller, J. P., & Seller, W. (1985). *Curriculum: Perspectives and practice.* New York: Longman.

Morgan, H. L. (1981). *Learning styles: The relationship between need for structure and preferred mode of instruction for gifted elementary students.* Unpublished dissertation, University of Pittsburgh.

Morgan, M. J., & Foot, H. C. (1990). *Children helping children.* New York: John Wiley.

Morrison, H. C. (1926). *The practice of teaching in the secondary school.* Chicago: University of Chicago Press.

Mruk, C. (1995). *Self-esteem: Research, theory, and practice.* NY: Springer.

Myers, I. B. (1993). *Gifts differing: Understanding personality type.* Palo Alto, CA: Consulting Psychologists Press.

Myers, I. B., & Briggs, K. (1976). *The Myers-Briggs Type Indicator.* Palo Alto, CA: Consulting Psychologists Press.

Naigle, R. J., & Thwaite, B. C. (1979). Modeling effects on impulsivity with learning disabled children. *Journal of Learning Disabilities 12,* 331-336.

Nelson, K. (1988). Where do taxonomic categories come from? *Human Development 3,* 3-10.

Newman, J. (1985). *Whole language: Theory in use.* Exeter, NH: Heinemann.

Nickel, H. (1984). *Begriffsbildung im Kindesalter: zum Verhältnis von Stilen und Fähigkeiten* [The relationship of abstraction in childhood to style and ability]. Bern: H. Huber.

Nunan, D. (1988). *The learner-centered curriculum: A study in second language teaching.* New York: Cambridge University Press.

Nyikos, M. (1987). *The effect of color and imagery as mnemonic strategies on learning and retention of lexical items in German.* Unpublished dissertation, Purdue University, West Lafayette, IN.

O'Malley, J. M., & Chamot, A. U. (1990). *Learning strategies in second language acquisition.* Cambridge, UK: Cambridge University Press.

Osmond, H., with Osmundsen, J. A., & Agel, J. (1974). *Understanding understanding.* New York: Harper & Row.

Oxford, R. L. (1989). Use of language learning strategies: A synthesis of studies with implications for strategy training. *System, 17,* 235-247.

Oxford, R. L. (1990a). Language learning strategies and beyond: A look at strategies in the context of styles. In S. S. Magnan (Ed.), *Shifting the instructional focus to the learner* (pp. 35-59). Middlebury, VT: Northeast conference on the Teaching of Foreign Languages.

Oxford, R. L. (1990b). *Language learning strategies: What every foreign language teacher should know.* New York: HarperCollins.

Oxford, R. L., Ehrman, M. E., & Lavine, R. (1991). Style wars: Teacher-student style conflicts in the language classroom. In S. S. Magnan (Ed.), *Challenges in the 1990s for college foreign language programs* (pp. 1-25). Boston: Heinle & Heinle.

Oxford, R. L., & Leaver, B. L. (1996). A synthesis of strategy instruction for language learners. In R. L. Oxford (Ed.), *Language learning strategies around the world: Cross-cultural perspectives* (pp. 227-246). Manoa: University of Hawaii Press.

Paredes, J., & Hepburn M. (1976). The split-brain and the culture-cognition paradox. *Current Anthropology, 17,* 1.

Parrill-Burnstein, M. (1981). *Problem solving and learning disabilities: An information processing approach.* New York: Grune and Stratton.

Pask, G., &Scott, B.C.E. (1975). Learning strategies and individual competence. In J. M. Whitehead (Ed.), *Personality and learning 1: A reader prepared by the personality and learning course team and The Open University* (257-287). London: Hodder and Stoughton.

Pellegrino, V. (1997). Risk Taking. In PRC, Inc., *Language awareness course* [CD-ROM]. Prepared under contract to the Central Intelligence Foreign Language Committee under the direction of the Defense Language Institute, Monterey, CA.

Piaget, J. (1967). *Biologie et connaissance* [Biology and knowledge]. Paris: Gallimard.

Piaget, J. (1974). *Adaptation vitale et psychologie de l'intelligence* [Life adaptation and the psychology of intelligence]. Paris: Hermann.

Piaget, J., & Inhelder, B. (1959). *La genèse des structures logiques élémentaires* [The genesis of elementary logical structures]. Neuchâtel: Delachauz and Niestlé.

Piaget, J., & Inhelder, B. (1973). *Memory and intelligence.* New York: Basic Books.

Pierce, C.S.S. (1935). *Collected works of Charles D. Pierce, Volume 5.* Cambridge, MA: Harvard University Press.

Plant, J. S. (1966). *Personality and the cultural pattern.* New York: Octagon.

Pool, C. R. (1997). Maximizing learning. *Educational Leadership, 54,* 11-15.

Poulisse, N. (1989). *The use of compensatory strategies by Dutch learners of English.* Unpublished doctoral dissertation, The Catholic University of Nijmegen, Nijmegen, The Netherlands.

Poulisse, N., Bongaerts, T., & Kellerman, E. (1984). On the use of compensatory strategies in second language performance. *Interlanguage Studies Bulletin 8,* 70-105.

Pressley, M., Burkell, J., Lynschuk, T., McGoldrick, L., Schneider, J. A. , Snyder, B., Symons, B. L., & Woloshyn, V. E. (1990). *Cognitive strategy instruction that really improves children's academic performance.* Cambridge, MA: Brookline Books.

Quotes from previous Superbowls. (1997, January 26). *Portland Press Herald,* p. D1.

Ramirez, M., &Castaneda, A. (1974). *Cultural democracy, biocognitive development, and education.* New York: Academic Press.

Reder, L. (1980). The role of elaboration in the comprehension and retention of prose: A critical review. *Review of Educational Research, 49,* 5-53.

Reiff, J. (1992). *Learning styles.* Washington, DC: NEA Professional Library.

Reiser, M. (1991). *Memory in mind and brain.* New Haven: Yale University Press.

Reynolds, M. C., & Birch, J. W. (1977). *Teaching exceptional children in all America's schools.* Reston, VA: Council for Exceptional Children.

Ross, A. O. (1976). *Psychological aspects of learning disabilities and reading disorders.* NY: McGraw-Hill.

Ross, D. F., Read, J. D., & Toglia, M. P. (Eds.). (1994). *Adult eyewitness testimony: current trends and developments.* New York: Cambridge University Press.

Saracho, O. N. (1988). Cognitive styles and young children's learning. *Early Child Development and Care, 30,* 213-220.

Scales, A. (1987). Alternatives to standardized tests in reading education: Cognitive styles and informal measures. *Negro Educational Review 38,* 99-106.

Scarr, S. (1981). *Race, social class, and individual differences in I. Q.* Hillsdale, NJ: Lawrence Erlbaum.

Schmeck, R. R. (1988a). Individual differences and learning strategies. In C. Weinstein, E. Goetz, & P. Alexander (Eds.), *Learning and study strategies: Issues in assessment, instruction, and evaluation* (pp. 171-191). New York: Academic Press.

Schmeck, R. R. (1988b). *Learning strategies and learning styles.* New York: Plenum.

Serrapere, P. F. (1977). *A rationale and design to train adults to develop their non-dominant learning styles.* Unpublished dissertation, University of Pittsburgh.

Sharron, H. (1987). *Changing children's minds: Feuerstein's revolution in the teaching of intelligence.* London: Souvenir.

Sinatra, R., & Stahl-Gemake, J. (1983). *Using the right brain in the language arts.* Springfield, IL: Charles C. Thomas.

Slavin, R. R. (1985). An introduction to cooperative learning research. In R. Slavin, S. Sharan, S. Kagan, R. H. Lazarowitz, C. Webb, & R. Schmuck (Eds.), *Learning to cooperate, cooperating to learn* (pp. 177-210). New York: Plenum.

Snow, T. (1997, March 5). Mediocrity taints teachers' ranks. *The Californian.*

Solomon, Daniel. (1989). *Teaching styles and learning.* Chicago: Center for the Study of Liberal Education for Adults.

Spear, K. (1993). *Peer response groups in action: Writing together in secondary schools.* Portsmouth, N.H.: Boynton/Cook.

Spearman, C. (1927). *The abilities of man: Their nature and measurement.* New York: Macmillan.

Springer, Sally P. (1981). *Left brain, right brain.* San Francisco: W. H. Freeman.

Stephens, T. M. (1970). *Directive teaching of children with learning and behavioral handicaps.* Columbus, OH: Charles E. Merrill.

Sternberg, R. J. (1985). *Beyond IQ: A triarchic theory of human intelligence.* London: Cambridge University Press.

Sternberg, R. J. (1986). Intelligence is mental self-government. In R. J. Sternberg, & D. K. Detterman (Eds.), *What is intelligence?:Contemporary viewpoints on its nature and definition* (pp. 141-148). Norwood, NJ: Ablex.

Sternberg, R. J. (1989). *The triarchic mind.* New York: Penguin.

Sternberg, R. J. (1990). *Metaphors of mind: Conceptions of human intelligence.* Cambridge: Cambridge University Press.

Sternberg, R. J. (1997). What does it mean to be smart? *Educational Leadership, 54,* 20-24.

Stilgenbauer, R. (1995, June 27). Discussion on "Ed Talk: The Radio Show," KNRY, Monterey, CA.

Stryker, S. B., & Leaver, B. L. (1997). *Content-based instruction: Models and methods.* Washington, DC: Georgetown University Press.

Sylwester, R. (1995). *A celebration of neurons: An educator's guide to the human brain.* Alexandria, VA: Association for Supervision & Curriculum Development.

Terman, L. M., & Oden, M. H. (1947). *The gifted child grows up.* Stanford, CA: Stanford University Press.

Torrance, E. P. (1980). *Your style of learning and thinking, Forms B and C.* Athens: University of Georgia.

Torrance, E. P., Reynolds, C. R., Riegel, T., & Ball, O. (1977). Your style of learning and thinking. *The Gifted Child Quarterly, 21,* 565-573.

Torshen, K. P. (1977). *The mastery approach to competency-based education.* New York: Academic Press.

Tsang, S. (1983). *Mathematics learning styles of chinese immigrant students: Final research report.* Oakland, CA: ARC Association.

Vygotsky, L. S. (1982). *Sobranie sochinenii v shesti tomakh* [Collected works in six volumes]. Moscow: Pedagogika.

Wallace, A.F.C. (1970). *Culture and personality* (2nd ed.). New York: Random House.

Washburne, C. W. (1922). Educational measurements as a key to individualizing instruction and promotions. *Journal of Educational Research, 5,* 195-206.

West, T. G. (1991). *In the Mind's Eye.* Buffalo, NY: Prometheus.

Whittlesea, B.W.A., Jacoby, L. L., & Girard, K. A. (1990). Illusions of immediate memory: Evidence of an attributional basis for feelings of familiarity and perceptual quality. *Journal of Memory and Language, 29,* 716-732.

Williams, L. V. *Teaching for the two-sided mind: A guide to right/left brain education.* Englewood Cliffs, NJ: Prentice Hall.

Witkin, H. A. (1975). Research on cognitive style. In J. M. Whitehead (Ed.), *Personality and learning 1: A reader prepared by the personality and learning course team and The Open University* (pp. 257-287). London: Hodder & Stoughton.

Wolf, G., & Koff, E. (1978). Memory for pure and verb-derived nouns: Implications for hemispheric specialization. *Brain and Language, 5,* 336-341.

Woo, E. Y., & Hoosair, R. (1984). Visual and auditory functions of Chinese dyslexics. *Psychologia: An International Journal of Psychology in the Orient, 27,* 164-170.

Yong, F. L., & McIntyre, J. D. (1992). A comparative study of the learning style preferences of students with learning disabilities and students who are gifted. *Journal of Learning Disabilities, 25,* 124-32.

Young, A. W. (1983). *Functions of the right cerebral hemisphere.* New York: Academic Press.

Zelniker, T., & Jeffrey, W. E. (1976). Reflective and impulsive children: Strategies of information processing underlying differences in problem solving. *Monographs of the Society for Research in Child Development, 41,* Serial No. 168.

Index